CERVANTES

CERVANTES

RUDOLPH SCHEVILL

FREDERICK UNGAR PUBLISHING CO.
NEW YORK

Republished 1966

Reprinted
from the edition of 1919

Printed in the United States of America

Library of Congress Catalog Card No. 66-19467

CONTENTS

PAGE

PREFACE   i

CHAPTER I. ALCALÁ DE HENARES AND THE FAMILY OF CER-
VANTES.—Birth of Cervantes. Alcalá to-day. The University of Alcalá. Its curriculum in the sixteenth century. Life of the students. The family of Cervantes.
His father: a poor hidalgo; imprisoned for debt. His
grandfather: lawyer and magistrate; involved in law-
suits. His brother Rodrigo. Mother and sisters: their
character and history   3

CHAPTER II. THE YOUTH AND EDUCATION OF CERVANTES.—
Absence of facts regarding his youth. Plausible theories. His schooling. Whereabouts in 1566-68. Probable enlistment in military service. Autobiographical
references in his works. *The Story of the Captive, Don
Quixote, The Licentiate of Glass.* First reliable date:
1568. His earliest printed verse. Living in Madrid.
Pupil of López de Hoyos. In Italy: 1569. Relation
with Acquaviva. Reasons for leaving Spain . . .   33

CHAPTER III. SOLDIER AND SLAVE.—Ottoman Empire and
Christian Powers at war. Seizure of Cyprus and fall
of Nicosia. Cervantes' Italian campaigns. Juan de
Austria. Battle of Lepanto. Cervantes wounded. Campaigns of 1573-74. Garrison duty. Influence of Italian
culture and literature: slight evidence in works. Miguel
and Rodrigo set out for Spain. Captured by pirates.
Slavery in Algiers. Cervantes' captivity: 1575-80. References to it in his works. Plots to escape. He is ran-

CONTENTS

somed by Trinitarian monks. Important document on
his life as slave. Juan Blanco de Paz. Return to his
native land 58

CHAPTER IV. THE ENTRANCE OF CERVANTES ON HIS CAREER
OF LETTERS; "LA GALATEA."—Conditions at home. Poverty of his family. Brief employment in the King's
service. First literary ventures. Madrid as a center
of letters. Cervantes known as a writer of satiric
verse. References to contemporaries in the *Song of
Calliope*. *La Galatea*. Origin and nature of pastoral
stories. Montemayor. Gaspar Gil Polo. Gálvez Montalvo. Story of *La Galatea*. Episodes. Discussions
of shepherds. Neo-platonism. Verse of *La Galatea*.
Final verdict of Cervantes on the pastoral type . . 93

CHAPTER V. MARRIAGE; FIRST PERIOD AS PLAYWRIGHT;
GOVERNMENT COMMISSARY AND PREPARATIONS FOR "DON
QUIXOTE."—Literary activity. Ana Franca de Rojas.
Birth of Isabel de Saavedra. Marriage. Esquivias and
the family of his wife. Home of the newly married
couple. The theatres at Madrid. Cervantes writes for
the stage. *Pictures of Algiers*. *Numantia*. Character
of these plays. Dramatic art of his early contemporaries. Abandons literature. Commissary of the Government. Vexatious duties. Intermittent literary
efforts. Financial difficulties. Imprisonment. Subsequent occupation uncertain. At work on *Don Quixote* 129

CHAPTER VI. THE RELATION OF CERVANTES TO THE CULTURE
OF THE RENASCENCE AND THE FICTION OF THE SIXTEENTH
CENTURY.—Cervantes a wide reader. His relation to
the intellectual forces of his times. Renascence culture. Humanism. Cervantes not a classical scholar.
His indebtedness to well known works. Influence of
drama and fiction. *The Celestina*. *Lazarillo de Tormes*.
Realism based on human experience. The romance of
chivalry. Its character as a tale of adventure. Its
popularity. Cervantes criticizes the romance of chiv-

CONTENTS

alry. His final verdict recorded in *Don Quixote*. His
conception of fiction as an art. His classic qualities.
Publication of *Don Quixote* 167

CHAPTER VII. "THE RESOURCEFUL KNIGHT, DON QUIXOTE
DE LA MANCHA." (PART I).—Original purpose of Cervantes. Growth in the plan of his novel. Original
outline of Don Quixote's character. The first quest of
adventures. Pure burlesque. Return of Don Quixote
and the creation of Sancho Panza. Adventures of the
second sally. Their meaning and interpretation. Development of the character of both protagonists. Vast
material for comedy in *Don Quixote*. Large canvas of
the story. Its numerous characters. The serious portions of the novel. Discourses. Novelistic incidents.
Stories of love and adventure. Personal reminiscences.
The hero's return. Cervantes criticizes his own book. 204

CHAPTER VIII. "THE RESOURCEFUL KNIGHT, DON QUIXOTE
DE LA MANCHA." (PART II.).—Composition of the second part. Relative merits of the two parts. Concentration of the reader's interest in the protagonists.
Amplification of their character. Happy balance between burlesque and sanity. Sancho becomes a philosophical squire: the voice of humor and wisdom. Examples of the dialogues between master and servant.
Conversation more highly developed as a vehicle of
expression. Delineation of specific characters. Teresa.
Sansón Carrasco. Don Diego de Miranda. The wedding feast of Camacho. The sojourn at the palace of
the Duke and Duchess. Sancho as governor. Final
adventures. The spurious *Don Quixote*. Final defeat
of the hero. His return and death. Popularity and
influence of *Don Quixote* 250

CHAPTER IX. "THE EXEMPLARY NOVELS."—Imagination and
style of Cervantes. The rare inventor in *Don Quixote;*
the conscious literary artist in the *Novels*. Their Span-

CONTENTS

ish character. Difficulty of translating them. Cervantes' claim to be the first to write novels in Spain. Comparison with Boccaccio. Beauty and harmony in Cervantes' art. His rejection of coarseness. His originality. Old-fashioned traits in the manner and method of both novelists. Résumé of the twelve *Novels*. Popular and traditional elements of love and adventure in *The Little Gypsy*. Defects in the less original stories. Improbable occurrences and coincidences. The skillful delineation to be found in *The Illustrious Kitchen-maid*. Its graceful narratives and humorous episodes. *Rinconete and Cortadillo:* a genre picture of the highest order. Three realistic tales based on amorous intrigues: *The Force of Blood, The Jealous Estremaduran, The Deceitful Marriage.* Two masterpieces: *The Licentiate of Glass, The Colloquy of the Dogs.* The former another study of partial insanity. Its analysis of life. The sententious or philosophic discussions in the *Colloquy of the Dogs.* A rehearsal of many kinds of human experience. A picture of Spanish life and culture. Influence of the *Novels* 292

CHAPTER X. THE CLOSING YEARS OF CERVANTES; HIS LAST WORKS; HIS ACHIEVEMENT.—Residence at Valladolid. Assassination of Ezpeleta. Removal to Madrid. *A Journey to Parnassus.* References to poets of the time. Autobiographical details. Occasional passages of eloquence. The *Postscript. Eight Plays and Eight New Interludes.* The second dramatic period. Characterization of the *Eight Plays.* Verse and structure. Absence of genuine dramatic instinct. Lope and Cervantes contrasted. Dramatic theories of Cervantes. Humor and realism of the *Interludes.* Last works. *Persiles and Sigismunda.* Character of its episodes. *Dedication* and *Prologue.* Death. His achievement 330

PREFACE

Berkeley, January, 1919.

Sr. D. Adolfo Bonilla y Sán Martin,
      Madrid, Spain.

My Dear Friend:

You will remember how after completing the first part of *Don Quixote* Cervantes confided to his reader that although the composition of his story had cost him much labor, he nevertheless experienced none greater than the making of his Preface. By this admission, the truth of which has been questioned by no writer of books, he permits the inference that whatever may be the purpose or the claim of a literary work, its author cannot hope to deceive the shrewdness of "that ancient lawgiver called the Public": for it may presently prove to him that he has neither fulfilled the one, nor justified the other. I shall, therefore, refrain from betraying in a perfunctory manner my original design, and thus invite no contradiction; my protagonist will speak for himself as far as possible, and explain to the reader the extent of his achievement.

It is now three centuries since Cervantes was laid away in the grave, and in Spain, at least, he has had his reward: there his name has become one to conjure with,

i

he has attained a veritable apotheosis, and the mention of no other writer is joined with as much unqualified praise. Among English-speaking people he has also been honored from time to time by a scholarly investigation or an appreciative essay; but the adventures of Don Quixote, or the noble *Exemplary Novels* have not occupied the leisure moments of the average reader according to their merits.

The assertion is entirely justified that if Cervantes had never written immortal books, his remarkable career and rare personality would still deserve our admiration and esteem. No estimate of his work can, therefore, be complete without a rehearsal of the chief events of his life, and of his manifold experiences. I have attempted to include the latest discoveries of importance as far as they were known to me, yet the interrupted communications of these troublous times made it impossible to obtain all the material that has come to my notice. On the other hand, the burden of presenting the main facts of Cervantes' biography was substantially lightened by Professor Fitzmaurice-Kelly's compendious *Memoir* of the great Spaniard's life. Mr. Fitzmaurice-Kelly has also done the English public a service in making accessible under his general editorship the satisfactory translation of *Don Quixote* by Ormsby, of the *Exemplary Novels* by Maccoll and of *La Galatea* by Oelsner and Welford. They have been printed in a useful form by Gowans and Gray of Glasgow. My quotations from *Don Quixote*, the *Novels* and the *Galatea* are taken from these

translations, not because they are wholly free from grave
defects—no English translation of Cervantes can boast
that—but because they are within easy reach of the
general reader in every library. I have taken the liberty, although rarely, of altering an occasional word, of
dividing long sentences for the sake of clearness, and of
suiting the punctuation to the change. Notably with
Ormsby's *Don Quixote* I attempted to avoid the bookish
flavor of *thou* by letting Don Quixote address Sancho
with our more normal *you*. The passages from the *Journey to Parnassus* and the *Letter to Mateo Vázquez* are
from the admirable versions of Gibson. The extracts
from *Lazarillo de Tormes* are by Roscoe; although his
translation is exceedingly free at times, it is spirited and
adequate. For all other translations I am responsible.

I have been most fortunate in having at my disposal
the advice of the general editors of this series, Professor
Noyes and Professor Hart, to whom I cannot adequately
express my gratitude for their numerous scholarly sug-
gestions. I am also indebted to my friend Dr. Morley,
and especially to my wife for constant and substantial
help. It is idle to add, my dear friend, how much improved this little book would have been, if I had had the
benefit of your sane judgment, your limitless store of
knowledge, your rare understanding of our favorite
author. If the defects of what I venture to offer to the
public seem to you very glaring, your friendship and
charity will at once recall how common is the victory of
our shortcomings over our best-laid schemes and pur-

poses; and if you give this book your approval, I shall indeed feel that it may stimulate many of our readers to become more deeply acquainted with your great fellow countryman.

Devotedly yours,

R. S.

CERVANTES

CERVANTES

CHAPTER I

ALCALÁ DE HENARES AND THE FAMILY OF CERVANTES

LITTLE more than twenty miles northeast of Madrid, in the midst of a rolling yellow plain, near the banks of the insignificant stream Henares, lies Alcalá, famous to-day chiefly as the birthplace of Spain's most illustrious man of letters, Miguel de Cervantes Saavedra. No other town of Spain is so intimately connected with his name, for, although the sojourn of Cervantes in the more important centers, Madrid, Seville, Valladolid, is well attested, his native town, nevertheless, represents something which other cities cannot boast: it is the cradle of his genius, it recalls the origin of his family and his own youth. Alcalá de Henares was also the site of one of the most famous universities of the world, an academic center of vast influence and the alma mater of many famous men.

The picturesque remains of the little town at the present time enable us to visualize what it was during Cervantes' earliest years. Its chief square, called properly enough, **Plaza de Cervantes**, is surrounded by a number of low, picturesque houses with dingy old patios, but its greatest attraction is the parish church of Santa María. Here, in a side chapel, Cervantes was baptized on Sunday, October 9, 1547. The day of his birth is not known, although it may have been on, or near, Michaelmas, September 29th, the Feast of San Miguel, his patron saint. The baptismal document, first printed in 1753, reads:

On Sunday, the ninth day of the month of October, in the year of our Lord, 1547, was baptized Miguel, son of Rodrigo de Cervantes and his wife, doña Leonor; his godfather was Juan Pardo, the Rev. Sr. Bachiller * Serrano, parish priest of Our Lady, baptized him, the witnesses being Baltasar Vázquez, sacristan, and myself who baptized him and signed my name, El Bach. Serrano.

This precious document, which decided all disputes concerning Cervantes' native town, may still be seen, even if not deciphered, in the parish register on folio 192 v. where it was scribbled in a crabbed and illegible hand.

From the Plaza de Cervantes leads the only prominent street of Alcalá; its houses, hanging over the sidewalks, are fronted by arcades or covered walks where somber shops display their wares. During the period of Alcalá's greatness, this street was the main artery of traffic. An old saying reads: "Alcalá, thou dost boast more than thou art worth, for were it not for that one

---

* Bachelor, in those days a high academic degree.

street of thine, thou wouldst not be worth a maravedí."
By this street one reaches the College Church, once filled
with a brilliant clergy because of whose learning the
title of the Magistral was conferred upon it. Near by
is the noble palace of the archbishops, with spacious
halls and corridors, besides decorative courts and stair-
cases, all indicatory of the faded glory of Alcalá, when
the town was under the loving protection of the Archbishops of Toledo. Now these sumptuous quarters house
the dusty archives of the War Department, and a drowsy
keeper opens a shutter to let in a ray of light for the
intruding visitor. Not far from the palace may be seen
the remains of a city wall, with the plains beyond.
Occasional striking façades of the sixteenth century,
remnants of older buildings, indicate the wealth and
prosperity of days when Alcalá was still the home of
many noble families.

But the name of Alcalá is most closely bound up with
the famous university founded there by Cardinal
Ximénez de Cisneros at the beginning of the sixteenth
century, and transferred to Madrid in 1836, leaving only
the hollow shells of buildings and empty court-yards.
The main façade, of regal splendor and profuse decora-
tion, gives an idea of the wealth and ambitions of its
chief protectors and fosterers. Three courts may still be
seen: where now absolute silence reigns were once heard
riotous crowds of disputatious students. Of the University proper, the chapel, with its rare carving on the ceiling and the magnificent iron grating, is an excellent

example of the fusion of Christian and Moorish styles; and the abandoned hall of ceremonials, with ornate galleries and dignified ceiling, still suggests its former lavish beauty.

It would be misleading to suppose that Alcalá was ever a large city, or that it harbored the excessive number of students attributed to it by some writers. As a matter of fact, no two statements agree on the attendance at any university. Thus Cervantes in an offhand way tells us on one occasion, that of five thousand students pursuing courses at Alcalá more than two thousand were enrolled in medicine; while the unidentified author of *The Feigned Aunt,* a tale of student life at Salamanca—attributed by some to the pen of Cervantes —gives the exaggerated figures of ten or twelve thousand students for the latter institution. These two universities of Spain were smaller during the sixteenth century than is generally believed. In the last third of the sixteenth century Alcalá is mentioned by a pilgrim, Villalva, as a town of four to five thousand inhabitants, and a trustworthy account by a Portuguese traveller, Barreiros, who visited Alcalá in 1546, the year before Cervantes' birth, contains the following interesting details: "If we except those who attend the colleges of Latin Grammar, the majority of students, including those who are housed in the town, attend their lessons at the Colegio Mayor. Some told me that there were more than one thousand students, others that there were in all three thousand. The village has scarcely more than one thousand inhabitants. In the summer the majority of students leave for their homes, and Alcalá becomes very quiet. Many are housed under one roof for lack of lodgings.'' In 1551 the number of students who matriculated at Salamanca reached 5856, three times as many as those of the sister University. We therefore have a fair estimate of Alcalá during the years of Cervantes' boyhood, while his family was still residing in the University town. Its outer aspect must have been wholly that of a community filled with schools and convents, students and clergy, yet by no means free from that antagonism between town and gown which has characterized every center of learning the world over.

The serious life of its curriculum and classroom need occupy us only briefly, since we are more interested in the life of the student world as it is occasionally reflected on the page of Cervantes. No evidence has yet been discovered to prove that Cervantes was ever definitely enrolled at any University, and his own writings lead us to infer that many features of its training were distasteful to him. He, therefore, occupied himself with the life which the students lived rather than with what they endeavored to acquire from books. Within the classroom the scholastic system was still dominant: the text-books used spoke with unassailable authority, and criticism of the contents was not permitted. The treatment of the matter before the student consisted of an attempted elucidation, phrase by phrase, with constant reference to other accepted and interdependent authorities. The language of the classroom was almost entirely Latin, which in spirit gave the atmosphere a certain uniformity not free from monotony or pedantry. The subject was ventilated as far as possible by argumentation and dispute, that peculiar system of dialectics based on affirmation and refutation, keeping the student in the channels of a certain mental routine, highly objectionable to original minds, but satisfying to all of average ability. The demands on the memory were unusually great because authorities were quoted verbatim, and a student who learned an elaborate system of commentaries by heart easily stood high among his classmates. On Saturdays especially we are told the halls resounded with arguments and discussions of theses. Alcalá was famous for its courses in the humanities and in theology, and inasmuch as the character of a university in those days was predominatingly ecclesiastical, no faculty was wholly free from the churchman's authority. The most important subjects taught were law, notably canonical, theology and medicine, so that the courses in the arts and sciences were subsidiary and supplementary. Among these were logic, physics, metaphysics and philosophy, and the three languages, Latin, Greek and Hebrew, taught especially in the famous Trilingual College of San Jerónimo. That the chief requirements for the degree of Bachelor of Arts were then somewhat different may be seen from the fact that the chief subjects were Latin, to be passed as a preliminary subject, followed by logic, philosophy, the physics of Aristotle and ethics.

A visitor to Alcalá in the middle of the sixteenth century would have been struck by a sharp contrast between the outward formality of university activities and the liberty, bordering on license, of the students themselves. He would have seen processions of faculty and student body, picturesque in their colored gowns and academic caps, long lines of candidates for the priesthood, or for the career of law or medicine proceeding to mass, or to their lecture rooms. He might have entered the courtyards of the Colleges and heard the students discuss either a prank of the night before or dispute over some phrase from Plato or Virgil. Concerning the student life at Alcalá an infinite number of details have been preserved for us in fiction, drama, letters, and university statutes and regulations. The intellectual revival of the Renascence had spurred on the youth of the land to seek more and more the fruits of a higher education; for this was a stepping-stone to the best posts in the Church and in the offices of the Government. As was natural in such an influx, the majority of students were poor, and frequently not to be distinguished from vagabonds and adventurers. Cervantes speaks of them on various occasions as indigent, unwashed and afflicted with the itch. In this he is corroborated by many contemporaries, and, although the assertion may be taken with a grain of salt, there must have been some truth in it. "If the itch and hunger were not such constant companions of students," he tells us in *The Colloquy of the Dogs*, "there would be no existence of greater pleasure and pastime, for virtue and pleasure have an equal share in it, and youth is spent in learning and in enjoying oneself.'' On another occasion, in the *Persiles and Sigismunda,* the father of a truant student is reproaching a young girl for admitting his son's courtship, and he asks: ''And where did you meet my son Andrew? Was it at Madrid or Salamanca?'' ''It was at Illescas,'' she replied, ''picking cherries early one St. John's morning, and ever since that, I see him before me, and have him engraved on my soul.'' ''Well, I am surprised,'' says the father, ''that my son should be occupied in picking cherries rather than catching fleas, which is more characteristic of students.'' Another result of the students' poverty was the springing up of a class who lived on alms, who wandered from place to place, often getting their food at convent doors, and beguiling their idle hours with music on the guitar. A certain student, according to a current story, we may assume either through ignorance or folly, knocked at the door of a professor to ask for an alms. The latter appeared and asked gravely: ''Brother, what is the preterite of *conquinisco, conquiniscere* (to stoop)?'' And the poor fellow answered, ''I don't know.'' Whereupon the master said, ''The preterite is *conquexi; there's* an alms for you. Good-by.''

But if the life of the majority of students was one of privation and discomforts, the sons of wealthy parents, scions of aristocratic houses, enjoyed relatively many comforts and luxuries. The difference made itself felt

at once on their arrival, when the poorer newcomer
sought a boarding-house, while the young man with
means, who generally brought furnishings, servants and
tutor with him, proceeded to rent quarters and set up
housekeeping. Frequently the indigent students entered
the service of the rich. Little did they know what was
in store for them at the hands of owners of boarding-
houses, vendors and shop-keepers, that element which in
all college towns profits at the expense of the bodily
well-being of its victims. Many authors, especially the
writers of the picaresque novels, have left us minute
details in this matter. The soups were so clear that the
boarder while eating them ran as great risk as did Nar-
cissus when he was drowned in the fountain. The chick-
pea broth was a delusion, for no diver, however skilful,
could, even after four plunges, bring up a chick-pea.
Of the meat we learn that it consisted of delicate fibers,
so that between the grease clinging to the fingers and
the shreds remaining between the teeth, the stomach
was easily absolved from any participation. Bread was
served stale and hard so that less of it would be eaten.
The fruit course consisted of three or four cherries for
each, or a few grapes picked from the bunch, but both
were never served at the same meal. For dessert there
was at times a slice of cheese, quite transparent and
resembling the shavings of a carpenter's shop. On fish
days a small sardine was each hungry boy's share, and
the less said of the eggs the better, for they had been
stored by the dozens in ashes or salt for six months or

more. Thus the world has remained much the same. The portraits preserved for us of heads of boarding-houses, both men and women, are in keeping with the meals they serve. No chronicler tires of disclosing their pettinesses, their dishonesty, their corruption, their slovenliness and greed. No private stores of food or personal possessions were safe under their roofs. Especially the ruinous state in which the laundry was returned brings this academic life home to us.

Other features of the student's experiences have their corresponding traditions among us, such as that of hazing the latest arrivals. In many cases the customs seem to us brutal or repulsive, filthy and disgusting rather than witty or amusing, although not a few pastimes and hoaxes were worthy of recording. No doubt the boys made life sufficiently wretched for the town folk, if we are to give any credence to the stories so often repeated of the filching of pies and sweets, executed with unsurpassed skill at Alcalá, of serenading, of hideous caterwaulings at night to disturb innocent sleepers, of heckling and harassing the unpopular professors, of gambling, of journeys to Madrid in good or bad company to see the bull-fights or the jousts. A characteristic joke may be worth repeating. A student much given to pranks, so the narrative runs, desired to "treat" his companions; he entered a confectioner's shop, drew his sword, and shouting to the proprietor, "Die, villain," at the same time made a pass at him. The poor man fell down on his knees saying, "Let me first confess my sins," while the student stabbed a box of conserves and, running it through, carried it off on his sword amid the jubilant shouts of his comrades. Never, so the tale ends, did anything taste better. Cervantes tells us, in *Persiles and Sigismunda*, of two students, who, eager to see a little of the world, abandoned their books, and, having dressed as ransomed slaves and bought a canvas depicting the city and port of Algiers, set it up in the market-places through which they passed and exhibited it to gaping and credulous throngs for an alms. In a certain village the stories of their experiences, especially the terrible hardships which they had endured as slaves, drew the rapt interest of two aldermen, one of whom had been a captive among the Turks of Algiers, and their fraud was discovered. The alderman was about to sentence them to one hundred stripes, but the glib tongue of one of the boys, who was very witty and persuasive, changed his mind, and instead of a severe punishment he gave them a lesson in the real Algiers and his own experiences, so that they might on no future occasion be caught selling the public a hare for a cat.

The pastimes at the Spanish universities were numerous and diversified. The bull-fights and jousts, especially attractive at the capital, have already been mentioned. At Alcalá common sports or games were bowling, *argolla* (a kind of croquet), displays of prowess in arms, races, jumping, throwing a heavy bar, to say nothing of the popular festivities which were enlivened by dancing, mummeries and masquerades. As will be considered natural among students who lived without the proper restraint, there was also the accompanying element of songs of questionable propriety, and irreverent travesties of subjects of a religious import. Popular, indeed, according to one writer, was the mail which arrived Tuesdays and Saturdays; candles were lighted and the letters burned until one was reached which said: "My dear son, the muleteer is also bringing you money and provisions, and so on," which resulted in a general rejoicing at the prospect of further distractions and less study. Of a more serious and academic character were occasional theatrical performances in which not only the comedies of Terence and Plautus, but Latin plays written at that time were presented amid general applause.

In the course of their long history the Universities of Salamanca and Alcalá had occasionally to use drastic measures to curb the excessive license of the student body, which considered itself quite immune from the ordinary course of justice, even if guilty of felony and crime. As the custom of carrying arms was unrestrained for a period of many years local statutes, directed against this ever-growing danger, had to be reinforced by royal decrees and penalties prescribed for the infringement of the new laws. These precautions were required, since duels, bloodshed and murder were not of rare occurrence, and the local police found themselves so greatly in the minority as to be at the mercy of the student body. In proportion as the organization at the universities improved, the authority of the rector and faculty was more able to curb these evil features of an academic career.

But many evidences of a serious and earnest occupation at the University, with ample opportunities for real achievement are also to be found among famous writers on life at Alcalá. Mateo Alemán, the author of the picaresque tale, *Guzmán de Alfarache,* tells us:

Where is greater liberty to be enjoyed, or who lives a life of such repose? What distractions of any kind whatever were lacking? If the students are retiring they find their equals, if ne'er-do-wells they are never without companions, like finds like, and the studious have those with whom to discuss their studies. Wherever the student may find himself, although he has left home with the sole purpose of seeking recreation along the spacious and cool bank of the stream Henares, still, while there he will store up knowledge, he will reason, and take counsel with himself without feeling any solitude, for truly, men well-occupied are never lonesome. Where can you find such gifted men in the arts, in medicine and theology as at Alcalá? Where can we equal the education given by the theological and Trilingual Colleges whence issue every day so many and such rare talents? Where such competition? And where such friendship? O mother Alcalá, what shall I say to do thee justice?

In this city, then, Cervantes was born. We have no information regarding the number of years during which he remained in his native town. Many documents discovered in recent times show that his father,

Rodrigo de Cervantes, resided in various places, that he was an unfortunate, harassed individual, who found a prolonged sojourn anywhere impossible; there is no evidence, however, that on every one of his frequent migrations he took his large family with him. Strangely enough, Miguel, in whom we are most interested, is never mentioned as living with his father. It would thus be misleading to assume that the University of Alcalá had any profound effect on the early education of Cervantes. On the other hand, through associations maintained by the members of his family and from what he could have learned later about his native town, in his mind the constant connection of his boyhood days with Alcalá was assured.

With the growth of the University, Alcalá had arisen anew, and from the constantly increasing number of its colleges, its two score churches and convents, its resident nobility, bourgeoisie and student body, we may gather that it was a place of infinite activity. In this city, somewhere, no longer to be definitely determined, lived the family of Rodrigo de Cervantes, who calls himself on several occasions *médico cirujano,* a practitioner of little authority, without the training of a physician and presumably acquainted with a few simple remedies, capable of setting bones and alleviating mild injuries. The son had no high regard for his father's profession, for, in one of his amusing interludes, *The Divorce Court,* an irate wife appeals to the judge in the following words:

Your honor, listen to me, and note that if my husband seeks divorce for four reasons, I seek it for four hundred. The first, because every time I see him it is like seeing Lucifer himself; the second, because I was deceived when I married him: he told me he was a genuine doctor and he turned out to be a *cirujano*, a fellow who cures sprains and other trifling ailments, and from that to being a real doctor is like getting half the worth of your money; the third, because he is jealous of the sun which shines upon me; the fourth, because I can't see him and would like to be separated from him two million leagues; the fifth, —— *The Judge. Madam,* if you think you are going to recite your four hundred reasons, I am in no mood to listen to them.

We also infer that the father Rodrigo was not successful in his profession from the fact that his career has throughout the stamp of poverty, that he was hard of hearing, and that he was a restless wanderer from place to place. If we scrutinize the pay-roll at the University of Alcalá, we shall find that a *cirujano* was among those who received the lowest remuneration. A comparison of the daily wages paid early in the sixteenth century is illuminating. A professor of medicine received about one hundred and forty-five maravedís, and a professor of Latin one hundred and nine, while the majordomo was paid fifty, the laundress forty-eight, the barber sixteen, the janitor eleven, the cook seven, and the *cirujano,* who brings up the rear, six maravedís! A recent authority, taking the price of staples as a basis, gives to the money of that period about

twenty times the purchasing power of today, which
would make the daily payment of a *cirujano* about one-
fifth of a real, roughly equivalent to less than twenty-
five cents. If Rodrigo was ever in the University's
employ, and even if an occasional student entrusted
himself to his mercy, it is not likely that the perquisites
made a comfortable living for his family.

There seems, however, to have been no inconsistency
between great poverty and a claim to nobility. Both
Rodrigo de Cervantes and his famous son frequently
asserted their undisputed right to be considered *hidalgos*,
of gentle blood. But Cervantes on various opportune
occasions refers with deep feeling to the apparent injustice of fortune which prevents a gentleman from being
one by afflicting him with poverty. When Don Quixote's
niece remonstrates with him for his mad notions about
chivalry and his pretence of being a knight, she adds,
that although *hidalgos* may be so, ''when poor they are
nothing of the kind.'' And again later Don Quixote
apostrophizes poverty in words which may well have
applied to Cervantes' father as well as himself:

Why dost thou love to fall out with gentlemen and men of
good birth more than with other people? Why dost thou com-
pel them to smear the cracks in their shoes, and to have the
buttons of their coats, one silk, another hair, and another glass?
Why must their ruffs be always crinkled like endive leaves, and
not crimped with a crimping iron? . . . Poor gentleman of good
family! always cockering up his honor, dining miserably and in
secret, and making a hypocrite of the toothpick with which he

sallies out into the street after eating nothing to oblige him
to use it! Poor fellow, I say, with his nervous honor, fancying
people perceive a league off the patch on his shoe, the sweat-
stains on his hat, the shabbiness of his cloak, and the hunger of
his stomach! [II, 44.]

It is not known how far back the nobility of the Cervantes family goes, and it would, therefore, be interesting to discover more detailed information regarding
Cervantes' ancestors and the origin of the distinction.

From the records of a law case tried at Valladolid in
1552-1553 we learn that Rodrigo de Cervantes, who had
been imprisoned for debt in that city, determined to
make use of an old law still in force, that a man who
was a recognized *hidalgo* was thereby exempt from that
penalty. A number of witnesses were brought in, residents of Valladolid, but formerly citizens of Alcalá and
friends of the Cervantes family. The gist of their
testimony, couched in the stereotyped phraseology of the
notary, is that Rodrigo and his father, the Licentiate
Juan de Cervantes, were known to all their acquaint-
ances as *hidalgos*, that they had servants, took part in
jousts and other sports of gentlemen, and enjoyed the
hidalgo's best privilege of paying no taxes. Juan de
Cervantes, Miguel's grandfather, is represented as a man
of considerable means, and both he and his son, we
may infer, possessed property in various places. It must
have been, however, of that unfortunate kind that
yielded little or no income. Further details of this suit

against Rodrigo are perplexing, but they are important in so far as they throw light on the early years of our protagonist. A father in jail, and for financial reasons, indicates generally that an unhappy family remains at home. In this case it is uncertain where that home was. Rodrigo, when imprisoned, was residing at Valladolid, but was his own family with him? The evidence seems to indicate that Rodrigo's wife, even if she visited Valladolid, was still living with her little ones at Alcalá. His own statement is: "I have no residence in this town, for I am a native of Alcalá de Henares and there and in other places I have property out of which I could pay my creditors." When the plaintiff in the suit wished to attach Rodrigo's personal property, he found nothing, and seized certain articles which were assumed to belong to María de Cervantes, Rodrigo's sister, but by a subsequent action all were claimed by his mother, Leonor de Torreblanca. From this confusion it is apparent that the family of the Cervantes lacked cohesion. Thus we find the mother of Rodrigo dwelling with her daughter in Valladolid, while the father, Juan de Cervantes, is in Córdoba. There are various other documents which permit the inference that while Rodrigo is in one place, his family is resident in another. It is therefore reasonable to suppose that Rodrigo, when in Valladolid, lived with his mother and sister, and that he may have gone there chiefly to practice the profession of *cirujano* among people to whom he was less known than at Alcalá. This may be gathered from the household goods attached and claimed by his mother, among which we find some curious articles. These without argument would seem to have belonged to Rodrigo, to wit, one pair of yellow breeches, a volume on the practice of surgery, a volume on "the four diseases"— which possibly represented the extent of the good Rodrigo's information—a Latin grammar, presumably to help him decipher his Galen, if he ever had one, to say nothing of a sword and a guitar. Quite naturally he claimed in court that possessions really worth attaching were elsewhere. On the testimony of his witnesses he was released, only to be reincarcerated, and then definitely freed early in 1553, an acknowledged *hidalgo*, but with his debts unpaid. A vast unstudied portion of Spain's history during the sixteenth century lies buried in her archives, and to one who can find time to read the scores of protocols, law suits, cases tried before the Inquisition, royal grants, and the like, one thing is apparent, that there was a constantly growing desire among individuals of all kinds to be rated as *hidalgos*. In the case of Rodrigo, we are convinced that he based his defense on a righteous claim; still the frequency of the plea of a defendant in court, without documentary corroboration, will account for the fact that Rodrigo was not instantly set free on presenting his claim.

In the records there is no mention of Rodrigo's little ones, at that time five in number, ranging from three to ten years, but, even if they were not in Valladolid, it is not likely that they were wholly spared the squalor of the father's situation. This atmosphere of penury, alas, envelopes Rodrigo's mother and his sister, María, as well. The case speaks of numerous household and personal articles pawned by them, we must presume, to alleviate immediate needs; María, although called a minor, has apparently been living as an independent woman, and leasing a house in her own name. Upon finding herself without funds to pay her rent, she gives her creditor as surety some personal wearing apparel to cover the sum of twenty ducats due for one-half of her indebtedness. At this juncture, the owner of the house learns that she is about to leave for Madrid, and, asking for surety to cover the other half of his rent, he receives a tapestry, a mantle and a promise that money would be sent as soon as she reached her destination. Such evidences of poverty unfortunately recur again and again in the history of Cervantes' family, and, while of secondary interest, cannot be neglected if we wish to understand the probable reasons which launched young Miguel on his rare and adventurous career. The father, Rodrigo, will turn up again on a few of our pages, a troubled, indefinable and vague character.

Of far greater interest is the grandfather, Juan de Cervantes, already mentioned, a man who during a long life filled important public posts in which he attained considerable distinction. The date of his birth is not known, but at his death, on March 11, 1556, he was presumably seventy, or more, years old. As far as our limited information permits, we may infer that he was

a native of Córdoba, for we know that his parents, one
Bachiller Rodrigo de Cervantes and Catalina de Vera
(or de Cabrera, since both forms occur), resided there
in 1489 and 1493. The great grandparents of Miguel
de Cervantes are as yet only names to us. The wife of
Juan de Cervantes, Leonor de Torreblanca, is thought
by some to have been a gentlewoman, and, although she
was unable to sign her own name, according to the
records of the suit at Valladolid in 1552, too much importance must not be attached to illiteracy, a common
thing in those days, even among the nobility. But if
we are to see in this marriage another evidence that
Juan de Cervantes was a *hidalgo,* it is worthy of note
that his signature never occurs with *don* prefixed to it.
Nor are the names of his son Rodrigo or his grandson
Miguel ever found with this title. Indeed Cervantes
makes his attitude clear now and then by ridiculing the
abuse of *don* on the part of those who had no right
to it.

Juan de Cervantes had the title Licentiate, and, we
may assume that it was of law, for we learn that he was
an advocate at Córdoba in 1508, and that among the
prominent positions which he filled was the office of
acting chief magistrate of Córdoba in 1516, deputy
magistrate of Cuenca in 1523, judge at Plasencia in
1538, chief magistrate of estates possessed by the Duke
of Sesa, 1541-1545—a position which he seems to have
resigned to become governor of the lands of the Count
of Ureña—and, toward the end of his life, that of city

attorney at Córdoba. Everything seems to indicate that he died enjoying the respect of his fellow citizens and wearing his honors thick upon him.

But dusty archives and notary's records have an impartial way of dealing with the best of men, and posterity is obliged to weigh objectively the evidence which survives. Thus two curious suits filed against Juan de Cervantes, when he had ceased to be deputy magistrate of Cuenca in 1524, have come to light very recently, and are not yet generally known to those interested in all that concerns the name of Cervantes. The first is a complaint by one Diego Cordido that he had been unjustly hurried into the torture chamber of the prison at Cuenca, disrobed and tormented inhumanly under the direction and with the assistance of the magistrate himself, and that he had been subsequently kept in jail for three months without cause. In pronouncing sentence, the judge stated that Juan de Cervantes had manifestly violated the usual process of the law, and fined him twenty ducats to be paid to Cordido, and costs. Both sides appealed the case, but its subsequent history is not known to us. This unfortunate episode has all the earmarks of numerous cases inspired by the Inquisition during the early half of the sixteenth century, and if we recall that among the offices filled by Juan de Cervantes may be found that of inquisitorial judge, some weight is given to the suspicion that the magistrate of Cuenca may have been acting, even in a secular capacity, under the express orders of that institution. The wording of the sentence seems to imply that Diego Cordido had been unjustly treated as though he were a "suspect," while his own complaint was that he had been asked to give information which he did not possess. This method of extracting accusations under torment in order to incriminate even innocent men and women in some form of heresy was by no means uncommon in those days. It would, therefore, be absurd to condemn Juan de Cervantes for what we naturally consider an arbitrary and inhuman action without taking into consideration the history of his times and also the fact that we have not his side of the case.

At about the same time another suit was brought against Juan de Cervantes by a servant residing in Cuenca, who had been jailed for more than ten days for using improper language to her mistress. She had called her "Jewess," and thus made herself liable also to inquisitorial investigation. Her complaint was that she had left a ducat in deposit with the bailiff, and that having thereupon been freed, the Licentiate Cervantes had pocketed the coin, although she had not been condemned to pay it by law. The judge decided that the servant was partially in the right, but in so far as she had been guilty of misdemeanor and had been fined to pay the costs, these were to be deducted from the sum taken from her, and the remainder was to be paid by Juan de Cervantes within fifteen days. The episode cannot be clearly made out from the record, but it seems to imply that the late magistrate of Cuenca had been found guilty of malfeasance in office. This is somewhat unjust to the memory of Cervantes' grandfather since we have not his version of the facts. At all events, it appears to be on the face of it a mild example of corruption in high office, a condition common enough in those days to make Cervantes refer to it again and again in his writings. Among the maxims which Don Quixote teaches Sancho, when he is about to be made governor of an island, we find: "If you permit the staff of justice to swerve, let it not be by weight of a gift, but by that of mercy." And on the occasion of a certain suit introduced into *Persiles and Sigismunda*, in which the judge kept for himself the object in dispute, Cervantes remarks that it was in the natural course of things for the judge to keep something. There is no reason for thinking that in all this he recalled the action of his own grandfather, because with this slight exception, the career of Juan de Cervantes was, as far as our knowledge goes, one of which to be proud.

The only other male relative of Cervantes who is more than a mere name to us is his brother, Rodrigo, born in June, 1550, and consequently by three years his junior. The careers of the two brothers are for a number of years intimately connected, since both chose the life of a soldier, and only when the older brother definitely renounced the sword for the pen did their ways part. Rodrigo seems to have been through and through a man devoted to arms, and was probably imbued with the same love of adventure which characterized Miguel.

From 1572, or earlier, to 1577, his career is bound up with that of his brother and will be referred to in a later chapter. He was a slave in Algiers for two years, and after his return to Spain in August, 1577, he re-enlisted as a soldier, for he took part subsequently in Spain's campaign against Portugal and the Azores. On this occasion Rodrigo was promoted to the rank of Ensign for bravery displayed in a battle fought at Porto das Moas, near Angora, in July, 1583. He had a soldier's end, for he was killed on July 2, 1600, at the battle of Nieuport, in Flanders, where the Spanish under the Archduke Albert, nephew of Philip II and military Governor of the Low Countries, were defeated by Dutch and Flemish troops under the command of Maurice of Nassau, who led the struggle for independence from Spanish rule. As was generally the case, a soldier's pay was several years in arrears, and Rodrigo's was no exception. At his death a considerable sum was still due him for his devoted services, and during the next fifty years we hear of intermittent efforts made by his heirs to recover what was their right. How successful they were is not evident, for an installment which does not seem to have covered the whole indebtedness of the government was paid as late as 1654.

The biographer of Cervantes would be happy if he could set down a number of satisfactory and illuminating pages dealing with the chief women who played a part in the great novelist's career. They are known to us chiefly through protocols, deeds, suits, donations, lists of household goods, or an occasional last will and testament which in a thoroughly objective way leaves a bedstead or a worn piece of apparel to the nearest of kin and the soul to the Creator. Nothing denatures men and women more than the monotonous, impersonal language of the acts executed before a notary, and only now and then do we succeed in lifting the veil of our ignorance and discovering human vicissitudes underneath, grief, privation, failure, or, less frequently, a measure of well-being and success.

We know very little of Cervantes' mother, Leonor de Cortinas, except that she must have been a woman acquainted with grief and that she died at an advanced age in the fall of 1593, having outlived her husband, the *cirujano,* by more than eight years. We should like to know something of her personality, for she cannot have been without influence on her distinguished son. Her lot and the character of her husband would engender above all a gift of patience; the instability of her home life and the frequently disorganized character of her hearth must have made her the more practical of the parents, and, perhaps, on critical occasions, the mainstay financially. The mother of many children brought up with inadequate means has numerous daily problems to solve, and if Leonor de Cortinas failed to bring success to all of her family, it must be admitted that her task was too burdensome for her shoulders alone. Her sons, Miguel and Rodrigo, cannot have been of any effective material assistance to the household, having left home definitely at the close of their boyhood years. The mother's attitude of loyalty and acquiescence in the face of her husband's inefficiency recalls an amusing dialogue between Sancho Panza and his wife, Teresa, who remonstrates with him for his inflated notions and ridiculous ambitions. Sancho tells Teresa that when he has been made governor of an island he will confer nobility upon their daughter Sancha, who shall be called My Lady, make a high match, wear fine clothes and ride in a coach. To this Teresa objects that Sancha shall marry her equal, that she shall not exchange her wooden clogs for high-heeled shoes, nor be subjected to the whims of the aristocracy who would be sure to recall to her that she was a clodhopper's daughter and a spinning-wench, and she closes significantly: ''The day that I see her a countess it will be the same to me as if I were burying her. But once more I say, do as you please, for we women were born to the burden of being obedient to our husbands, even if they are blockheads.''

Leonor de Cortinas had the sorrowful experience of having both sons, Rodrigo and Miguel, carried into slavery in Algiers, and when she learned of their captivity, probably a number of months after the event, she made heroic efforts to gather sufficient funds to free them. She brought forward such sureties as she could out of her meagre possessions to guarantee certain small government grants which were intended to swell the sums demanded for their ransom. And if, under these difficult and pathetic circumstances, she gave herself out

on various occasions as a widow—we may assume to ex-
cite greater compassion among the government officials
with whom she had to barter—her statement reveals not
only the afflictions of a helpless mother, but it also makes
clear the incompetence of her husband, who at this time
of life, no doubt, had definitely shelved his volume on
the four diseases, and taken his place by the fireside in
innocuous desuetude.

The sisters of Cervantes were Andrea, born in 1544,
Loisa, in 1546, and Magdalena, about 1553. Loisa entered a nunnery of the order of the barefooted Carmelites at Alcalá de Henares, in February, 1565, and
consequently plays no part in the biography of her
younger brother, Miguel. Within the convent walls she
was known as Sister Louise of Bethlehem, and among
the posts she filled were those of sacristan, treasurer, sub-
prioress and prioress, to which latter position she was
elected three times. From her history we may assume
that to the usual virtues of an exemplary nun, devotion
and piety, she added a practical sense which justified
her choice for a place of responsibility among her sister
nuns. She was thus spared the disillusion of a worldly
career, and the perplexing revelations of contemporary
documents which, in the case of her sisters, Andrea and
Magdalena, give the biographer of Cervantes vexatious
problems to solve. Men and women who live a normal
existence, blessed by a reasonable portion of life's gifts
in health, good will and happiness, go their way leaving
very little for the chronicler to glean, while those who

become entangled in our social fabric of misfortune, cross purposes, petty wrong-doings, recriminations and sorrow, are fairly certain to leave a trail which is quickly taken up by the pitiless seeker of cold, and, too often, unproductive facts. But the injustice of details gathered from archives is often apparent, when, after casting up our account, we find that most of the features necessary for an accurate moral portrait can no longer be clearly detected. This applies to the women of Cervantes' family, who lived in a circumscribed world of daily routine the incidents of which we can frequently guess; but we cannot find in our sources the more important record of those actions or habits of thought which not only would make them interesting as near relatives of a great man, but which could speak of possible personal charms worthy of rehearsal for their own sakes.

We have thus been introduced to some of the members of Cervantes' immediate family, and although the careers of his brother and sisters, as contemporaries, are occasionally interwoven with his own, the scope and character of this book do not permit our dealing with them extensively. But a clearer picture of the type of family from which he has sprung has been here attempted by presenting it as a unit, by showing not only the continuity of the atmosphere which characterizes it from one generation to the next, but also the presence of certain traits which Cervantes may have shared with his nearest of kin. A more profitable achievement, however, than the discovery of more relatives would be the finding of a single document of a personal character, something that would present to us the great novelist in his habit as he lived. Perhaps a kind fortune will some day crown the efforts of his devotees with a genuine discovery which shall reveal to us more of the facts of his youth and his early education, to which we now turn.

CHAPTER II

T HE biographer of Cervantes who approaches the story of his youth, his education, and the beginnings of his career of arms and letters, must hesitate before setting down any theories, however plausible they may seem. Yet, regarding the first twenty-one years of his life, there are only theories; on precisely the formative period of his mind no documentary evidence has ever produced a single fact. A good deal has been discovered in protocols and law-suits about certain members of his family, their unstable residence or occupation, and not a few facts related to the very period under consideration, but the name of Miguel de Cervantes never appears; and if inferences have any weight, he was not living with those members of his family whose activities have been preserved for us. There is no convincing reason for believing that Leonor de Cortinas and her large family of little children left Alcalá before 1560-1561, although the statement is frequently made that the Cervantes family resided at Valladolid at some time between 1552 and 1560. This assertion is based chiefly on the suit against the father, dis-

33

cussed in the previous chapter, and on an assertion made in the will of Magdalena, sister of Cervantes, that she was a native of that city. Her death certificate states, however, that she was born in Madrid. Nor did she ever have any more definite opinion as to her age, a fact which discredits her testimony. In the face of all this uncertainty it seems more reasonable to believe that Magdalena, as well as the other children of Leonor de Cortinas, was born in Alcalá de Henares. To reach any more conclusive evidence on the migration of the family to Madrid we must depend on an act executed in that city in 1569, and recording the depositions of two witnesses who were brought in to testify to the good name and purity of blood of the Cervantes family. These witnesses, apparently residents of long standing in the capital, state that they had been acquainted with the Cervantes for eight years, and if their affirmation refers exclusively to a friendship formed at Madrid, the inference is permissible that the family removed to Madrid about 1560-1561. This conclusion is strengthened by the fact that at this time Madrid was made the only capital of the Spanish realms, and that the definite removal to that city of the court and numerous members of the aristocracy attracted many citizens from all over Spain.

The opinion has also gained support that the Cervantes family as a whole lived in Seville about 1564; there is no convincing evidence for this supposition, but it may be worth while to state upon what grounds it is based. Rodrigo, the father, may be found there at that date, involved as usual in some suit regarding the rent due on certain house property which may or may not have been his, as the wording of the record is not clear. But we do learn that Rodrigo's financial state could hardly have been equal to the needs of a large family. It certainly cannot be definitely determined that his wife also was residing in the same city. Be this as it may, the assumption that all of the children were living in Seville during this period has given rise to the belief that Cervantes, at the time a youth of seventeen, was educated at the College of the Jesuits in the Andalusian capital. This institution is mentioned in very flattering and affectionate terms in one of his novels, *The Colloquy of the Dogs;* and whether or not Cervantes was recalling experiences of his early education, it is interesting to learn what he says of a boy's school days, presumably not unlike his own. Berganza, one of the canine interlocutors, is speaking of a merchant who had two sons—

one twelve years old and the other nearly fourteen, who were studying grammar in the school of the Company of Jesus. They went with some display, with tutor and pages who used to carry their books and what they call a *vademecum*, or portfolio. The sight of their going with such pomp, in chairs if it was sunny, and in a coach if it rained, made me consider and think of the great simplicity with which their father went on 'Change to transact his business, for he took no other servant than a negro, and sometimes he even rode a mule by no means well caparisoned. . . . The sons of my master left one day a portfolio in the court where I was at the time, and as I was taught to carry the basket of the butcher, my master, so I did with the *vademecum,* and I went after them with the intention of not letting it go until I reached the school. All turned out as I desired, for my masters, when they observed me coming with the *vademecum* in my mouth, craftily seized by the ribbons, bade a page take it from me; but I did not agree to that, nor did I let it go till I entered the hall, a thing which made all the students laugh. I went up to the elder of my masters, and, to my thinking, with much politeness I put it in his hands, and I stayed, sitting on my haunches at the door of the hall, watching with close attention the master who was lecturing at the desk. I know not what there is about virtue that, although so little or nothing of it has fallen to my share, I straightway derived pleasure from seeing the love, the discreet behavior, the anxiety and industry with which those blessed fathers and masters taught those children, strengthening the tender shoots of their youth so that they might not bend or take an evil direction in the path of virtue, which conjointly with letters they kept pointing out to them. I began to consider how they rebuked their pupils with sweetness, chastised them mercifully, animated them with examples, stimulated them by rewards, and overlooked their shortcomings with judgment; and finally, how they described to them the ugliness and horror of vice, and sketched for them the loveliness of virtue, in order that loathing the one and loving the other they might attain the end for which they were educated.

If this passage is sufficiently convincing to justify the belief that Cervantes attended the Jesuit College at Seville, careful reading of the works of the great narrator and an examination of the rest of his career must incline to the conclusion that his sojourn under the rigid and capable Jesuit fathers was brief. His writings give no evidence that he was ever well grounded in the studies which constituted the fundamentals of their curriculum, or that he was ever a student of the classics. In this field, which naturally involved a comprehensive study, as well as the constant practical use, of the Latin language, the Jesuits were unexcelled. But such evidence as may be deduced from Cervantes' literary ideas makes it not only likely that he never drank deeply at classical fountains, but that he even broke off his preliminary training, to use his own phrase, "at the very threshold of the study of Latin." Moreover the conditions of his home life can have permitted the parents to give their boys no more than a desultory, or haphazard, education.

In the absence of any definite facts regarding the whereabouts and education of Cervantes during his boyhood, other sources of information must be sought on which to base admissible theories. In 1566 Leonor de Cortinas, the mother of Cervantes, was residing at Madrid, where she signed a document empowering her husband, at that time with her, to take over the estate of her mother, recently deceased. The act is signed by her son Rodrigo, the younger brother of Miguel, but of the latter there is again no mention. Neither in this year nor in the following one of 1567 do we hear of him, and it is unlikely that he was living with his mother. A solution of the difficult question of his activities at this time may, however, be attempted. In 1576 a royal permit, issued at the request of Leonor de Cortinas, and granting her sixty crowns toward the ransoming of her two sons then in slavery, states that both had served in Italy and in Flanders, while the father, Rodrigo, asserted in March, 1578, that his son Miguel had been serving the king for ten years past. There is no reasonable ground for doubting these affirmations. Let us now look in the writings of Cervantes, our only source of information, for something which may be interpreted as corroborating the probability that he had already seen military service as early as March, 1568, and that he had served in Flanders as well as Italy. It must be always borne in mind that Cervantes' writings, more than those of most men of supreme genius, are so completely fused with the externals of his career, that a thorough appreciation of his creation is impossible without complete knowledge of the events of his life. In so far as there are in his works numerous autobiographical details which can be controlled and verified by other sources of information, the belief is justifiable that many personal experiences and actual episodes, unrecorded in any chance document, have found mention, however veiled or modified, in the course of his fiction. And where these supposed experiences are not in contradiction with the character, the history, or the general assertions of the author they are worthy of consideration.

From the career and unsatisfactory financial state of Rodrigo, the father, it is evident that he must have found it increasingly difficult to keep his growing boys at home, at least as unproductive or idle members of his household. For not only was this household at times migratory; but it was hardly productive of ease and comforts, and perhaps not always of the bare necessities of life. Any property which the father may have inherited from older, well-to-do generations must have passed out of the family's possession in Cervantes' youth. From the documents which have been preserved regarding the good practitioner, it is clear that he was not very skillful in managing his affairs, and this stricture is perhaps borne out by a statement in *Don Quixote*, in *The Story of the Captive*, a narrative admittedly full of autobiographical details and personal recollections. Here the Captive, a ransomed slave, as was Cervantes himself, says of his father, that in the general poverty of the community in which he lived, he passed for a rich man,

and he would have been so in reality, had he been as clever in preserving his property as he was in spending it. . . . My father went beyond liberality and bordered on prodigality, a disposition by no means advantageous to a married man who has children to succeed to his name and position. [I, 39.]

It is then natural to assume that young Cervantes was forced to look for some decent means of earning his own bread; and the usual course taken by families

who prided themselves on being of hidalgo extraction
was to avoid a trade, and to enter the services of some
aristocrat, or in default of that, some office of the government. An entertaining episode in the second part of
Don Quixote, the substance of which has all the marks
of a personal reminiscence, makes it seem possible that
Cervantes entered the household of some nobleman as
servant or page, that he found the service unremunera-
tive, and thereupon decided to enlist as a soldier. After
Don Quixote's descent into the cave of Montesinos,
where he witnessed such unexpected wonders, he, his
squire, Sancho Panza, and the cousin of an acquaintance
proceed along the highway in search of a resting place
and refreshments.

They pushed on towards the inn, and soon came upon a youth
who was pacing along in front of them at no great speed, so
that they overtook him. He carried a sword over his shoulder,
and slung on it a budget, or apparently a bundle of his clothes,
probably his breeches or pantaloons and his cloak and a shirt
or two; for he wore a short jacket of velvet, with a gloss like
satin on it in places, and his shirt hung out; his stockings were of
silk, and his shoes were square-toed as they wear them at court.
His age might have been eighteen or nineteen; he was of a
merry countenance, and to all appearance of an active habit,
and he went along singing a roundelay to beguile the weari-
someness of the road. As they came up with him he was just
finishing one, which the cousin got by heart and they say ran
thus:

> "I'm off to the wars
> For the want of pence,
> Oh, had I but money
> I'd show more sense."

The first to address him was Don Quixote, who said, "You travel very airily, sir gallant; whither bound, may we ask, if it is your pleasure to tell us?"

To which the youth replied, "The heat and my poverty are the reason of my travelling so airily, and it is to the wars that I am bound."

"How poverty?" asked Don Quixote; "the heat one can understand."

"Señor," replied the youth, "in this bundle I carry velvet pantaloons to match this jacket; if I wear them out on the road, I shall not be able to make a decent appearance with them in the city, and I have not the wherewithal to buy others; and so for this reason as well as to keep myself cool, I am making my way in this fashion to overtake some companies of infantry that are not twelve leagues off, in which I shall enlist. After that there will be no want of baggage trains to travel with to the place of embarcation, which they say will be Cartagena. I would rather have the king for a master, and serve him in the wars, than serve a court pauper."

"And did you get any bounty, now?" asked the companion of Don Quixote.

"If I had been in the service of some grandee of Spain or personage of distinction," replied the youth, "I should have been sure to get it; for that is the advantage of serving good masters, that out of the servants' hall men come to be ensigns or captains, or obtain a good pension. But I, to my misfortune,

have always served place-hunters and adventurers whose keep
and wages were so miserable and scanty that half went in paying
for the starching of one's collars; it would be a miracle indeed
if a fortune-hunting page ever found anything like reasonable
good luck."

"And tell me," asked Don Quixote, "is it possible, my friend,
that all the time you served you never received any livery?"

"They gave me two," replied the page, "but just as when one
quits a religious community before making profession, they strip
him of the dress of the order and give him back his own clothes,
so did my masters return me mine; for as soon as the business
on which they came to court was finished, they went home and
took back the liveries they had given merely for show."

"What niggard treatment," said Don Quixote; "but for all
that, consider yourself happy in having left court with as worthy
an object as you have, for there is nothing on earth more honorable or profitable than serving, first of all God, and then one's
king and natural lord, particularly in the profession of arms,
by which, if not more wealth, at least more honor is to be
won than by letters, as I have said many a time; . . . and remember, my son, that it is better for the soldier to smell of
gunpowder than of civet, and that if old age should come upon
you in this honorable calling, though you may be covered with
wounds and crippled and lame, it will not come upon you without honor, and that of such a kind as poverty cannot stain;
especially now that provisions are being made for relieving old
and disabled soldiers; for it is not right to deal with them after
the fashion of those who set free their black slaves when they
are old and useless. . . . Get up behind me on my horse as far
as the inn, and sup with me there; tomorrow you shall pursue
your journey, and may it be crowned with success." [II, 24.]

Manifestly we have in this episode something more than a mere "adventure." In the first place, the boy appears without any further reason than to permit Cervantes to express some personal ideas or recollections, the dialogue is a pure digression, for the youth after following Don Quixote to the inn plays no part there, and subsequently goes on his way. Again, not only the boy's age is striking, but the manifest connection which Cervantes establishes between the youth's choice of a career and his own past; it is no longer Don Quixote speaking, but Cervantes, who wishes to recall to the reader his unrequited services as a soldier, his scars, his poverty, his old age. None of these things apply to Don Quixote, nor to his purely bookish interests. Cervantes never tires of telling us that he was a soldier from the days of his youth, and the probability is very great that his first enlistment antedates any known facts of his career. A statement, no doubt emanating from his mother, that he had served in Flanders, was referred to above, and this possibility is greatly strengthened by numerous passages in his writings. The battle of Lepanto (October 7, 1571) may have been his first great action, but it is not unlikely that he had previously seen military activity of a desultory character. The Captive, in *Don Quixote*, already quoted, while speaking of his enlistment as a youth, tells of what befell him on leaving his father's house:

My own adventures during that period I will now briefly

relate. I embarked at Alicante, reaching Genoa after a prosperous voyage, and proceeded thence to Milan, where I provided
myself with arms and a few soldier's accoutrements; thence it
was my intention to go and take service in Piedmont, but as I
was already on the road to Alessandria della Paglia, I learned
that the great Duke of Alba was on his way to Flanders. I
changed my plans, joined him, served under him in the com-
paigns he made, was present at the deaths of the Counts
Egmont and Horn, and was promoted to be ensign under a
famous captain of Guadalajara, Diego de Urbina by name.
[I, 39.]

There may be something more personal in this than
we know. The growing opposition of the Netherlands to
Spanish rule, the famous "League of Breda," formed
in 1566 to wrest from the obdurate Philip II a recognition of their rights, and the departure for Flanders
of the noted Duke of Alba to crush the insurrection,
would, no doubt, inspire many an adventure-loving, patriotic lad to enlist in the king's service. Alba left for
the Netherlands in the fall of 1567, Egmont and Horn
were executed in June, 1568. It is not impossible that
Cervantes actually witnessed this act.

The selection of these particular features as of possible autobiographical value, is, no doubt, arbitrary, but
Cervantes has such a disconcerting way of mingling
fact and fiction that the reader is obliged to choose,
and his choice naturally falls upon statements to which
the author gives prominence by repeating them many
times in various parts of his works. Among them is that

relating to the young soldier, who, upon enlisting, has his first experiences in Flanders and Italy. But we know that Cervantes must have been in Madrid in the fall of 1568, as we shall see presently, and it is therefore essential, if he actually was in Flanders, that his own words should make plausible his return to Madrid, and thus give us some acceptable reason for it. To this feature of a return to the capital after his first military venture there are so many references in his writings that they cannot fail to attract attention. In *The Licentiate of Glass*, a story which has drawn a great deal upon the author's experiences, the hero, Tomás, a young student at Salamanca, is induced by a Captain of Infantry in his Majesty's service to go with him to Italy and enjoy the freedom of the soldier's life:

The Captain, who was called Don Diego de Valdivia, highly pleased with the good presence, ability, and frankness of Tomás, asked him to go with him to Italy, if only for the curiosity of seeing it, and offered him his table, and if necessary his flag, for his ensign had to leave him shortly, he said. Little was necessary to induce Tomás to accept the invitation, after holding, for a moment, a brief argument with himself that it would be well to see Italy and Flanders and divers other lands and countries, since long travels make men shrewd. In this journey he could at the most spend three or four years, which, added to the few that he had, *would not be so many as to prevent him from returning to his studies;* and, as if all was bound to turn out as he wished, he said to the Captain that he was content to go with him to Italy. But it must be on the condition that he had not to engage under the flag, nor place himself on the list of soldiers, that he might not be compelled to follow his banner. And although the Captain told him that it would not matter if he placed himself on the list (for in that case he would enjoy the aids and pays which would be given to the company), because he would always grant him leave as often as he chose to ask it, Tomás nevertheless replied: "That would go against my conscience and yours, Captain, and so I prefer to go unattached, rather than under restraint."

And a little later, after a detailed description of some Italian cities and an account of some experiences which befell him in journeys from Genoa to Naples, Venice, Milan and other cities, the author continues:

Thence he went to Asti, and arrived the day before the regiment began its march to Flanders. He was very well received by his friend, the Captain, and in his company and society he journeyed to Flanders, and reached Antwerp, a city not less of a marvel than those he had beheld in Italy. He saw Ghent and Brussels, and perceived that the whole country was getting ready to take up arms and enter on a campaign in the following summer: and having satisfied the desire that compelled him to see what he had seen, *he determined to return to Spain and to Salamanca in order to complete his studies.*

In this portion of the narrative, which is merely introductory to the story of the Licentiate, the details given have an importance for the reader only because they reflect the intense interest of the author in telling about them. Another reference to a preliminary campaign in the North of Europe and a return to Madrid previous to prolonged absence from home, may be found, as we shall see presently, in an important passage of Cervantes' *Persiles and Sigismunda;* and the idea of fortune-hunting in Flanders is brought out very prominently in *The Little Gypsy.* Preciosa, the heroine, tries to induce young Andrés, her lover, to give up his intended journey to Flanders:

I should like to succeed in persuading you not to depart, but to quiet your aspirations and to tarry with your parents to give them a good old age, for I am not in accord with these goings and comings to Flanders, especially in lads of such tender years as yours. Allow yourself to grow a little older, that you may be able to endure the toils of war; besides, you have sharp war in your house and sharp amorous combats assail your bosom.

It is, therefore, tempting to infer from all this that there is, indeed, a possibility that Cervantes as a youth enlisted in military service, that he saw some campaigning in Flanders and perhaps in Italy, and returned after a brief period to Madrid to continue his interrupted studies.

Whatever may have been the facts of his early career, we come now to the first reliable date, the autumn of 1568. At that time Cervantes was a student in the City School of Madrid, and although his advanced age of twenty-one makes his enrollment unusual, it would appear to be a very striking justification of the belief that he was merely continuing the studies interrupted some years previous. Could he not, as did the Licentiate of Glass, have returned to his country to exchange the lot of a soldier for that of a student or writer? At all events we now have some of his earliest poetic productions in a miscellany of memorial verses written in honor of Isabel de Valois, the third wife of Philip II, who died October 3, 1568. As was usual at the death of an important personage, many poets exercised their skill to commemorate the deceased, their productions being displayed in solemn public obsequies and not infrequently later printed in a collection. The latter was the case with the verse of Cervantes, which appeared in a volume edited by Master Juan López de Hoyos, giving an account of the Queen's last illness, her demise and the solemn funeral rites. This López de Hoyos was professor of Latin and of the humanities at the City School, and in the volume mentions Cervantes as his dear and beloved pupil. It is not known when the young poet entered his classes, although it has been ascertained that López de Hoyos's incumbency dates from January 7 of the same year, 1568.

The poems by Cervantes need detain us but a moment. They are, with the rest of the volume in which they are included, of mediocre quality, and, like most occasional compositions, have lost today such vitality as they may once have had. The longest contribution is an elegy, "written in the name of the whole school," and dedicated to Cardinal Espinosa; "in it, in elegant style, are

recorded things worthy of memory.'' The elegy, however, is full of commonplace sentiments. Invincible
death, we are told, has again won the victory over life,
spring has turned to cold winter, and while the Queen's
soul rejoices in perpetual glory, her body has returned
to earth. There is also the usual admixture of classical
references, which, according to the taste of the times,
did not seem to jar by the side of devout Christian sentiments. Apart from this influence of the ancients, it is
not evident that Cervantes copied with any conscious
effort such Spanish poetry as may have been known to
him at that time, with the exception of Jorge Manrique,
famous for an elegy on the death of his father, and the
great Garcilaso, remarkable for his purity of diction and
fine lyric gift. Cervantes imitated the technical and material features of Garcilaso all his life, without, however, equalling him in skill or inspiration. For Cervantes was never destined to earn any laurels as a poet,
however much he strove in this field to the end of his
career.

We know nothing farther of Cervantes' whereabouts
until December, 1569, when we hear of him in Italy.
Previous to this date, perhaps in the fall, he had written
home to Madrid asking that information be obtained
and legally recorded before a notary, to establish the
purity of his line, to show that he was of legitimate birth,
and without trace of the blood of Moors, Jews or con-
verts, that his family had never been investigated by the
Inquisition, and that he was of good old Christian stock.

The document, drawn up at the plea of his father, tells us nothing of the son's occupation in Rome, where he was at the time, but the request may have had the object of obtaining some worthy post. Years later he tells us he was chamberlain in the household of Cardinal Acquaviva. This statement has always been seized upon as the reason for his departure for Italy, the motives for which have never been made clear. Presumably by a mere coincidence, the same Giulio Acquaviva had visited Spain in the fall of 1568, as papal delegate, entrusted with a message of condolence from Pope Pius V to Philip II upon the occasion of the untimely death of the latter's son, Prince Carlos. Acquaviva returned to Rome in December, 1568, and most biographers of Cervantes have accepted without question the supposition that he accompanied the Italian prelate on this journey. But it is likely that Rodrigo de Cervantes, in drawing up, in the following year, the information regarding his son, would have made some mention of such an employment, had young Cervantes already been admitted to the service of Acquaviva. It is not possible to affirm that his acquaintance with the papal delegate dates from the fall of 1568.

Is it not conceivable that some other cause may account for his discontinuing his studies at the City School? Through a curious document first discovered some sixty years ago in the archives at Simancas, but generally disregarded because of the unquestioned acceptance of the above theory as to his departure, we learn of a grave occurrence at Madrid about this time. On

the fifteenth of September, 1569, a police order was issued to lay hands on a certain Miguel de Cervantes, condemned by default to have his right hand cut off, to exile
from the kingdom for ten years, beside other penalties,
''for having inflicted certain wounds on Antonio de Sigura'' while in the capital. The document adds that
according to information received the said Cervantes
was at large in Spain, and that he had been seen in
Seville and other places. The order permits the inference that the offense, a duel of some kind, had taken
place on an unknown previous date, that the offender
had successfully concealed every trace of his flight, and
that his whereabouts at that time were unknown. We
should not refuse to admit that this culprit is our Miguel de Cervantes, if the occurrence falls in with the
known chronology of his life, especially when his writings are full of references to just such an escapade and
to the subsequent flight from the country. The belief
that there was another man with the same name guilty
of the crime is based entirely on the theory that Cervantes had already left for Italy with Acquaviva in
December, 1568, and in an honored employment. It is
wholly unlikely that there was at Madrid and at the
same time another young man named Miguel de Cervantes whose offense should fit so admirably into the
career of López de Hoyos's pupil. When Cervantes returned to Spain twelve years had elapsed; and, owing
to the frequency of these quarrels, it is not likely that
the case was again brought out against him. Moreover,

the interesting episode of a similar duel and flight is
recorded, as we shall see, in the *Persiles*, the last novel
of Cervantes.   There we are told with great precision
that the culprit's escape from punishment after his return to Spain may be explained on the ground that his
opponent had died after becoming reconciled with the
offender's father, and that subsequently it had been established that no affront had been inflicted upon the
wounded man by the supposed offender.

In the course of the narrative of *The Little Gypsy*,
Cervantes introduces as a pure digression the story of a
young page, who, having been obliged to flee from Madrid because of the part he played in an unfortunate duel,
comes by chance upon the camp of the gypsies.   Preciosa,
the heroine, had seen him before in the capital, where
he presented her with some verse.

He spoke to me two or three times at Madrid, and even
gave me a very good ballad.   There he went dressed as a page
to my thinking, none of your ordinary pages, but one of those
favored by some prince, and in truth I tell you, Andrés, that
the lad is clever, well spoken and beyond measure upright, and
I know not what to think of his arrival in such costume.

This reveals nothing contrary to Cervantes' early literary inclination or a possibility of his employment in
some noble house, hinted at before.   The youth tells his
own story in these words:

I was in, Madrid, in the house of a man of title, whom I
served, not as a master, but as a relative.   He had an only

son and heir, who, both on account of the relationship, and because we were of the same age and in the same circumstances, treated me with familiarity and great friendship. It chanced that this gentleman fell in love with a lady of quality, whom he would, with the utmost willingness, have chosen for his wife, if his wishes had not been, as is the duty of a good son, subservient to those of his parents, who hoped to make a more exalted match for him. Yet in spite of all this he paid her court, out of sight of the eyes of all whose tongues could publish his inclinations. I alone was witness of his intentions. One night, which misfortune must have chosen for the fatality which I shall now relate to you, passing by the door and street of this lady, we saw close to it two men, apparently of good presence. My relative wished to reconnoitre them, but scarcely had he stepped towards them, when with much agility they laid hands on their swords and their bucklers, and advanced towards us. We did the same, and with equal weapons we engaged. The fight lasted only a short time, for the lives of our two opponents lasted not long, since they lost them by two thrusts which the jealousy of my relative directed, and by the defense that I made for him—a strange chance, and seldom witnessed. Then, having won a success for which we did not wish, we returned home, and secretly taking what money we could, we made off to the monastery of St. Jerome, waiting for day, which would reveal what had happened and lead to conjectures regarding the slayers. We knew that we had left no trace of our presence, and the prudent monks advised us to return home, and not by our absence to cause or awaken any suspicion against ourselves. Just as we had made up our minds to follow their advice, they warned us that the Alcaldes of the Court had arrested the parents of the damsel and the damsel herself in their house, and that among other servants whose depositions they took was a servant of the lady, who said that my relative used to wait on her mistress night and day. With this indication they had set off to search for us, and since they did not find us, but several indications of our flight, it became recognized throughout the capital that we were the murderers of the two gentlemen, as they indeed were, and men of rank. Finally, by advice of the Count, my relative, and of the monks, after we had been concealed a fortnight in the monastery, my comrade went off in the dress of a friar, and accompanied by a friar, in the direction of Aragon, with the intention of passing into Italy and thence to Flanders, until he saw how the matter ended. I sought to divide and separate our lot, so that it might not run the risk of taking the same road. I followed another direction different from his, and, putting on the dress of a servant of a friar, I set out on foot with a religious person, who left me at Talavera. Thence I came to this spot alone and avoiding the road.

Whatever modification of the real occurrence this tale may show, it is worth considering in the light of the above royal order and of other references to duels and flights. In one of the plays of Cervantes, *The Gallant Spaniard*, certain adventures of one Fernando de Saavedra—the name is worthy of note—are narrated by Margarita, whose brother has been wounded by him in a duel. Into this play Cervantes wove a number of personal experiences. Margarita's words are:

I told you, if my memory does not fail me, of an angry reply which my proud brother gave to a gentleman of rank, who to avenge himself, inflicted on him a grave wound. He thereupon fled, as I learned afterwards, and went to Italy.

The last romance which Cervantes penned, his *Persiles and Sigismunda,* was written with more warmth, more apparent interest in the narrative, than any other of his works, not even excepting *Don Quixote,* and it is, therefore, not surprising to find the story full of autobiographical details. This is especially the case with the history of one Antonio, a portion of whose career, although placed in the days of Charles V, must have been intended to reflect that of the author.

"As a good fate willed," says Antonio, "I was born in Spain, in one of the best provinces. My parents were of the lesser nobility; they brought me up in wealth, and I arrived at the threshold of my Latin studies, over which one enters into the rest of the sciences. But my star inclined me, although in part to a career of letters, still more to one of arms. At no period of my youth was I given to riotous living. Carried away, therefore, by my natural inclination, *I left my country, and entered service in the war* which the Emperor Charles V was at that time waging against some potentates of Germany. Mars showed himself favorable to me, I earned the reputation of a good soldier, the Emperor honored me, I acquired friends, and, above all, I learned to be liberal and courteous, for these virtues are learned in the school of Christianity's wars. *I returned to my country* honored and with means, intending to remain there some days in the company of my parents, who were still alive, and of friends whom I had left there. But that which they call fortune, I know not what it may be, envious of my peaceful existence, turned her wheel and plunged me from the top where I was placed into the depths of the misery in which I see myself. To accomplish her purpose she selected a gentleman, the second son of a nobleman, who had an estate near my native town."

Then follows a detailed description of a quarrel which ensues between Antonio and the young gentleman over an insulting manner of address which the arrogant nobleman uses in speaking to the narrator. There are again several references to campaigning in Flanders and in Italy, and Antonio continues:

"I, because I am the son of my deeds and of *hidalgo* parents, deserve to be addressed 'your grace' by any lordship, and whoever maintains the opposite—here I laid hands on my sword— is far from being a gentleman. Thus speaking and acting, I gave him two blows upon the head, so well directed that he was stunned and did not know what had happened, nor could he undertake his defense and avenge his injury."

The bystanders now take part in the quarrel, and Antonio is obliged to make his escape. After due preparation and having taken leave of his parents, he flees from the country and re-enters military service. With this last important detail the story of Antonio again becomes interwoven with the narrative of the whole romance, of which the reader will hear more in a later chapter.

The evidence is thus very greatly in favor of the theory that Cervantes was a soldier at an earlier date than known facts would indicate, and that his departure

for Italy in 1568 or 1569 may very easily be accounted
for if the affair of the duel fought in the Court, and referred to again and again in his writings, be given fair
consideration.   Although it cannot be stated for what
object Cervantes required the legal information, mentioned above, regarding his blood and family, nor at
what date he entered the service of Giulio Acquaviva,
the temptation to connect the two circumstances is very
great.   At all events, subsequent developments make it
likely that Cervantes was chamberlain to the Roman
prelate before the period of his Italian campaigns, that
the latter were not interrupted until 1575, and that he
entered his household in the spring of 1570 or a little
earlier.   He frequently refers to the limitations and
degradations incurred by one who serves in the ante-
chambers of the privileged classes, and it is not likely
that his stewardship with Acquaviva was of long duration.   It is certain that the enthusiasm for an effective
campaign against the arrogant encroachments of the
Turk, which was spreading at this time through Rome
and into many Christian countries, reawakened in Cervantes the spirit of the soldier and adventurer, for we
next find him enlisted as a man of the ranks in a Spanish
regiment in Italy.

CHAPTER III

OWING to profound racial and religious antagonism and to numerous political differences of long standing, the middle of the sixteenth century witnessed one of the many crises in the relations between the Ottoman empire and the Christian powers of the Mediterranean. When Selim II, who had become Sultan in 1566, determined on the seizure of Cyprus, at that time under Venetian rule, the Republic of the Adriatic, unable to withstand the Turkish power single-handed, turned at once for aid to the Pope and other Christian potentates. France and Austria were disinclined to take part in the quarrel, but the fervent plea of the Pope Pius V, an able and energetic personality, moved Philip II of Spain to promise Venice both naval and military assistance in her ensuing struggle with Islam. After some delay the fleets of the Holy See, Venice and Spain, at first united under the supreme command of Marco Antonio Colonna, attempted a preliminary campaign against the Turk in the summer of 1570, but the apparent lack of harmony among the Christian forces had proved fatal and they were unable to prevent the fall of Nicosia, the capital of Cyprus. This occurred in the month of September and was immediately followed by the investment of the fortress of Famagusta by the Moslem army under Mustafa Pasha. In the face of this irremediable disaster, and on account of the advanced season, the allied fleet broke off the expedition and returned to winter quarters at Messina and Naples.

It is not possible to determine whether Cervantes took part in this futile campaign, nor whether he had already enlisted at that time. His novel, *The Liberal Lover,* opens with a pathetic apostrophe to the fallen Nicosia, which has given rise to the supposition that he recalled therein the failure of the Allies to prevent its capture, and his own participation in the attempt. The most reliable information which we have regarding Cervantes' Italian campaigns must be gleaned from a bare outline of their history included in his memorial to the King; this was drawn up at his request twenty years later, and speaks of his services on sea and land, "particularly of the Naval Battle, where he received many wounds and lost a hand. And the following year he went to Navarino, and later with the expedition against Tunis and Goletta." Of these three events a few details may now be given.

With an outward semblance, at least, of harmony and unity of purpose the Allies proclaimed a Holy League at Rome in May, 1571, and the three fleets, Venetian, Papal and Spanish, were once more united, this time

under the supreme command of Juan de Austria, the
enthusiastic and popular half-brother of Philip II.
Their common leader was a youth whose personality
filled his men with religious fervor and stimulated them
to practical efficiency. The assembled armada left the
harbor of Messina in the middle of September, 1571, and
sailed east in search of the Turkish fleet. Cervantes,
then a young man of twenty-four, was enrolled in the
company of one Diego de Urbina, which formed part
of the regiment of Miguel de Moncada, and was embarked on the galley *Marquesa*. The Christian forces
were arranged in three divisions of the line, with one
reserve division, the right wing being commanded by
the Genoese Giovanni Andrea Doria, the left by the
Venetian Agostino Barbarigo, and the center by the commander-in-chief, Juan de Austria. One of the greatest
of Spanish sea captains, Álvaro de Baxán, Marqués de
Santa Cruz, commanded the reserve division. The *Marquesa,* at first a part of Doria's division, was before the
battle transferred to the left wing and shared with the
Venetians in the fiercest part of the attack. The fleets
met in the Gulf of Patras (an arm of the Ionian Sea, on
the west coast of Greece), near the mouth of the Gulf
of Lepanto, on Sunday, October 7, 1571. According to authoritative details the Allied forces consisted
of about two hundred and eight galleys, together with a
number of galleasses and sailing-ships, and carried between twenty-five thousand and thirty thousand troops.
The Ottoman fleet numbered more vessels, but they were

smaller and not so well equipped as the armada of the Christians. But a few days previous to the battle, the Allied soldiers had been informed of the surrender of the brave garrison at Famagusta, and of the unspeakable atrocities committed by the Turks, all of which may have been influential to no small degree in making them fight with unusual ardor and bravery. Before nightfall the victory of Juan de Austria was complete. The majority of the enemy's vessels had been sunk or captured, and Cervantes, writing with feeling of the episode in his old age, says that "there were fifteen thousand Christians, all at the oar in the Turkish fleet, who regained their longed-for liberty that day."

Cervantes never tired of referring with pride to that famous event and to the fact that he was present as a witness. We are fortunate in having some details of the part which he played, and since the importance of the action was greatly overestimated in his day, and its effect on the Ottoman power was practically negligible, the battle of Lepanto now owes its fame almost entirely to the participation of Cervantes. When the signal to open fire was given he was ill with fever and lying below decks, but he could not be kept out of the fray, and having been entrusted with the command of twelve soldiers at a post of importance and danger, he fought with great skill and valor. If he was proud of the share he had in the victory—"the grandest occasion the past or the present has seen, or the future can hope to see," as he says in his preface to the second part of *Don Quixote*—

he was even prouder of the gun-shot wounds which he received, two in the chest, and another which maimed his left hand.   Of this incident he says, while drawing a portrait of himself in the noted prologue to his *Novels*:

He lost in the naval battle of Lepanto his left hand, which was struck by a shot from an arquebuss,—a wound which, although it appears ugly, he holds for lovely, because he received it on the most memorable and lofty occasion that past centuries have beheld, nor do those to come hope to see the like —when serving beneath the victorious banners of the son of the thunderbolt of war, Charles V, of happy memory.

Before the end of October the Allied fleet had returned to its base at Messina, and Cervantes had to look after his wounds.   From statements made by companions it is probable that he passed a part of his convalescence at Reggio in Calabria.   His services had been marked by effective fighting and by gifts of leadership.   During the following year, 1572, he received on various occasions honorable mention in the more acceptable form of special grants of money, and an increase of pay.   In March his wounds were not yet fully healed.   But in April he had again enlisted in the service, presumably at Naples, as a member of the company of Manuel Ponce de León, which formed part of the regiment of a noted military leader, Lope de Figueroa.

Another campaign against the sea power of Selim was planned for the summer, and Cervantes' company put out to sea under the command of the Marqués de Santa

Cruz, who scoured the bays and inlets of the Greek Archipelago in search of the Turk. There is nothing more exasperating than an enemy who refuses to come out and be trounced; the wary Uluch Ali, mindful of the disaster at Lepanto, kept his fleet safely stowed in the harbor of Navarino, on the western coast of Greece, and neither there nor at Modoni, farther to the south, were the Allies able to approach his forces. Cervantes, who speaks with much regret of the failure of these operations, mentions with satisfaction and in some detail the capture of a hostile galley, the *Prize,* commanded by a certain Hamet. We may infer from his narrative in *Don Quixote* that he actually witnessed this victory:

On this expedition was taken the galley called the *Prize,* the captain of which was a son of the famour corsair Barbarossa. It was taken by the chief Neopolitan galley the *She-Wolf,* commanded by that thunderbolt of war, that father of his men, that successful and unconquered captain Don Álvaro de Bazán, Marqués de Santa Cruz; and I cannot help telling you what took place at the capture of the *Prize.*

The son of Barbarossa was so cruel, and treated his slaves so badly, that, when those who were at the oars saw that the *She-Wolf* galley was bearing down upon them and gaining upon them, they all at once dropped their oars and seized their captain, who stood on the stage at the end of the gangway shouting to them to row lustily; and, passing him on from bench to bench, from the poop to the prow, they so bit him that before he had gone much farther than the mast his soul had already gone to hell; so great, as I said, was the cruelty with which he treated them, and the hatred with which they hated him. [I, 39.]

The League was now dissolved owing to the defection of Venice and the incessant discord between the contracting parties. But Spain determined to continue the struggle, and in the summer of 1573 Juan de Austria set out to attack the Turks at Tunis. His squadron reached the coast of Africa in October, and captured both Tunis and its citadel, La Goletta. After reënforcing the garrison and erecting fortifications, on all of which items Cervantes dwells with apparent interest in his *Story of the Captive*, Juan de Austria returned with his fleet to Palermo. The precise location of Cervantes' company during the winter of 1573-1574 cannot be exactly determined, but it is probably that he did garrison duty at Naples and at Genoa in the spring and summer of 1574.

In the meantime the Turk had made ample preparations for the recapture of Tunis. Juan de Austria attempted to frustrate these plans, but was unable to succor the Spanish garrison in time, and both Tunis and La Goletta again fell into Moslem hands. Of no event does the Captive speak with more regret, and in his sorrow Cervantes no doubt bemoaned the fate of many a soldier known to him personally.

The Turks had to win the fort inch by inch, for the soldiers who defended it fought so gallantly and stoutly that the number of the enemy killed in twenty-two general assaults exceeded

twenty-five thousand. Of three hundred that remained alive not
one was taken unwounded, a clear and manifest proof of their
gallantry and resolution, and how sturdily they defended themselves and held their post.

The news of the disaster reached the expeditionary
force in October and there was nothing to do but disem-
bark the troops and send them to winter quarters. Cervantes was apparently stationed first at Palermo and
then at Naples, his regiment having been transferred
to the command of the Duke of Sessa, viceroy of Italy,
who in November, 1574, signed an order for the payment
of Cervantes' salary at Palermo. He was to participate
no further in campaigns against the Ottoman fleet, but
another year passed before his Italian sojourn came to
an end. In fruitless voyages and expeditions the Allies
had reaped the inevitable results of various years of
quarreling amongst themselves, and Juan de Austria,
with his hopes and ambitions of crushing the Turk shattered, and with anguish in his heart was transferred to
Flanders; the Turk, now unmolested, continued his ag-
gressions and piracies as before.

Thus there was nothing in sight for Cervantes but
garrison duty, and he was no doubt eager for promotion
and active service elsewhere. Having obtained leave of
absence, he was given not only a letter of recommenda-
tion to the King by the Duke of Sessa, but Juan de Austria, his commander-in-chief, also wrote to Philip II,
commending him for his merits as a soldier and urging

that he be granted the command of one of the companies about to be organized in Spain.

It is not possible to make any definite assertion regarding the amount of time which Cervantes spent during these latter years in the study of Italian culture and literature.   Occasion will arise later to speak of the distinct traces left by certain works in poetry and fiction, but it may be worth while stating here, that the influence of Italian society and learning on the works of Cervantes is easily overrated.   Nor would it be safe to assume that he had had the time to become profoundly acquainted with all things Italian.   His career had been that of a simple soldier, and his writings again and again indicate that he had neither the leisure nor the opportunity to study Italian letters.   He tells us that "he trod the streets of Naples for more than a year," he writes of visits to many beautiful cities, Genoa, Milan, Venice, Florence, Rome and others, he speaks casually of current customs; but woven into the pleasant sketches of what he saw may be discerned a trace of his chief recollections:

the cold endured by the sentries, the peril of the assaults, the terror of the battles, the hunger entailed by sieges, the devastation caused by the mines, and other things of this description which some consider as supplements to the burden of the military career—while they really are the chief constituents of it.

It was characteristic of the genius of Cervantes that he should, first of all, observe, and his mind more than

aught else was a repository of infinite pictures. But
they were moving pictures. He was concerned with the
details of the lives of men and women wherever he found
leisure to study them, and in his narratives regarding
things Italian he quickly abandons mere description in
order to take up the more pleasant rehearsal of life and
action. In *The Licentiate of Glass*, which contains more
of Italy than any other single story, we have some amusing descriptions of tavern life, of the movement and
color in the streets, of the outward appearances of har-
bors and cities; we meet references to church festivities,
to the routine observations of pilgrims in their rounds
to specific shrines, and to compliance with church cere-
monies, but nowhere do we find any extensive assimilation of the culture of the Italian Renascence. It is the
vast spectacle of existence that holds Cervantes' attention, it is the spirit of constant motion, the traveling of
his characters which interests him. From the nature of
his position his reading and study must have been of a
desultory kind. Perhaps all this can be best demon-
strated by giving the reader the pleasure of examining
for himself one of Cervantes' most characteristic pages
taken from *The Licentiate of Glass*. Of his hero Tomás
we are told that—

he admired the fair tresses of the Genoese women, the gentility
and gallant disposition of the men, and the admirable beauty
of the city, which seems to have its houses set in those rocks
like diamonds in gold. Next day all the companies came on

shore which had to march to Piedmont. However, Tomás did
not care to make that journey, but decided to go by land from
Genoa to Rome and Naples, as indeed he did, intending to
return by the famous city of Venice and by Loretto to Milan
and Piedmont, where Don Diego de Valdivia said he would find
him if they had not by that time carried off his men to Flanders, as it was said they would. Two days afterwards Tomás
took leave of the Captain, and in five he arrived at Florence,
having first seen Lucca, a small city, yet excellently built, in
which Spaniards are better regarded and indeed received better
than in other parts of Italy. Florence pleased him extremely,
both for its agreeable situation and for its cleanliness, sumptuous edifices, fresh stream and quiet streets. He stayed four
days there, and then set out for Rome, queen of cities and
mistress of the world. He visited her churches, adored her
relics, and admired her greatness, and as by the claws of the
lion his size and ferocity are known, so he inferred that of
Rome from her fragments of marbles, her broken and entire
statues, her shattered arches and ruined baths, her magnificent
porticoes and great amphitheatres, from her famous and sacred
river, which always fills its banks with water, and blesses them
with the numerous relics of bodies of martyrs who found burial
on them, from her bridges, which appear to be gazing one at
the other, and from her streets, which by their names alone
assume authority over those of any other city in the world, the
Via Appia, Via Flaminia, Via Julia, and others of the same kind.
Then the division of the hills within the city excited in him
no less admiration, the Cælian, Quirinal, Vatican, and the other
four whose names indicate the greatness and the dignity of
Rome. He also remarked the authority of the College of Car-
dinals, the majesty of the chief Pontiff, the concourse and
variety of races and nations. All this he admired and observed,

and gave to it due meed of praise. And after visiting the
stations of the Seven Churches, confessing to a penitentiary
and kissing the foot of His Holiness, laden with images of the
agnus dei and beads, he determined to go to Naples, and as it
was then a change of season, unhealthy and obnoxious to all
who enter into, or leave Rome, by the land route, he proceeded
thither by sea.

To the admiration which he felt from having seen Rome
he added that which the sight of Naples caused: a city in his
opinion and in that of all who have beheld it, the finest in
Europe, and indeed in the whole world. Thence he went to
Sicily and saw Palermo, and subsequently Messina. The situation and beauty of Palermo pleased him greatly, and so did the
harbor of Messina, and the fertility of the whole island, on
account of which it is rightly and truly styled the granary of
Italy. He returned to Naples and Rome, whence he repaired to
Our Lady of Loretto, in whose sacred temple he saw no walls,
because all were covered with crutches, grave-clothes, chains,
fetters, hand-cuffs, hair, waxen busts, and paintings. These
gave manifest proof of the innumerable favors which many had
received from the hand of God by the intercession of His
Divine Mother, who desired to magnify and stamp with authority
that holy image of hers by a multitude of miracles, in recom-
pense for the devotion which those pay to her who have
adorned the walls of her house with canopies of this description. He beheld the very room and apartment where was received the most exalted embassy, and the most important that
ever occurred, which all the heavens and all the angels, and
all the dwellers in the eternal mansions beheld, and comprehended not. Thence, embarking at Ancona, he went to Venice,
a city that, had not Columbus been born, would have had no
parallel in the world; thanks be to heaven and the great Her-

nando Cortés, who conquered great Mexico, that illustrious Venice might have some sort of rival. The streets of these two famous cities resemble each other, for they are both watery ways; the European, the admiration of the old world, the American, the marvel of the new. It appeared to him that the wealth of Venice was infinite, its government prudent, its situation impregnable, its prosperity great, its neighborhood cheerful, and, in short, all of it in itself and in its parts deserving the reputation of its worth, which extends to all parts of the globe; the workshops of its famous arsenal, which is the place where its galleys are constructed, along with innumerable other vessels, especially giving cause to accept this truth. The enjoyments and diversions which our curious traveller found in Venice came nigh to being those of Calypso, since they almost induced him to forget his original purpose. However, after he had been a month there, he returned by Ferrara, Parma and Piacenza to Milan, the workshop of Vulcan, coveted by the kingdom of France, a city, in fact, of which is said whatever can be said, its size and that of its cathedral making it magnificent, and its marvellous abundance of all things that are necessary for human life.

We have here impressions, penned many years later, of an Italian journey and nothing more. The translation, unfortunately, does not give an adequate idea of the quality of Cervantes' style, but the thought permits us to form a fair estimate of the response which his sojourn in Italy had awakened; it tells us what aspects of Italian culture must have aroused his sympathy or curiosity sufficiently to live on among the memories which he had retained. It is, therefore, not an injustice to Cervantes if the reader does not detect in such typical passages a marked trace of any historical or humanistic interest. Even the artistic features which he mentions are superficially treated. It is the same with the fourth book of *Persiles and Sigismunda,* in which the reader is taken through northern Italy to Rome. But this romance was written almost forty years after Cervantes' Italian experiences, and his reminiscences had acquired a vague and shadowy character. His attitude of mind toward Italian culture would, however, seem very natural in a young soldier who had, on the one hand, an incomplete academic training and, probably, slight learning, and, on the other, a surpassing interest in all the aspects of life about him. Yet it is not unlikely that during occasional hours of leisure Cervantes gave expression to his love of letters in writings now lost to us. This is to be regretted, for they would have thrown light not only on this question of Italian influence, but have revealed something of the course his genius was to take later to reach its prodigious height.

Thus Cervantes brought his experiences as a soldier to a close and, in September, 1575, together with his brother Rodrigo, embarked for Spain on the galley *El Sol,* belonging to a small squadron in charge of a prominent naval commander, Sancho de Leiva. We have had no occasion to mention Rodrigo since an earlier chapter, because his share in the Italian campaigns has not been definitely determined. Whether he was attracted to Italy by his brother's account of the glory gained at

Lepanto, or whether he too had a share in that action, is not known. We have Miguel's statement that Rodrigo took part in later campaigns, and it would be interesting to learn whether the brothers were enlisted in the same company. At all events, for a while longer both were to share the same fortune. They had not seen their native land for a number of years and were, no doubt, devising many plans to improve their careers at home; they were still young, Miguel being twenty-eight and Rodrigo twenty-five years old:

> The world was all before them, where to choose
> Their place of rest, and Providence their guide.

But an adverse fortune, by a single stroke, overwhelmed their hopes and expectations. The European powers, engrossed in constant quarrels with one another, had left the Mediterranean to the mercy of thieves and pirates whose raids obliged the people dwelling along the shores of France and Spain to live in constant terror. The galley, *El Sol*, which carried Cervantes and his brother, was proceeding westward along the coast of France in the neighborhood of the islands Les Saintes Maries, not far from one of the mouths of the Rhone, when, presumably by winds and rough weather, it became separated from the rest of the flotilla. It was beset by a number of vessels manned by Algerian pirates, and after long and valiant resistance, Cervantes, his brother, and such companions as had survived the unequal battle,

were made prisoners and taken to Algiers. The captain
of the Turkish flotilla was one Arnaute Mamí, while Dalí
Mamí, a Greek renegade, commanded one of the raiding
vessels; to the latter Cervantes fell as a prize of the battle. The letters which he carried from Juan de Austria
and the Duke of Sessa, and upon which he had, no doubt,
founded high hopes of preferment, proved his undoing,
for Dalí Mamí inferred from them that his captive was
a man of rank and importance.

Cervantes pathetically recalls this streak of ill-luck in
one of the many passages inspired by these tragic experiences. In his novel, *The Spanish-English Lady,* he
gives what must be considered a fairly accurate account
of the capture:

We embarked, and coasted along close to the land with the
intention of not running into danger, but when we arrived at a
place called The Three Maries, which is on the French coast,
while our first felucca was going ahead reconnoitring, unluckily
two Turkish galliots shot out of a creek, the one taking the
open sea, and the other keeping inshore; and when we were
going to beach our vessel, they cut off our course and took us
prisoners. When we went on board the galliot, they stripped
us to the skin. They plundered the feluccas of all they contained, and left them to run ashore, not sending them to the
bottom, but remarking that the vessels might do another time
to bring fresh plunder. You can well believe me, when I say
that I felt in my soul my captivity, and above all the loss of the
certificates from home, which I carried in a tin case, together with
the draft for sixteen hundred ducats.

And in his pastoral romance, *La Galatea,* we have a vivid narrative of a sea fight, and of the capture of Christians by this same terrible Arnaute Mamí. The episode, stripped of the novelistic variants with which it is mingled, was undoubtedly based on the fate of the galley *El Sol.* It is one of our best sources of information concerning her fate.

It happened then, that at the time the wind began to freshen, the busy sailors hoisted all the sails higher and assured themselves of a safe and prosperous voyage to the general joy of all. One of them, who was seated on one side of the bow, discovered by the brightness of the moon's low rays that four rowing vessels with long-drawn-out strokes were approaching the ship with great speed and haste. Instantly he knew that they were an enemy's, and with loud cries began to shout: "To arms, to arms, for Turkish vessels are in sight." This cry and sudden alarm caused such panic in all the crew of the ship, that without being able to take thought for the approaching danger, they looked at one another; but its captain, coming to the bow, sought to learn how large the vessels were and how many, and he discovered two more than the sailor, and recognized that they were galliots with slave crews, whereat he must have felt no small fear. But, dissembling as best he could, he straightway ordered the guns to be prepared and the sails to be trimmed as much as possible, to meet the opposing vessels; for he wished to see whether he could go between them and let the guns play on every side. Straightway all rushed to arms. . . . The enemy did not delay much in approaching, and the wind grew calm, which was the complete cause of our ruin. The enemy did not dare to board, for it seemed to them better to wait for the day in order to attack us. . . . As soon as morning came, a boat was lowered from the hostile flagship, sent to tell our captain to surrender, since he could not defend himself against so many vessels, and to threaten him on behalf of Arnaute Mamí, his general, that if the ship discharged a single piece he would hang him from a yard-arm when he caught him. . . . The Turks in four hours attacked us four times and as many times retired with great loss on their part and no small loss on ours. But not to weary you by relating in detail the things that happened in this fight, I will only say that after we had fought sixteen hours, and after our captain and nearly all of the crew had perished, and at the end of nine assaults they at last furiously boarded the ship. . . . Unconscious, I was carried to the enemy's flagship, where I was straightway tended with some diligence, for the captain had been told that I was a man of rank and of great ransom. Thus tempted by the bait of covetousness and of the money they might get from me, they looked after my health with somewhat more care. It happened then that, as my wounds were being tended, I returned to consciousness with the pain of them, and turning my eyes in every direction I knew I was in the power of my enemies.

Ransomed captives who returned to Spain were wont to give harrowing accounts of the slave trade of Algiers, of the wanton cruelty and merciless hardships to which slaves were subjected. Cervantes, as far as the available evidence shows, was spared these extremes, and even goes so far as to hint in his story of the Captive in *Don Quixote* that one of his masters, Hassán, never even struck him a blow. This may be fiction and not fact, but we have no reason to doubt it, and Cervantes, when he reached Algiers, probably fared better than he could have hoped. The number of slaves there at the time is not readily ascertained, but well-informed writers place it at more than twenty thousand Christians. Those who were expected to yield a large ransom, as was the case with Cervantes, were kept in prison, chained, or under duress and constant vigilance; others were given rude employments in the city or in the fields. They carried wood and water, they toiled on the highway and in the quarries, they cleaned the streets, and, yoked with the cattle, they worked on the farm lands, they were engaged in private service as well as public works. No punishment seemed too severe for untractable or fugitive slaves; Cervantes mentions on various occasions the horrors of crucifixion, impaling and mutilation.

In these new surroundings the adaptability and the experience that Cervantes had gained in a world of changing fortunes stood him in good stead, and he was soon recognized as a leader of men. No period of his life is better known to us, and the narrative of his activities during the five years of his slavery is worthy of a place by the side of the best adventures of his own creation. So far as our knowledge goes, he was never engaged in hard daily labor, from which he may have been spared by striking personal qualities, by his supposed social rank, and perhaps also by his maimed left hand. He seems to have found time for an occasional poetic effort, and he took part in the recreation of the captives, who organized theatrical performances and were glad to have the aid and contribution of literary talents. Dances and games relieved the hours of toil, and upon the days of important church festivities, such as Christmas, we are told by Cervantes himself in *The Prisons of Algiers,* the religious service was enhanced by music and followed by a play. He contributed two dedicatory sonnets to the work of an Italian fellow prisoner, Bartolomeo Ruffino, who in 1577 wrote a history of the capture of La Goletta and Tunis; he composed a letter in *terza rima* addressed to the secretary of the King, Mateo Vázquez, which will be mentioned later, and some stanzas directed to an Italian slave, Antonio Veneziano, and occasioned by a collection of the latter's verse. But he was chiefly occupied in devising means of escape for himself and his comrades, and the deep impression left by these schemes may still be traced years later when in *The Story of the Captive* he says:

In Algiers I resolved to seek for other means of effecting the purpose I cherished so dearly; for the hope of obtaining my liberty never deserted me. When in my plots and schemes the result did not answer my expectations, without giving way to despair I immediately began to search out, or conjure up some new hope to support me, however faint and feeble it might be. In this way I lived on immured in the building or prison in which they confined the Christian captives.

Cervantes' first attempt at flight was probably made in the spring of 1576, and the bitter memories of its failure are reflected in his play, *Pictures of Algiers.* The text of this drama has come down to us in a very unsatisfactory condition, but there can be no doubt that the sentiments voiced in it by captive slaves are throughout those of Cervantes. One of these slaves has resolved to run away owing to his insufferable existence. In the following scene he discusses his plan with a fellow slave:

First Slave: When I realize that I have a master as cruel as thou well knowest, and that he takes me for a gentleman, and that I have no means of gathering through alms the money which he demands of me, when I consider the unendurable life I suffer in hunger, nakedness, weariness and cold, I am determined to die by flight rather than to live this life of misery.

Second Slave: Hast thou thy knapsack ready?

First Slave: Yes, and I already have almost ten pounds of good biscuits.

Second Slave: But from here to Oran is sixty leagues, and thou thinkest of taking only ten pounds?

First Slave: No, because I have also made a paste of flour and eggs, mixed with honey and well baked, a little of which they tell me affords much nourishment; and if that fails me, I shall eat some herbs with salt, which I also carry.

Second Slave: Hast thou any shoes?

First Slave: Yes, three good pairs.

Second Slave: Dost thou know the way well?

First Slave: Not at all.

Second Slave: And how dost thou think of going?

First Slave: Along the shore.

This passage reflects the actual scheme according to which Cervantes and some of the fellow-slaves whom he wished to serve and liberate set out by land for Oran. He had hired a Moor as guide, but after the fugitives had journeyed several stages, they were abandoned by the fellow, and obliged to return to Algiers. There Cervantes was cruelly treated by his owner, loaded with heavy chains and guarded more closely than before. In *Pictures of Algiers,* the slave who flees to Algiers also fails, and the opening scene of the fourth act depicts him without shoes, his garments torn, and his feet lacerated by thorns and brambles. He laments his fate in a monologue which is deeply moving, if it be recalled that we are reading Cervantes' own experience:

This long road, this incessant passing through thickets and over mountains, the constant howling of wild beasts have brought me to a plight which can only end in death. My bread is soaked through, my garments and shoes torn, my courage spent; footsore and tormented by hunger and thirst, with failing strength I can no longer advance. My only refuge is renewed slavery under any one who desires again to capture me. I no longer know the way to Oran; neither path nor road can my sad lot discover, and too weary am I to follow it now. O thou, blessed and beautiful Virgin, that healest the human race, be thou the star to lead my poor bark out of the many dangers that beset it in this sea of pain and anguish.

In the summer of 1577 the family of Cervantes sent a sum of money for his ransom, but the amount, three hundred crowns, was considered insufficient for the older brother, and at his request it was used for the release of Rodrigo. The younger brother thus obtained his freedom in August, and returned to Spain with the secret plan of sending an armed frigate to carry away a number of Christians of repute, among them noblemen, priests, and men of learning with whom Cervantes had arranged the entire plot. Rodrigo carried out his part of the undertaking faithfully, and by the end of September a Spanish frigate appeared off the coast of Algiers to rescue his brother with his friends. The Christians had in the meantime been concealed in a cave dug for this purpose in a garden about three miles east of the city, and during a number of months their food was provided for them by the efforts of Cervantes himself. This difficult occupation seems almost incredible under the circumstances, and we are obliged to believe that the scheme was known to a number of Christians, perhaps to some well-to-do merchants who were willing and able to lend him substantial assistance in his plot without betraying it. A week before the vessel was due, Cervantes joined his companions in the cave. Upon its arrival the frigate failed to make an immediate landing, and the slight delay was fatal to the whole project. When a portion of the rescuing party went ashore two days later the plot had already been betrayed to Hassán Pasha, Dey of Algiers, by a Spaniard, El Dorador, whereupon Hassán sent "a large number of armed Turks and Moors on horse and on foot to capture Miguel de Cervantes and his accomplices." All who were found in the cave were seized and bound, and their ring-leader, Cervantes, who at once assumed entire blame for the plot, amid jeers and insults, was haled into the presence of the Dey. According to the affirmation of Cervantes himself, "the said Dey, with threats of death and torture, demanded the details of that business, but he [Cervantes], with much persistence, repeated that he was the contriver of the affair; and he begged his Highness, that if anyone were to be punished it should be only himself, for he was to blame for it all; and however many questions he was asked, he never named or incriminated any Christians." This statement, made before a notary, may, after this long lapse of time, have in it a slightly sanctimonious ring; but, as we shall see presently, it was made a few years later when Cervantes was on the defensive, and felt that he had to justify his conduct in Algiers. We may infer, nevertheless, that Hassán was greatly impressed by the culprit, for he bought him from Dalí Mamí and kept him under guard in his own prison, saying, that so long as he kept the maimed Spaniard under vigilance his Christian slaves, his ships and the whole city would be secure. This interesting bit of information has been preserved by a contemporary writer, Diego de Haedo, who, in his *Topography and General History of Algiers* (Valladolid, 1612) speaks at some length of Cervantes' deeds as a captive. The reflections for which Cervantes had ample time during the next months may have inspired the following memories of his experiences preserved in *Don Quixote*:

I passed my life in prison with several other gentlemen and persons of quality marked out for ransom; but though we almost always suffered from hunger and scanty clothing, nothing distressed us so much as hearing and seeing at every turn the unexampled cruelties which my master inflicted upon the Christians. Every day he hanged one man, impaled another, cut off the ears of a third; and all with so little provocation, that the Turks acknowledged that he did it merely for the sake of doing it, and because he was by nature murderously disposed towards the whole human race. The only one who fared at all well with him was a Spanish soldier, a certain Saavedra by name, to whom he never gave a blow himself, or ordered a blow to be given, or addressed a hard word, although the Spaniard had done things that would dwell in the memory of the people there for many a year—and all to recover his liberty. For the least of the many things he did we all dreaded that he would be impaled, and he himself was in fear of it more than once. [1, 40.]

The question arises, did Rodrigo or the other relatives of Cervantes make any immediate effort to repeat the attempt of freeing the captives? His family, although exceedingly poor, and though they had given abundantly of what they had to effect the release of Rodrigo, were making such additional efforts as they could to ransom Miguel. But they required time, and the renewed hardships, the confinement and the constant delay of the relief so ardently hoped for may have filled Cervantes with disappointment not unmixed with bitterness. For he says in *The Story of the Captive,* apropos of this very plan of securing liberty by purchasing a vessel in Spain:

Captives of distinction frequently had recourse to this scheme, paying the ransom of one who was to go to Valencia or Majorca with money to enable him to arm a bark and return for the others who had ransomed him. But he never came back as a rule, for recovered liberty and the dread of losing it again efface from the memory all the obligations in the world. [1, 40.]

It is generally assumed that in this year, 1577, Cervantes sent to Spain his famous plea in verse directed to Mateo Vázquez, urging that something be done by the Spanish Government to release the many Christians languishing in Algiers. The poem was discovered about sixty years ago, in some private archives and, if authentic, is the most worthy inspiration of all the longer efforts of Cervantes. It is characterized by striking sincerity of feeling, sonorous and lofty diction, and a spontaneity very rare in his lyric productions. The passage referring to his share in the battle of Lepanto may give an idea of the whole poem:

> These ten years gone I led a soldier's life
> > In our great Philip's service; now in state
> > Of sweet repose, now worn with toil and strife;
> And on that happy day when dubious fate
> > Looked on the foeman's fleet with baleful eye,
> > On ours with smiling glance and fortunate,
> Inspired with mingled dread and courage high,
> > In thickest of the dreadful fight I stood,
> > My hope still stronger than my panoply.
> I marked the shadowed host melt like a flood,
> > And thousand spots upon old Neptune's breast

Dyed red with heathen and with Christian blood;
Death, like a fury, running with foul zest
Hither and thither, sending crowds in ire
To lingering torture, or to speedy rest;
The cries confused, the horrid din and dire,
The mortal writhings of the desperate,
Who breathed their last mid water and mid fire;
The deep-drawn sighs, the groanings loud and great
That sped from wounded breasts in many a throe,
Cursing their bitter and detested fate.
The blood that still was left them ceased to flow,
What time our trumpets, pealing far and near,
Proclaimed our glory and their overthrow;
The sounds triumphant, ringing loud and clear,
Bore through the smitten air, in jubilant flood,
The Christian's victory from ear to ear!
At this sweet moment I, unlucky, stood
With one hand buckled firmly to my blade,
The other dripping downward streams of blood;
Within my breast a cruel thrust had made
A deep and gaping wound, and my left hand
Was bruised and shattered past all human aid;
Yet such was the delicious joy and grand
That thrilled my soul, to see the faithless foe
Crushed by the valor of the Christian band,
I hardly knew if I were hurt or no. . . .

Having for reasons unknown to us been spared the usual punishments, Cervantes continued to meditate over plans of escape. Five months after the abortive effort just described, he sent letters to the commanding general off the Spanish garrison at ·Oran as well as to others in authority, asking that trustworthy persons be sent to contrive his escape together with that of three others in the prison of the Dey. The Moor who carried the letters was captured and promptly impaled by Hassán, while Cervantes was sentenced to receive two thousand blows. We learn from his companions, however, that this punishment was not carried out, owing to the intercession of influential mediators.

One last effort to escape may be briefly recorded here. In the fall of 1579 a plan was hatched with some merchants from Valencia to purchase a frigate and rescue sixty Christians from among the foremost at that time in captivity. But the entire scheme was betrayed to Hassán by a mysterious personage, one Dr. Juan Blanco de Paz, a monk of the Dominican order at Salamanca. It is impossible to determine what grounds prompted the ugly act of the monk, but as a result of his treachery Cervantes, who had taken shelter with a friend, was again forced to appear before Hassán. This time he had his hands bound behind his back and a rope around his neck as if he were about to be hanged, and the Dey asked him to give an account of his actions. He again assumed all responsibility for the unfortunate plot, and, as on previous occasions, his life was spared, but he was remanded to further close confinement for a number of months thereafter. We have no reason to believe that it was anything else but his resourcefulness and undaunted courage which prompted his master to grant him his life. As a compensation for his act of treachery, Blanco de Paz received an escudo of gold (a crown, approximately $5 today) and a jar of butter, the latter having more the character of a penalty to those who know oriental butter.

In the spring of 1580 the clouds of Cervantes' imprisonment began to lift, and his fervent hope of release was slowly realized. In May two monks of the Trinitarian order, Juan Gil and Antonio de la Bella, landed in Algiers with the noble mission of freeing first those captives for whose release certain particular sums had been entrusted to them, and, thereafter, as many slaves as could be purchased out of the funds gathered for this purpose by their order. Hassán demanded five hundred crowns in gold for Cervantes, under which figure none of his slaves were to be had, since he rated them all as gentlemen and valuable prizes. In the meantime, through personal sacrifices and loans, through grants and impractical business schemes of which we have only imperfect details, Leonor de Cortinas and her daughter Andrea had succeeded in accumulating the sum of three hundred ducats (a ducat was worth five-sixths of a crown), destined for the ransom of Miguel. This sum was entrusted to the Trinitarians as early as July, 1579. To complete the whole sum necessary for Cervantes' release, one of the monks, Juan Gil, was able to add about forty-five ducats out of two special funds, and the remainder, amounting to two hundred and twenty crowns in gold, was obtained from merchants residing in Algiers. Hassán's tenure of office as Dey of Algiers came to an end in September, 1580, and he was about to leave for Constantinople; his slaves, among them Cervantes, had already been embarked when, at the last hour, Juan Gil was enabled to pay him the sum required. Thus the definite release of Cervantes was at last effected. The events just narrated seem more like features of a romantic drama than reality, and the timely salvation of Cervantes for a famous career of letters would be difficult to believe, had we not all the details from reliable contemporary evidence, especially from an account drawn up at the instigation of Cervantes himself, as we shall see. On September 19, 1580, exactly five years after his capture, the certificate of his ransom was signed, and he was free to make preparations for his return to Spain. The document adds the interesting personal touches that he was a man of medium size, with a goodly beard, and that his left arm and hand were crippled.

Another month elapsed before Cervantes set sail for home, and to the delay we owe the existence of a priceless document, which not only gives us infinite details concerning his life during the years of his captivity, but is the most reliable and complete picture which we have of the man and of his character. Juan Blanco de Paz, the monk who betrayed the last plot to escape from captivity, does not seem to have spent all the venom of his enmity in that inexplicable act of treachery toward his fellow Christians. He determined, now that the opportunity of ransoming a number of important slaves had come, to ruin by slander and blackmail the prospective career of Cervantes and others when, as free men, they should again set foot on the soil of Spain. "For the said Doctor Juan Blanco, seeing himself abhorred by all, shamed, insulted, and blinded by passion, threatened Miguel de Cervantes, saying that he would gather information against him, to make him lose all credit together with the pretensions which he had of getting preferment from His Majesty for what he had done and attempted to do in Algiers." To accomplish his purpose, he gave himself out as a commissary of the Inquisition, making inquiries into the lives and customs of those whom he hated, and he went even so far as to bribe those who could give him such information as he desired. Cervantes, no doubt, believed that such machinations might prove effective and destroy his chance for a career at home; he decided, therefore, to nullify them without delay. Before a notary apostolic who held his position by authority from the King of Spain, he asked that a series of twenty-five interrogatories be drawn up, itemizing the details of his life and illustrating his character from every point of view. The interrogatories have the prolix and monotonous character of all such acts, but they serve to make clear the circumstances of his captivity and his actions as a slave, notably his numerous efforts to liberate himself and many Christians in Algiers; they give an account of unusual acts of courage and self-sacrifice, and reveal Cervantes as a recognized intellectual and spiritual leader; they make

plain especially the facts that he had led a life above
reproach and remained loyal to the faith of the Spanish
Church, that he was held at all times to be of old Christian stock and a gentleman, and that he had associated
only with the worthiest Spaniards at that time in captivity. Twelve witnesses testified to the correctness of
Cervantes' history as embodied in these interrogatories,
at the same time discrediting the character and activities of Juan Blanco de Paz. But the motive for the
monk's enmity and betrayal, the history of his sojourn
in Algiers and his subsequent career still remain obscure. Nor do we know whether Cervantes ever saw fit
to make use of the evidence of this information to obtain
preferment at home.

On October 24, Cervantes was at last ready to
leave Algiers, in November he was at Valencia, where
he must have spent several weeks before undertaking the
last stage of his journey. At that city ransomed captives
were taken in charge by monks of the order of Redemptionists, and donning the pilgrim's long garment they
marched with bare heads in solemn procession to the
cathedral and gave thanks for their liberation. By the
middle of December Miguel de Cervantes had returned
to his family at Madrid. From Valencia he had written
the news of his arrival to his father, and we have in the
Persiles and Sigismunda a scene undoubtedly based upon
his own home-coming, although modified according to
his usual custom when incorporating personal recollections. Antonio, who in other respects embodies in his

career episodes from the life of the author, tells us how
after years of absence he again reached his home. He
plans to make himself known to his aged parents by de-
grees, lest the sudden shock of his coming prove too much
for them to bear:

One day, at dusk, the pilgrims arrived at Antonio's native
town, and at the house of his father, who, together with his
mother, was seated at the street door. Antonio addressed him:
"Is there, perchance, sir, in this place, an abode for pilgrims?"
"As the people who live in it are Christians," replied his father,
"all houses are so, and if there were none other but mine, it
would be large enough for you all. I, too, have some one near
and dear to me out in the wide world and I know not whether
at this moment he may not be looking for some one to shelter
him." "Perchance, sir," replied Antonio, "is not this place called
Quintanar, and do there not live here members of a noble family
called Villaseñor? For I knew a certain Villaseñor in distant
lands and if he were here, my comrades and I would quickly
find a lodging." "And what was the name of the Villaseñor you
mention?" said the mother. "His name was Antonio," replied
Antonio, "and his father, as I remember, was called Diego de
Villaseñor." "Alas, sir," said the mother, rising from her seat,
"that Antonio is my son, who, on account of an unfortunate
event, left his home sixteen years ago. I have ransomed him by
dint of tears, weighed my loss in sighs, benefited him by my
prayers. May it please God that my eyes see him again, before
I behold the night of eternal shade! Tell me," she added, "is it
long ago that you saw him, and left him? Is he well? Is he
coming back to his country? Does he think of his parents whom
he can see again, now that no enemies prevent? For those who

exiled him from his home have become our friends." The aged
father of Antonio was listening to this conversation; and, calling in a loud voice to the servants, he bade them bring lights
and introduce into the house these honorable pilgrims. Thereupon, approaching his unknown son, he embraced him closely,
saying: "For your sake alone, sir, and the good news you bring,
I gladly shelter you in my house, impelled by the custom which
I have of receiving all the pilgrims who pass." [III, 9.]

The final recognition scene is woven into the fabric of
the story. From the biographical details of Cervantes'
life thus far given, it is clearly apparent that he cannot
have had a large share in the customary routine education afforded by schools and universities. The completion of such a curriculum would have consumed a number of years, and it would be manifestly impossible to
find room for it. But many of his devotees seem loath
to consider the scanty education and haphazard culture,
which must be inferred from his career, an adequate
foundation for his enduring achievement. They consequently insist on seeking out some other period at which
Cervantes could have attended a university, and place
it at some time within the years immediately following
his return to Spain. The university selected for him is
that of Salamanca, because he refers to it several times
in his writings. There is, however, no sufficient evidence
upon which to base such a theory.

It would also be unwise to assume that Cervantes'
life as soldier and slave is indicatory only of an adventurous career. His extremely alert power of observa-

tion and his profound knowledge of humankind form the most acceptable substitutes for an acquaintance with books; his natural gift of expression which ripened steadily with the years was the sole medium he required to preserve for us the rare creations of his personality and of his experience.

CHAPTER IV

HE return of Cervantes to Madrid brings him to one of the most important moments of his career, the decision to substitute the fortunes of literature for those of military service. His choice cannot have been made immediately. Only the pressure of circumstances too great for him to resist must have forced him to adopt such a course. At home he could not have found those alluring conditions of ease and cheer which depend on entire freedom from financial embarrassment. His father and mother had grown old, and the distressing failure of Rodrigo de Cervantes to secure a hold, however precarious, on a few of the world's goods, had been further emphasized by the natural, but none the less deeply pathetic sacrifices of the family to obtain sufficient funds for ransoming the two boys from slavery. In this act of self-denial, the sisters, Andrea and Magdalena, had been involved, for Cervantes affirmed in 1590, in his memorial to the King, that not only his own patrimony and that of his brother Rodrigo had been spent on their liberation, but that "the entire property of his parents, as well as the dowries of his two sisters, now left in poverty, had been sacrificed." Though this was probably a slight exaggeration, his own situation was unquestionably difficult, for he returned from captivity heavily in debt. He owed money especially to Algerian merchants, of whom some had been instrumental in securing him his liberty, and others had advanced loans to him for food and clothing, "since his master left him to shift for himself." His first thoughts must now have been how to remedy the immediate necessity of his straitened circumstances. His brother Rodrigo had proved no breadwinner, and after his return from slavery had re-enlisted in the army. The social position of Andrea and Magdalena must have been as perplexing to the brother as to his biographers. Both had been involved in financial and other entanglements with a number of men, and though in justice to them any adverse judgment must be withheld, their relations with the defendants of the cases in which their history is preserved are not clear, and are somewhat disquieting. Andrea, the older, was living with a daughter, Costanza de Figueroa, whose father was Nicolás de Ovando, but she called herself subsequently the widow of a Florentine, one Sante Ambrosio. Magdalena was unmarried, and her history is no less enigmatical than that of Andrea, but the suits to which she was a party lead us to believe that they were wholly based on some vague history of unfulfilled marriage prospects.

Cervantes did not make a sojourn of long duration at his father's house, and perhaps his first inclination was to continue indefinitely his military career. He had a splendid record to fall back upon, and there was no other course for which he had received special training. His chief sponsor, Juan de Austria, was dead; even so it seems that his knocking at the official doors in Madrid was effective, although the result seems out of proportion with his merits. For in May, 1581, we hear of him on the way to Oran (on the African coast, opposite Spain) in the King's service, as a messenger with despatches and reports, presumably of a military character. By June he had returned to Spain. The memorial of his services states that both brothers, Miguel and Rodrigo, after regaining their liberty, re-entered the service of the King, "in Portugal, and in the campaign of the Azores under the Marqués de Santa Cruz." This has been interpreted to mean that Cervantes took part at this time in the military expedition to the Portuguese islands. This is unlikely, but if so, his enlistment must have been brief, for it would otherwise be difficult to reconcile it with his other activities and sojourns. At all events, his military career, so full of stirring episodes and so barren of practical achievement, was now definitely closed.

It is thus of importance in the narrative of his life, that we find him again at Madrid, certainly before 1583, engaged in his first literary ventures on a large scale, in poetry, fiction and the drama. The world of letters at

the capital offered him ample inspiration in a wide range
of productions. Madrid was at that time not only
Spain's chief clearing-house for every kind of literary,
historical and scientific work, but also the political center of a realm which extended with its far-flung bound-
aries across two oceans, and fostered innumerable eco-
nomic and social activities. Productions in art and
letters which testify to the intense esthetic and mental
interests of the educated classes of the Renascence continually saw the light. Notably the love of verse was
becoming current in all walks of society: poetry was
composed by artisans, physicians, lawyers, priests, aris-
tocrats of every rank, no less than by professional writers. Much of it became known through published
collections, but the custom handed down from the Middle
Ages, of circulating manuscripts from hand to hand,
still survived on an extensive scale. Indeed, by far the
greater part of the verse of the times became known only
in this way. Owing to the gradual disappearance of
numerous private libraries, many of which had been
gathered by distinguished noble families through dec-
ades and even centuries of careful selection, the amount
which has survived is small in comparison with all that
was composed in that fecund age. Productivity on so
generous a scale created a kind of communal spirit
among men of letters, so that informal societies and literary gatherings sprang up after the fashion of the
Italian academies. At the time that Cervantes began
his career in Madrid these meetings were becoming more

and more popular and widespread; poets of all kinds
associated under the protection of some nobleman with
literary tastes, discussed the latest compositions and
through the vote of specially chosen juries, awarded
prizes to the best verse. A man with the mental keen-
ness of Cervantes, with his unusual experiences and his
literary ambitions, would strive to become known in
these circles, and there is some evidence that he not only
achieved a reputation at this period as a poet, but that
he made the acquaintance of men of various professions.
It was the custom of writers about to print a book, to
solicit or to receive unsolicited from literary colleagues
some complimentary verse which was prefixed to the
volume. A number of works in widely different fields,
published during the next few years, are thus adorned
with sonnets and other poems from the pen of Cervantes. This fact may fairly indicate that he lived on a
friendly footing with the authors. He appears also to
have won a reputation for a gift of pungent satire, a
quality which he may have indulged occasionally in
verse now lost. This is to be regretted, for his great
works are relatively free from any such manifestation,
and it would be illuminating to see his compositions in
that vein. In an action brought a few years later, in
1588, against the great playwright, Lope de Vega, for
libeling a certain actor and his family in a satirical
ballad, the question of identifying the unknown author
involved the name of Cervantes. One of the witnesses,
one Vargas Manrique, a well-known poet, was called to

testify and gave this interesting evidence. "This ballad is in the style of only four or five poets who could have written it; it could be by Liñán, who is not in Madrid, or by Cervantes, and he is not here, and since it is not mine, it may be by Vivar or by Lope de Vega." This testimony permits us to infer that popular opinion rated Cervantes not only among poets of unusual skill but already ascribed to him a gift of pat characterization. Nevertheless, the qualities of malice and slander of the ballad in question were never traits of any of the pictures which Cervantes drew of mankind. In his *Journey to Parnassus* he says to Apollo:

> From tender years I've loved, with passion rare,
> The winsome art of Poesy the gay,
> In this to please thee hath been all my care;
> My humble pen hath never winged its way
> Athwart the field satiric, that low plain,
> Which leads to foul rewards, and quick decay. [IV.]

This statement must not be accepted without due allowance for poetic license, since, as we shall see later, two or three of his best sonnets are in the satiric field.

The fullest evidence of the profound interest which Cervantes took in the literary activities of Madrid during these years, especially in 1583, may be found in the *Song of Calliope*, a long poem which he inserted in the last book of his pastoral romance, *La Galatea*. The composition, written in octaves, is an uninspired catalogue of one hundred illustrious names of men still living at the date of writing, men active in the field of arms and of letters both in Spain and the Indies. It constitutes a valuable presentation of Cervantes' favorite theme, the achievement that may be gained by sword or pen; it reveals not only to what a large extent he was endeavoring to identify himself with these two activities, but it contributes a noteworthy chapter to the history of contemporary literature. A great deal of the poem is meaningless, perfunctory praise bestowed on names now wholly unknown; not a little is the uncritical expression of an inexperienced newcomer, of one who has fallen into the current vogue of compiling purely complimentary lists of prominent talents. But the *Song of Calliope* is important for this period because it speaks in no uncertain terms of the wide acquaintance which Cervantes already had with prominent names and representative productions. In the forefront must be placed his rehearsal of the chief poets, as evidence that he was already wholly engrossed in what was being written at that time. The list includes such names as Ercilla, the author of Spain's noblest epic poem, *La Araucana,* a work rehearsing the deeds of Spaniards in their conquest of the warlike Araucanians in South America; it tells us of the eminent lyric singers of the period, of Fernando de Herrera, subsequently known as the greatest of the Sevillian school of poets, and esteemed for his sonorous and eloquent vein; of the spiritual Luis de León, loftiest of the group of mystic poets; of Vicente Espinel, Cervantes' intimate friend, a gifted versifier and noted mu-

sician; of Baltasar del Alcázar, graceful and witty; of
Pedro Laínez and the "divine" Francisco de Figueroa,
whom Cervantes unites in his eulogy because the verse
of both reveals an exquisite appreciation of nature, a
warmth of tone and a sensuous richness of color. The
young playwrights who contributed to the literature of
the theatre are not forgotten, and the particular praise
bestowed upon them shows that Cervantes' creative talent had already turned toward an art to which he
remained devoted all his life. We hear of the chief
dramatists of the older classical stage, Francisco de la
Cueva y Silva, Juan de la Cueva, Cristóbal de Virués,
and Lupercio Leonardo de Argensola, who had no slight
influence on Cervantes' early efforts in the drama; of
Rey de Artieda, noted in letters no less than in arms, and
like Cervantes a participant in the chief campaigns
against the Turk; and of the greatest of them all, Lope
de Vega, at that time still a youth, but already known
for his rare facility in lyric and dramatic composition.
Among the writers of romance Cervantes gives a place
of honor to two authors of pastoral stories, Gálvez de
Montalvo and Gil Polo. This is of special interest because at the time when the *Song of Calliope* was written
the admiration of Cervantes was directed chiefly to that
type of fiction. Of Montalvo, his friend and author of
Filida's Shepherd, he speaks in these terms:

> Who could the praises, shepherds mine, recite
> Of him ye love, a shepherd crowned by fame,

> Brightest of all the shepherds that are bright,
> Who is to all known by Filida's name?
> The skill, the learning and the choice delight,
> The rare intelligence, the heart of flame,
> Of Luis de Montalvo aye assure
> Glory and honor whilst the heavens endure.

And of Gil Polo we are told that he deserves in his single person all the eulogies bestowed upon other men of genius.

To the student of today the praise meted out indiscriminately to these hundred notables makes dry and repetitious reading, but it leads us naturally to a consideration of Cervantes' first literary publication of real worth, *La Galatea,* which included the *Song of Calliope,* and to a careful examination of the earliest fruits of his great narrative genius. The interesting question at once arises with regard to Cervantes' choice of the pastoral type as a vehicle for his effort as a novelist. The answer is not far to seek. Cervantes was still at the beginning of his literary career, he was as yet under the influence of his literary environment, restrained by the force of tradition and the prestige of the foremost narrative models of his day. It was hard to shake off the yoke of public taste or academic authority in a circle of writers whose efforts took color from one another's works. The external frame, as well as the thoughts, in short, the artistic formula which constituted the accepted mould for imaginative creations, was questioned by no one, nor was the genius of Cervantes mature enough to

break it. Nevertheless, the models from which he could
have obtained a suggestion for narrative fiction were
numerous and it is, therefore, of interest to speculate
why he chose the pastoral form.

Among the novelistic types popular at the time the
foremost place in bulk, if not in quality, was held by
the romance of chivalry, a form of tale widely read
throughout the sixteenth century. The clear vision of
Cervantes saw its approaching doom, to which he himself was to contribute so largely in the immortal satire
of *Don Quixote*. He, therefore, could never have
thought of imitating it in any serious vein, with its
fantastic and grotesque conception of individual prowess, its absence of truth in the delineation of martial
deeds, its formless and verbose prose. Nor was he as
yet attracted by two great realistic masterpieces of
which we shall hear more later, the famous love-story of
Calisto and Melibea, better known under the title of the
Celestina, and the earliest Spanish rogue story, the
Lazarillo de Tormes. Cervantes himself was to become
one of the noblest of realists in the history of the novel,
and it is thus astonishing that two such rare models in
dialogue and minute portraiture did not yet influence
his creation. It is likely that his recent experiences with
the world of action, with events and facts which involved
spiritual unrest together with physical and mental suffering of every description, impelled him to seek repose
in another extreme, in an idealized world of peace and
innocence, in the expression of a golden age conceived

in the dreams of harassed mankind and referred to by
Cervantes on many a page of his books. There is a very
manifest desire on his part to express himself for the
time being in some poetic form for which the accurate
psychological painting of character, the masterful dialogue, the natural and undisguised sentiments of the
Celestina could furnish inspiration as little as the worldliness, the bald, unadorned prose, the crass, unemotional
pen-pictures of the *Lazarillo de Tormes*. Other minor
types of fiction existed, such as jest-books and miscellanies, but in so far as they are utterly devoid of art
either in their diction or narrative, and are for the most
part little more than frigid compilations of unoriginal
material, it is natural that they were not taken seriously
by Cervantes at this or at any period of his career. For
the present he was dominated by his love for the pastoral
novel, and in this taste he was but one of the vast body
of Spanish readers of fiction, among whom prose and
verse of the bucolic strain had found sincere welcome
and appreciation.

The creation of works inspired by the life of shepherds, by the spirit of the woods and fields, by the contrast between the commonplace existence of towns and
cities and the charm, real or imagined, of rural life has
an extensive history in Spain as elsewhere. But we are
concerned with only such names or literary influences
as may be directly related to Cervantes and the origins
of *La Galatea,* and these do not take us far afield. In
poetry, Garcilaso had from Cervantes' early youth been

his foremost model in poetic expression of any kind. In particular his *Eclogues,* which embodied the choicest imitation of the bucolic vein of classic authors, especially of Virgil, and of prominent Italian poets of the Renascence, have merited their enduring fame. Nowhere has the pastoral spirit received a loftier expression, in no Spanish poet has beauty of style been more harmoniously fused with the tone and color, the serene air of sun-lit hillside or rolling meadow. Garcilaso gives typical expression to a shepherd's lament in the following song:

> Oh thou, more obdurate than marble to my complaint,
> And to the hidden fire in which I am consumed,
> Colder than snow art thou, oh Galatea!
> I am dying, but life I fear;
> I fear it rightly since thou leavest me,
> And without thee life no longer hath its lure.
>
>   *   *   *   *   *   *   *
>
> For thee the silence of the shady woods,
> For thee seclusion and the loneliness
> Of the solitary mountains I desired,
> For thee the green expanse, the freshening wind,
> The white lily and the glowing rose
> And sweet Spring I loved.

This is the spirit incarnate of the poetic tales of shepherds and shepherdesses, in which things of this world underwent a complete transformation into a life marked by simplicity, by the absence of corruption and common vice. In prose narratives, however, this presentation had to be given more body, and worldliness with its manifestations of jealousy, hatred and revenge, derived from other types of fiction, soon crept in.

In the field of the pastoral novel the best known work is the *Diana* of a Portuguese, Jorge Montemayor, who wrote his romance in Spanish about the middle of the sixteenth century. His story, by no means the best of its type, owes its wide reputation to two reasons. It was the first to transplant to Spanish soil the art of Boccaccio's *Ameto* and Sannazaro's *Arcadia*, which combined the novel procedure of mingling verse and prose; and, in the second place, as a pioneer, it exerted the widest influence upon subsequent pastoral tales, not only in Spain, but in France, England and Germany. The love story of Diana and Sireno has positive charms, and would be readable to-day if we could assume the uncritical point of view and enjoy the leisure of sixteenth-century readers. Montemayor has a gift of narrative, while lacking that of construction; individual episodes have merit, but his story as a whole is something of a labyrinth, and the plot cannot proceed without the usual borrowings of pagan touches, nymphs and satyrs, witchcraft and enchantment, together with the shepherd's crook and the pipe of Pan. Moreover, Montemayor was not a great poet; he lacked the profound sincerity of emotion necessary for a convincing interpretation of nature and the rural surroundings of his characters. He was purely an innovator in Spanish, and the source of inspiration in others. His story breaks off in an unsatisfactory way; the lovers are parted by enchantment, and Diana, instead of marrying her lover, Sireno, becomes united to Delio, a character of inferior worth and importance. This close is supposed to reflect an unhappy episode in the poet's life, and while it may constitute good realism, makes bad fiction. Don Quixote had the *Diana* in his library, and in the chapter which deals with the latter in detail Cervantes characterizes the romance with acumen, but with a severity unexpected from one who had freely imitated its diction and plot:

> Since we are beginning our examination with the *Diana* of Montemayor, I am of the opinion that it need not be burned, but that it be freed from all that portion which deals with the learned Fabia, and the enchanted water, and almost all of his verses of the *arte mayor,* and let the book retain its prose and the honor of being the first of similar books. [1, 6.]

The unsatisfactory close of the *Diana* immediately prompted other poets to write a continuation of the heroine's story, with the purpose of getting the intruding husband out of the way and uniting Diana with the hero of the tale. By far the best of these sequels is the *Diana in Love* of Gaspar Gil Polo, a genuine poet, who succeeded in composing the most exquisite of all Spanish pastoral romances. Cervantes, after damning Montemayor with faint praise, recommends in a characteristic pun that Gil Polo's work be preserved as though it were by Apollo himself. The romance is not superior to

Montemayor's *Diana* in construction, but the touch of the
poet, in his prose no less than in his unsurpassed verse,
gives the narrative a spirit of youthfulness, of sincerity,
of inspiration, of beauty, which the centuries that have
elapsed since it was written have hardly diminished.
Gil Polo's tale far more than Montemayor's belongs to
the class of the adventure story: its episodes tell of
violent separations and unexpected recognition scenes,
there are shipwrecks and combats with pirates, all of
which combined with Cervantes' own experiences to
prompt a number of similar events in *La Galatea*. In
Gil Polo the bucolic vein of Garcilaso is most worthily
continued:

> Come with me to the sweet woods,
> And to their welcome shade
> Filled with scented flowers,
> Where even on brightest days
> Summer cannot offend.
> And if cool waters please thee more
> I know of a rare fountain.

We may assume that Cervantes was already engaged
in writing *La Galatea* when his friend Luis Gálvez de
Montalvo printed a pastoral tale *Filida's Shepherd*
(1582), and the work is so unlike its predecessors that
it deserves mention. Although dealing with shepherds
and rural scenes, it has a more courtly, refined and original tone, because of its dignified, unemotional prose and
highly cultivated diction. Cervantes himself, aware of

its striking distinctiveness, says of Filida's lover in
Don Quixote: "This is no shepherd, but a very polished
courtier and the book deserves to be kept like a precious
jewel." Montalvo included in his book relatively more
verse than his forerunners in this genre, and manifested
great variety and skill in the meter; a number of the
poems reveal spontaneous inspiration and love of nature. But Montalvo was not free from the growing
vogue of figured and dark speech, conceits, artifical
thoughts and even metaphysical turns, thus furnishing
examples which Cervantes followed in his *Galatea*. The
prose narrative of Montalvo has the qualities of a contemporary tapestry, the rural landscape of which presents an admirable picture of faded woods and dimmed
sunlight, adorned but hardly animated by sitting and
standing figures; so greatly do reflection, description
and discourses in prose and verse dominate the little
action which the story contains. These three pastoral
romances, then, the *Diana* of Montemayor, the sequel by
Gil Polo, and *Filida's Shepherd* by Montalvo, were Cervantes' chief models; in them may be found an abundance of material which contributed to the composition
of *La Galatea*.

It is difficult to say when Cervantes began his tale.
It may be assumed that most, if not all of it, was written in 1582 and 1583. It was completed by February,
1584, when it was licensed for press, and a few finishing
touches may have been added between that date and its
publication in the spring of 1585. *La Galatea* was a

compromise between the natural dictates of Cervantes'
talent to express himself in prose and his incessant desire
to compose verse like every other poet; it was a *tour
de force* which tried out all the refinements and com-
plexities of Castilian speech in a select and poetic vein.
To the inexhaustible treasure of its unadorned, everyday language Cervantes was to give the most satisfactory expression only in his later masterpieces. His
taste at this period is illuminated by his preface, in which
he rebukes "the narrow souls who desire to check the
copiousness of the Castilian tongue by the conciseness
of our ancient speech," whereas they ought to "understand that it offers a field open, easy and spacious, which
they can freely traverse with ease and sweetness, with
gravity and eloquence, discovering the variety of acute,
subtle, weighty, and elevated thoughts which, because
of the fertility of Spanish men of genius, Heaven's favorable influence has produced with such profit in different
parts, and every hour is producing in this happy age of
ours."

In this spirit *La Galatea* was written, with the author's
attention fixed upon the language and thought rather
than upon its structure. The plot cannot be given in a
brief résumé, nor any adequate idea of the main characters. Of these there are many, but they are generally
marked by very few distinctive traits. The story turns
entirely upon the loves of shepherds and shepherdesses,
of whom the chief are Elicio and Galatea, Damon and
Amarili, Lauso and Silena, Tirsi and Fili, the course of

their affections being for the greater part inextricably interwoven. *La Galatea* is divided into six books and was left unfinished, perhaps in imitation of some of Cervantes' predecessors, notably Gil Polo, who promised a sequel to *Diana in Love*, and Montalvo, who does not bring the courtship of his hero, Siralvo, to any conclusion. To the very end of his long life Cervantes did not give up the idea of writing a second part, for on the last page which he penned, that noble dedication of his romance, *Persiles and Sigismunda*, to the Count of Lemos, he still expresses the hope of completing Galatea's story. Among the books of fiction possessed by Don Quixote was Cervantes' pastoral, and when it was brought out for scrutiny, he emphasized the unfinished character of the work, and humorously alludes to his difficulty of continuing a novel so wholly dependent on poetic inspiration:

"What book is the next?"

"The *Galatea* of Miguel de Cervantes," said the barber.

"That Cervantes has been for many years a great friend of mine, and to my knowledge he has had more experience in reverses than in verses. His book has some good invention in it; it presents us with something but brings nothing to a conclusion: we must wait for the second part it promises. Perhaps with amendment it may succeed in winning the full measure of indulgence that is now denied it. And in the meantime do you, my friend, keep it shut up in your own quarters." [I, 6.]

Nevertheless *La Galatea* had won favor among many

readers; it is mentioned in contemporary plays more than
any other of the author's creations. Its extensive popularity, even in foreign parts, is also vouched for by the
official censor who signed the approval to print the
second part of *Don Quixote* in February, 1615. In it
we are told that certain French gentlemen who had come
to Spain in the company of the Ambassador of France
showed themselves to be warm friends of polite letters.
They inquired what books of note were at that time
in favor:

Scarcely had they heard the name of Miguel de Cervantes,
when they grew lavish in their praises of him, dwelling upon
the esteem which his works enjoyed not only in France but in
neighboring countries, and they mentioned the *Galatea,* which
some of them knew almost by heart, the first part of *Don Quixote,* and the *Novels.*

Exaggerated as the praise of these foreign gentlemen
may seem to us now, there was, no doubt, a kernel of
truth in it, if we may judge from the popularity at that
epoch of D'Urfé's *Astrée,* Spenser's *Shepherds' Calendar,* and especially the poetic but fantastic *Arcadia* of
Sir Philip Sidney. A very brief description of *La
Galatea* may throw some light on the literary taste of
these readers. Its absence of plot may be amply illustrated by giving, as an example of its static qualities, a
single day out of the life of these shepherds. We first
hear of the love of Elicio for Galatea, both of whom
dwell on the banks of the Tagus. This stream was

chosen by Cervantes, no doubt, for the locality of his romance, because it is the only river in central Spain with any water in it all the year round:

It must not be thought of Galatea that she despised Elicio, still less that she loved him, for at times almost persuaded, as it were, and overcome by the many services of Elicio, she with some modest favor would raise him to heaven; and at others, without taking account of this, she would disdain him in such wise that the lovesick shepherd scarce knew his lot. The excellencies and virtues of Elicio were not to be despised, nor were the beauty, grace and goodness of Galatea not to be loved. On the one hand, Galatea did not wholly reject Elicio; on the other, Elicio could not, nor ought he to, nor did he wish to forget Galatea.

This makes the opening situation sufficiently indefinite not to compromise the author and oblige him to bring their loves to a hurried close. After Elicio has "communicated his complaints to heaven with a voice of exceeding beauty," another shepherd also in love with Galatea appears, and we have a dialogue in verse, accompanied by pipe and rebeck. Their idyllic strains are harshly and unexpectedly brought to a close:

Erastro was already setting himself to continue in his song when they perceived, on a thickly wooded hillock which was at their back, no slight clamor and sound. Both rose to their feet to learn what it was and they saw a shepherd descending from the mountain, running at the greatest speed in the world, with a naked knife in his hand, and the hue of his countenance changed; and coming after him, another shepherd, swift of foot, who in a few strides overtook the first, and seizing him by the collar of his leather coat, raised his arm in the air as high as he could, and a sharp dagger which he carried unsheathed, and burying it twice in his body he said:

"Receive, O ill-starred Leonida, the life of this traitor which I offer up in vengeance of your death."

This happened with such rapidity that Elicio and Erastro had not the opportunity to stop him; for they came up at the time when the stricken shepherd was already giving out his last breath, struggling to utter these few ill-formed words:

"Would that you had allowed me, Lisandro, to satisfy Heaven with a longer repentance for the wrong I did you, and had then taken from me the life which, for the reason I have said, now departs from this flesh ill-content."

And without being able to say more, he closed his eyes in ever-lasting night. By these words Elicio and Erastro fancied that for no small cause had the other shepherd inflicted on him so cruel and violent a death.

The astonished reader of *La Galatea* is inclined to agree with them, but is no less grateful for the interruption than he is shocked at the savage action of Lisandro, "for such is the murderer's luckless name." This bloodthirsty episode in a pastoral tale seems at first incongruous, but it was a distinct trick in the technique of bucolic narrative, derived from tales of adventure, to break off a quiet scene with something intended, no doubt, to stimulate the reader's interest, and to give the writer the opportunity of introducing a new tale. In this case it is the story of Lisandro's life which we

now hear, together with the cause of his unhappy deed.
His narrative is, in brief, a tragic love story, presumably based on some Italian tale in which the lovers belong to hostile families, as was the case with Romeo and Juliet in Shakespeare and in his Italian source.
The history of Lisandro and similar stories intercalated in *La Galatea* constitute its best parts and give the most satisfactory idea of Cervantes' beginning as a real narrator. His pen acquires genuine vitality and there are occasional pages not unworthy of his later *Novels*. The tears evoked by the story of Lisandro and by every tragic or pathetic event in *La Galatea* have been unduly criticized, for they are not only common in all tales of love and adventure of the Renascence, but they have a sound classic origin. The heroes of Homer and Virgil poured forth their tears by the waves of the resounding beach, the sturdy warriors of Italian and Spanish romances of chivalry wept copiously, and there is no reason for taking umbrage at these purely literary tears.

Galatea now enters with her flock, and after an amorous discussion there is another interruption by a pathetic shepherdess, Teolinda, whose tale forms a pendant to the episode of Lisandro. Her entrance is a stilted mixture of the pathetic and the dramatic for ''she stopped from time to time, and raising her eyes to heaven, uttered sighs so piteous that they seemed to be torn from her innermost soul.'' She proceeds to the brink of the stream and apostrophizes the water running by:

"How little avails your coolness to temper the fire I feel in my soul. Vain will it be to hope from you, or indeed from all the waters of the mighty ocean the remedy I need. . . . Ah, sad eyes, cause of my ruin! To how lofty a height did I raise you for so great a fall! Ah, fortune, enemy of my repose, with what haste didst thou hurl me from the pinnacle of my joy to the abyss of misery wherein I lie. . . ." All that the shepherdess said she mingled with such tears, that no heart could listen to her and not be moved with compassion.

Galatea and her companion, Florisa, show the required sympathy, and after the hapless Teolinda ''has calmed her sorrowing breast to the sound of the waves gently flowing by'' in a song adapted to her purpose from an older lyric of the fifteenth century, we have the story of her true love and how it failed to run smooth. Her tale is left unfinished, thereby giving the author an opportunity to continue the same thread on the following day.

Thus into the fabric of *La Galatea* are introduced, one after the other, a multitude of shepherds and shepherdesses who are all skilled in singing or reciting verse, and who discourse in the most carefully worded of Renascence styles. The chief characters seem devoid of any real blood because we are no longer aware of the secondary interest which attached to them in the days of Cervantes. This interest lay in the fact that they represented friends of the author's circle whom he introduced in a pastoral disguise. Thus Tirsi is Francisco de Figueroa; Siralvo, Gálvez de Montalvo; Crisio, Cristóbal de Virués; Artidoro, Rey de Artieda; Damón may be Pedro Laínez, and Lauso, Cervantes himself. This mystifying feature was no innovation on the part of Cervantes, for it had been employed by his predecessors, especially Montemayor and Montalvo, presumably because Sannazaro had done so in his *Arcadia*. Consequently, the first and most natural criticism that shepherds never spoke or discussed as do the characters of *La Galatea* is answered at the outset by Cervantes in his prologue:

I shall not have much fear that any one may condemn me for having mingled philosophical discourses with amorous dialogues of shepherds, who rarely rise beyond treating of things of the field, and that with their wonted simplicity. For when it is observed, as is done several times in the course of the work, that many of the disguised shepherds in it were shepherds only in jest, this objection falls to the ground.

It would be impossible to give an example of every kind of tale introduced into *La Galatea*, but it is of interest to note that among the shepherds there is one who tells an experience which incorporates for the first time in the writings of Cervantes the theme of the duel and flight discussed in a previous chapter. The allusion is framed in the typical language of the cultivated shepherd. A character named Silerio is speaking of himself and of a friend:

We two passed our youthful years in incredible joy and happiness, engaging ourselves now in the field, in the pastime of the chase, now in the city, in that of honorable Mars, until, one day of the many unlucky days that hostile time has made me to see in the course of my life, there happened to my friend Timbrio a weighty quarrel with a powerful knight, an inhabitant of the same city. The dispute came to such a pass that the knight remained wounded in his honor and Timbrio was obliged to absent himself, to give an opportunity for the furious discord to cease, which was beginning to kindle between the two families. He left a letter written to his enemy, informing him that he would find him in Italy, in the city of Milan or in Naples, whenever, as a knight, he should wish to have satisfaction for the insult done him. [II.]

This episode gave Cervantes occasion to transfer a part of his narrative to Italy, and thus enlarge the field of the romance for the benefit of the reader who would have grown weary of the banks of the Tagus. The love story which follows is not without interesting details, some having an autobiographical touch, but it is involved and controlled by the classic element Fortuna, by chance rather than the skill of the author. The elements introduced are those sanctified by tradition: long journeys, dangerous voyages, separations, shipwrecks, together with a few personal recollections of Algerian pirates already referred to above. In this way one shepherd no sooner completes the rehearsal of his experiences than a new one appears on the scene, for the author's imagination supplied and the rambling technique of the pastoral permitted this perpetual sequence.

The most difficult feature of La Galatea, the portion

which must trouble the modern reader most, is that which deals with the shepherds' discussions and their contests in mental ingenuity. They are the least original and the most vulnerable additions to *La Galatea;* they deal for the greater part with such subjects as the nature of love, the peculiar disease known as jealousy, the relative influence on a lover of death or absence of the beloved one; they ventilate such arguments as which is the greater tragedy, separation or the anguish of unrequited affection, themes that have a long history in the realm of fiction. They are nothing more than semi-academic subjects having their origin in scholastic discussions which left a distinct trace in numerous types of the Renascence novel. The most prominent theme in *La Galatea,* the discussion which attempts a definition of love, is couched throughout in subtle, metaphysical language derived from the doctrine of mystics and neo-platonists. Of these the chief exponent known to Cervantes was a Spanish Jew, León Hebreo, whose volume entitled *Dialogues on Love,* was posthumously printed in Italian in 1535. The dialogues were much read in Spain during the sixteenth and seventeenth centuries; their fusion of mysticism with neo-platonism, wrapt in a pleasant obscurity, was a potent influence on the language and and thought of innumerable poets.

According to the philosophy of the neo-platonists, the individual soul enters the body against its will, but in its prison house it is dominated by matter: an idea in which

the neo-platonists agreed with the philosophy of the
mystics, notably such authorities as Luis de León. By
its own intrinsic nature the soul would follow the dictates of divine reason from which it emanates, and love
the good and beautiful of the spirit world. Under the
influence of the body it inclines toward the world of the
senses. But the triumph of the spiritual or good over
the material or evil can be realized only by the annihi-
lation of our sensuous being; the ultimate liberation of
the soul from the body is achieved by visualizing the
highest Being in a mystic transfiguration called ecstacy,
a state in which the individual soul sees God and is reunited with the universal soul.

During the Renascence this philosophy, made dark to
the ordinary reader by more obscure commentaries, was
fused with other systems of similar thought which had
found expression in literature. One was that of the
mystics who strove for identification of the soul with the
Divinity, for the absorption of their individual being by
the highest Being. The aim of their philosophy could be
reached only by repudiating the flesh in an ecstatic
state which carried the soul into the presence of God.
Another doctrine related to asceticism arose in the Middle Ages and dealt with the nature of love, the relation
of the sexes, the justification of desire, the general worth
and position of womankind. It was frequently cast into
a semi-novelistic form and produced the fiction which
tells of the deeds of good and evil women. Of this literature all nations have well-known examples; from Eng-

lish literature it will suffice to recall Chaucer's *Legend of Good Women.*

Certain discussions in *La Galatea* have absorbed tangible elements from these types of philosophy and literature, to which Cervantes as well as his contemporaries was attracted because they represented our unending but futile attempt to reconcile the spiritual and material cravings of our being. For these will dominate us as long as we have to shape our existence according to the limitations imposed by being born at all. In the mature Cervantes the result of this reading was a very simple philosophy, that we must strike a balance between the dreams of the idealist and the bald facts of life accepted by the materialist. The portion of *La Galatea* which represents an imitation, an unoriginal incorporation of ideas taken from the exposition of León Hebreo is thus worthy of attention; the subject matter continued to interest Cervantes to the end of his life. It will be worth while to give a single example of the cultivated dialogue of these shepherds; one of them, Lenio, opens the discussion and discourses on the nature of love. He lays stress on one of its phases, desire, and the evils and crimes which earthly passion has occasioned among men:

Love, then, as I have heard my elders say, is a desire for beauty; and this definition, amongst many others, those give it that have advanced farthest in this question. Then, if it be granted me that love is desire for beauty, it must necessarily be granted me that such as is the beauty which is loved, will be the

love with which it is loved. And because beauty is of two
kinds, corporeal and incorporeal, the love which loves corporeal
beauty for its ultimate goal, such a love as this cannot be good,
and this is the love whose enemy I am. But as corporeal beauty
is divided likewise into two parts, namely living bodies and dead
bodies, there can also be a love of corporeal beauty which may
be good. The one part of corporeal beauty is shown in living
bodies of men and women, and this consists in all the parts of
the body being good in themselves, and altogether making one
perfect whole, and forming a body proportioned in limbs and in
pleasantness of hue. The other beauty of the corporeal part
which is not alive, consists in pictures, statues and buildings;
which beauty can be loved without the love with which it is loved
being blameworthy. Incorporeal beauty is divided also into two
parts, the virtues and the sciences of the soul. And the love
which cleaves to virtue must necessarily be good, and likewise
that which clings to virtuous sciences and agreeable studies.
Then, as these two kinds of beauty are the cause which begets
love in our breasts, it follows that whether love be good or bad,
depends upon loving the one or the other. But, as incorporeal
beauty is viewed with the pure and clear eyes of the understanding, and corporeal beauty is regarded with the corporeal eyes,
clouded and blind in comparison with the incorporeal, and as
the eyes of the body are quicker to regard the present corporeal
beauty which pleases, than those of the understanding are to
view the absent incorporeal beauty which glorifies, it follows
that mortals more usually love the fading and mortal beauty
which destroys them than the rare and divine beauty which
makes them better. [IV.]

Tirsi now takes up the defence of spiritual love; he
analyzes it carefully, laying stress upon its commendable
features and extolling its most perfect manifestations:

Though the definition you made of love may be the one most generally given, yet it is not so much so but that it may be contradicted; for love and desire are two different things, since not everything that is loved is desired, nor everything that is desired loved. The reasoning is clear in the case of all things that are possessed, for then it cannot be said that they are desired, but that they are loved: thus, he who has health will not say that he desires health, but that he loves it; and he who has children cannot say that he desires children, but that he loves his children; nor yet can it be said of the things that are desired that they are loved, as of the death of enemies, which is desired and not loved. And so for this reason love and desire come to be different passions of the will. The truth is that love is the father of desire, and amongst other definitions which are given of love this is one. Love is that first change which we feel caused in our mind by the appetite which moves us and draws us to itself, delighting and pleasing us. And that pleasure begets motion in the soul, which motion is called desire, and, in short, desire is a motion of the appetite in regard to what is loved, and a wish for that which is possessed, and its object is happiness. As there are found different species of desires, and love is a species of desire which looks to and regards the happiness which is called fair, yet for a clearer definition and division of love it must be understood that it is divided into three kinds, chaste love, useful love, and delectable love. To these three forms of love are reduced all the kinds of loving and desiring that can exist in our will. For the chaste love regards the things of heaven, eternal and divine; the useful, the things of earth, full of joy and doomed to perish, such as wealth, powers, and lordships; the delectable, things giving delight and pleasure, as the living corporeal beauties of which you, Lenio, spoke. Each form of these loves of which I have spoken ought not to be blamed by any tongue, for the chaste love ever was, is, and must be spotless, simple, pure and divine, finding rest and repose in God alone. Profitable love, being, as it is, natural, ought not to be condemned, still less the delectable, for it is more natural than the profitable. That these two forms of love are natural in us, experience shows us, for as soon as our daring first parent transgressed the divine commandment, and from lord was made a servant, and from freeman a slave, straightway he knew the misery into which he had fallen, and the poverty in which he was. So he at once took the leaves of trees to cover him, and sweated and toiled breaking the earth to sustain himself, and to live with the least discomfort possible. Thereafter, obeying his God therein better than in aught else, he sought to have children, and in them to perpetuate and delight the human race. As by his disobedience death entered into him, and through him into all his descendants, so we inherit at the same time all his affections and passions, as we inherit his very nature. [IV.]

The fundamental arguments of this discussion no doubt seem remote, and the involved conclusions may awaken little response in the modern reader, but the beauty and nobility of the style have retained their charm after the lapse of these many centuries.

The highly diversified metrical forms which Cervantes employs in *La Galatea* intimately connect his work with his predecessors in the pastoral type and with the many contemporary lyric poets who were highly skilled in using infinite varieties of verse. These practically all go back to Italian origins, and when employed by highly gifted and inspired poets such as Garcilaso, Gil Polo,

Luis de León, Lope de Vega, Herrera, Figueroa, and others, add greatly to the wealth of Spanish lyrics. But much of Cervantes' own verse is labored; when he attempts ornate expression he is apt to fall back upon artificial platitudes. Upon a number of occasions his inspiration had to be coaxed into being; he himself was the first to recognize that meter was not his real instrument of expression. In his *Journey to Parnassus* (chapter one) he admits this fact, saying with mingled humor and pathos: "I must ever toil and keep vigil, that I may seem to have of the poet those gifts with which Heaven did not wish to favor me." A fair estimate of his verse, however, must admit that some of his poems are pleasing; it could not be otherwise with one who had such profound love for the lyric art, and who did not hesitate to imitate the best verse of his day. His genuine bucolic compositions in *La Galatea* are not extensive. There are some devoted to themes of stream, meadow, woods and the rest, but the large majority deal with amorous lamentations or the subtleties of shepherds' discussions, those features which afford an opportunity for figured thoughts (conceits or *concetti*) and elevated or polished phrases. Of the best of these an English translation can give no adequate idea, just as no fair verdict on *La Galatea* can be set down by one who does not read it in Spanish.

Thus, the work, as Cervantes himself has declared, proposes far more than it fulfills, and it ends nowhere. Nor did Cervantes ever gather courage to complete it,

although his many references to a forthcoming sequel
lead us to surmise that he may have had in hand a manuscript fragment which continued the loves of his principal shepherds.   The influence of *La Galatea* as an individual work cannot be determined, for it was fused
with that of the whole type of pastoral romances.   Of
these many others appeared far into the seventeenth century, and their popularity found an echo in the literary
world of every civilized nation.   Yet practically the only
important Spanish pastoral mentioned outside of Spain
is the *Diana* of Montemayor.

In Spain itself many great writers attempted something in this rural genre, but almost invariably when
they were young and not yet inclined to sit in judgment
on its uncritical and false image of life.   It is, therefore,
of the greatest interest to find that men like Cervantes
and Lope de Vega, who during the first years of their
literary career indulged in the bucolic vein, realized
later, when they were creating the peculiar works for
which their genius was so admirably fitted, that the tale
of life among shepherds was an insincere form of literary art.   In his *Dorotea,* which he finished in his old age,
Lope remarks:

This business of shepherds is nothing but brooks and banks,
and they and their shepherdesses are forever singing; some day
I hope to see a shepherd seated on a bench, and not always upon
a rock or near a fountain.

And many years after writing *La Galatea* Cervantes

expressed his final verdict on the whole type, which has since been that of posterity. In the *Colloquy of the Dogs,* Berganza rehearses his many experiences, and among them he tells of his life as a herder of sheep:

In the silence and solitude of my siestas, among other things I took to considering that what I had heard say of the life of shepherds could not be true, at least of those of whom the mistress of my master used to read in certain books, which all treated of shepherds and shepherdesses, saying, that they were in the habit of passing their whole lives in singing and playing on pipes, bagpipes, rebecks, and hautboys, and other outlandish instruments. I used to stop to hear her read, and she read how the shepherd of Amphrysus sang exquisitely and divinely, praising the peerless Belisarda; and how there was not in all the mountains of Arcadia a tree under whose shade he had not sat singing, from the time that the sun emerged in the arms of Aurora, till he sank in those of Thetis. Even after dark night had stretched its black and obscure wings over the face of the earth, he ceased not from his well sung and better wept plaints. Nor did she pass in silence over the shepherd Elicio, who was more enamored than daring, for without attending to his loves or his flock, he meddled with the business of others. . . . All the reflections I have mentioned, and many more, opened my eyes to the difference between the ways and habits of my own shepherds and all of those of that countryside, and the customs of shepherds in books. If mine sang, it was not songs harmonized and well composed, but a "Ware the wolf," and "Where goes Juanica?" and other similar ditties, and this not to the accompaniment of hautboys, rebecks or pipes, but to the noise made by the clashing of one crook with another, or by some sherds placed between the fingers, and not with delicate, sonorous and admirable voices, but with harsh ones which, whether alone or joined with others, appeared not to sing, but to shriek or grunt. The most of the day they used to spend in getting rid of fleas or patching their footgear. Nor were there among them any named Amaryllis, Filida, Galatea and Diana, nor were there Lisardos, Lausos, Jacintos, nor Riselos. They were all called Antón, Domingo, Pablo or Llorente. From this I came to comprehend, what I think everybody must believe, that all those books are dreams well written to amuse the idle, and not truth at all; for, had they been so, there would have been some trace among my shepherds of that most happy life and of those pleasant meadows, spacious woods, sacred mountains, lovely gardens, clear streams and crystal fountains, and of those lovers' wooings as virtuous as they were eloquent, and of that swoon of the shepherd's in this spot, of the shepherdess's in that, of the bagpipe of one shepherd sounding here, and the flageolet of the other sounding there.

In this judgment, then, the mature genius of Cervantes appears to repudiate the early work of his hand, and if during the period of his immature literary venture he succumbed to a pseudo-classical tradition, to an artificial taste, he was to be the first to admit the error of his ways. We need not take his promise of a sequel too seriously, for it is not likely that his peculiar gifts which had at last found their true vehicle of expression in pictured reflections of real life, could again revert to the bucolic world so wholly static in its makeup, and removed by its speech from the plain language of the great majority of men and women. Shepherds and shepherdesses who are given to constant lamentation over their hard lot or sad fate, who had no sense of humor, could not hope to find a prominent place in the world which Cervantes created for us in his great pages, that world in which there is such an admirable balance between tears and laughter, between the heartless facts of life and the unattainable ideals which make them bearable. Yet *La Galatea* is, nevertheless, most illuminating in a study of Cervantes' achievement, for it contains in many portions the germs of his best gifts and the charms of his unequalled narrative style.

CHAPTER V

URING the years which immediately followed the return of Cervantes from slavery, he seems to have devoted himself to many activities, but to none with more youthful ardor than the pursuit of letters. He tells us on several occasions of the projects that must have occupied him at this time, and, as we shall see, not only the completion of *La Galatea* engrossed his attention. He was ever willing to embellish the forthcoming books of friends with laudatory sonnets, which, however, do not add to his fame as a poet. He had acquired a reputation as a writer of satirical verse; he was likewise being attracted more and more by the theatre, which was then growing rapidly in scope and popularity. With his unusual inventive gift he planned a number of dramas; he gained the friendship of prominent managers of theatrical companies, such as Jerónimo Velázquez, and was, no doubt, on a footing of intimacy with many of the young writers who frequented the company of actors and actresses.

To this period, probably before 1584, we must assign

the birth of Cervantes' natural daughter, Isabel de Saavedra, the child of one Ana Franca (or Francisca) de Rojas. The story of the relations between Cervantes and Ana Franca remains extremely obscure and would not detain us, if it were not for the fact that he had no children by his wife, and that Isabel de Saavedra played a prominent part in the routine life of her father. It has been ascertained that Ana Franca was also mother of a younger daughter (named after herself) by one Alonso Rodríguez, to whom she had been married before 1587. There was at this time a well-known actor, Alonso Rodríguez, "the Toledan," who is frequently mentioned as playing in both Madrid and Toledo between the years 1580 and 1587. If this particular actor became Ana Franca's husband, it would be permissible to surmise that she also was connected with the theatrical world, and that Cervantes may have become acquainted with her during his association with playwrights and stage managers. In all this, however, nothing definite can be asserted.

There is sufficient evidence that the family of Cervantes was still pursued by financial difficulties as of old, and it is therefore probable that, in addition to his literary activities, he was also engaged in some bread-winning occupation. His occasional writings, not extensive if compared with the productions of most of his prominent contemporaries, could not have been lucrative enough to keep body and soul together. His father was failing rapidly, and died in 1585; his brother Rodrigo, after a brief sojourn in Madrid in the same year, again resumed his military activities, which carried him to Flanders. We must, therefore, infer that the support of the women of the family fell chiefly upon the shoulders of the older brother.

While Cervantes was engaged in these various tasks, notably in finishing *La Galatea,* he became acquainted with doña Catalina de Palacios Salazar Vozmediano, a young girl of Esquivias, a village in the diocese of Toledo. Any one unacquainted with Spanish names would be tempted to surmise that she was of exalted origin. Yet she seems to have been a village maiden born of a simple but respectable family. It has too generally been assumed that Cervantes wrote *La Galatea* for her, that she masks in the pastoral tale under the title of the heroine, and that he won her consent to be his wife by this, his first literary work of note. Unfortunately one of the tasks of the biographer is to destroy pious legends, and in this particular case it becomes necessary to state that there is no evidence whatsoever for such an assumption, and that the publication of *La Galatea* and the marriage with doña Catalina must be considered a mere coincidence. There are but two events in the life of every man which may be considered inevitable, death and matrimony, and as Cervantes was reaching his fortieth year it is likely that his age quite naturally impelled him to seek a companion. Nor has it been ascertained where Cervantes met doña Catalina. She was born in November, 1565, in Esquivias. Her father, Hernando de Salazar Vozmediano had died in the spring of 1584, leaving to his wife, doña Catalina de Palacios, a small estate. They had had two sons and one daughter, Catalina, who was the oldest. We have no reason to believe that both branches of her family were other than well-to-do country bourgeoisie, but the proximity of Esquivias to Toledo and Madrid, in those days Spain's chief centers for both Church and State, and the importance of the town itself in the wine trade, may have given her family more than the usual narrow opportunities of culture which fall to villagers. We are also permitted to believe that the personal qualities of doña Catalina were sufficient to offset any limitations of her surroundings. Events of later years have given ground to the supposition that Catalina's relatives had no great esteem for Cervantes. There would be nothing improbable in an attitude of cool reserve on the part of matter-of-fact country folk toward a professional soldier and literary novice whose chief topic of conversation would be the victory at Lepanto, or his captivity in Algiers, and whose ideas about writing embodied themselves in such a preposterous tale as *La Galatea*.

Still Cervantes made an impression where it was most essential, and he and doña Catalina were married at Esquivias on the twelfth of December, 1584. It is likely that they set up housekeeping in that town, a thing made more possible by his wife's dowry, which was definitely made over to him by his mother-in-law in 1586. An itemized list with the appraised value of the objects which it contained has been preserved and gives an excellent idea not only of her property, but of the interior of Cervantes' home at perhaps the most flourishing period of his life.   Even so, the furnishings of his house seem very humble, but they are, no doubt, characteristic of village customs of those times.   In land Catalina brought to him some vineyards and an orchard, and among the household goods were included a variety of mattresses, pillows, spreads and the like, a few pieces of furniture, chests and clothes-presses, two ladders, some kitchen utensils, floor mats, one candle-stick and one brazier.   Many of the articles are called old and from their appraised value were of little worth.   The only ornaments mentioned are an alabaster image of the Virgin on a walnut stand, another of the Virgin in silver, an oil painting of the Virgin with a gold frame, a picture of St. Francis, a crucifix and two little representations of the Christ-child dressed "with his clothes and shirts." These items are not without interest because they confirm the impression gained from Cervantes' writing that he was a devout and loyal Catholic; and in this he and his wife must have been of one mind.   Furthermore the larder was supplied with six bushels of flour, a chicken-coop boasted forty-five hens and chicks with one rooster, and in the orchard were four bee-hives.   It is not improbable that Cervantes was occupied, partly at least, in looking after this estate, and perhaps selling its products, notably the wine, for among names of famous brands he occasionally mentions that of Esquivias.   Here he may have had his hearth a number of years, since in several documents he calls himself a resident of Esquivias; although he undoubtedly went to the chief centers, Madrid and Toledo, from time to time, there is no evidence that doña Catalina had transferred her household to another community.

Cervantes continued to remain in touch with the theatrical world, and in his preface to a volume of plays printed near the end of his life he says that he wrote at this time numerous dramatic works. The date of their production may be fixed between 1581, or 1582, and 1587, and represents the more important of two distinct periods in which he devoted a part of his time to writing for the stage. In the preface, written in 1615, he gives most interesting details of his early association with all things concerning actors and plays:

A few days ago I happened to be engaged in conversation with some friends, and the subject turned on plays and all matters concerning them; . . . and we discussed the question who was the first in Spain to rear them out of their days of infancy, to amplify them and dress them in gala and comeliness. I, as the oldest one there, said that I remembered seeing the great Lope de Rueda act, remarkable both for his playing and for his intelligence. . . . He was admirable in pastoral poetry, and in that vein nobody, either in his own day or since that, has surpassed him. Although I was a boy at the time and could not judge the excellence of his verses, some have remained in my memory, and today I am of the same opinion. . . . At the time of this celebrated Spaniard all the properties of a theatrical manager were contained in a sack and consisted of four white shepherd's cloaks adorned with gilded leather, of four beards and wigs and four crooks, more or less. The plays were dialogues, of the nature of eclogues, between two or three shepherds and a shepherdess. They were amplified by two or three interludes, the chief character of which was either a negress, a ruffian, a clown or a Basque: all of whom were excellently played by the said Lope. There was at the time no stage machinery, no duels between Moors and Christians, on foot or on horse. Nor was there any figure which came up or appeared to come out of the center of the earth through a hole in the middle of the stage, which consisted of four benches set up in a square and five or six boards on top, raising it above the ground four spans; nor did they lower from the sky clouds with angels or spirits. The furnishings of the stage consisted of an old blanket pulled by two ropes from one side to the other, forming a so-called dressing room, behind which sat the musicians singing some old ballad to a guitar. . . . After him came Navarro of Toledo, famous in the part of a cowardly ruffian; he improved the stage-setting, and exchanged the sack for chests and boxes, he brought the music out in front of the curtain, and he did away with the use of beards, for up to that time no actor appeared without a false one. Only those who took the parts of old men, or those who had to disguise their looks were permitted to wear them. He invented machinery, clouds, thunder and lightning, duels and battles, but none of these reached the high level on which we see them today.

This account has some inaccuracies characteristic of an old man who is setting down reminiscences of his boyhood and youth; it is, nevertheless, one of the most

important characterizations we have of the Spanish
drama as it was about the middle of the sixteenth century. It is of peculiar interest because it depicts the
state of the theatre up to the time when Cervantes first
contributed to its repertory a considerable number of
plays. We have no satisfactory contemporary evidence
on the success which these early efforts attained; but he
himself speaks of them with pride as real achievements,
notably at the end of his career, when he had grown out
of sympathy with the development of the national
drama, and he and the writers for the stage, who were
all of Lope de Vega's school, represented different points
of view. In the same preface he goes on to say:

There were enacted on the stages of Madrid *Pictures of Algiers* which I wrote, *The Destruction of Numantia,* and *The
Naval Battle,* in which I was bold enough to reduce the plays
from their customary five acts to three. I showed, or rather, I
was the first to present the conceits and thoughts hidden in the
soul, and I put on the stage moral personifications which met
with the approval and the applause of all. I composed in those
days between twenty and thirty plays and they were all acted
without any offering of cucumbers or any other things that can
be thrown; they went through their course without hisses, cat-
calls or turmoil. Then other matters occupied my time, and I
abandoned my pen and the writing of plays.

There is a ring of pathos in this last sentence, for it
not only permits the inference that Cervantes' literary
career was interrupted by the stress of poverty and the

need of a serious occupation, but it is a tacit admission
that he overrated his dramatic achievement. His plays
had gained him neither great popularity nor an adequate
income, and when competition increased he fell behind
in the race. This is evident from his own statement, for,
continuing the history of these times, he tells us:

Presently that monster of Nature, the great Lope de Vega,
appeared and made himself monarch of the theatrical world. He
subjected to his jurisdiction and made vassals of all the players;
he filled the world with dramas of his own invention, happily
contrived, and in such numbers that they amount to more than
ten thousand sheets; and all of them were put on the boards—
which is as far as any praise can go.

From this and other evidence we may infer that Cervantes was not so fortunate with all of the productions
which he offered to stage managers, that in spite of his
great love for the drama this could not have been considered his real medium of expression. Years of trial
and experimentation were yet to pass before he reached
the same conclusion.

Of the plays which Cervantes assigned to this period
three titles have been mentioned, and in the *Postscript*
to his *Journey to Parnassus* he speaks of seven additional dramatic works: *The Grand Sultana* (?) (*La
Gran Turquesca*), *Jerusalem, Amaranta, The Forest of
Love, The Only Play* (?), *The Matchless Arsinda*, and
one of which he was especially proud, *A Comedy of
Confusion* (?). To the latter alone a definite date may

be assigned, for on March 5, 1585, Cervantes made
a contract with one Gaspar Porras, a manager, to let
him have two plays, *A Comedy of Confusion* (?), to be
delivered eight days later, and *Pictures of Constantinople and the Death of Selim,* to be delivered by Easter,
each for twenty ducats. The meaning of these titles is
not always clear, because only two plays have survived
from the first period of his dramatic activity, *Pictures
of Algiers* and *The Numantia.* Of these, manuscript
copies were discovered and printed for the first time in
1784. The loss of the other plays is serious, because they
would permit us to form a far more definite estimate of
the dramatic creations of his first period. It would be
interesting, for example, to see *The Naval Battle,* written in three acts, an innovation tried, in spite of Cervantes' claim to priority, many years previous. As it
is, the opinions hitherto expressed represent the greatest
divergence possible. Some lovers of Cervantes, notably
those whose taste was nurtured by the romantic movement of the nineteenth century, have rated the *Numantia* not only as one of the greatest of Spanish dramas,
but as worthy of being placed among the foremost productions of all times. Other writers, especially those of
our own day, are more inclined to point out the numerous poetic and dramatic shortcomings of these early
plays. It will, therefore, be of interest to examine their
contents.

Pictures of Algiers may be considered, for two reasons, the oldest play which has survived from the pen

of Cervantes: first, because in it the memories of his
days of slavery are freshest; and second, because the
construction is absolutely devoid of skill, and the absence of any real plot is remedied by a loosely connected
series of pictures or scenes of life among the Christian
slaves in Algiers. The play is known through two manuscript versions which disagree on many passages and on
the construction in general, their apparent defects making it evident that the original version had been cut and
otherwise seriously marred. In one of the manuscripts
the play is divided into four acts, in the other into five,
a discrepancy easily accounted for by the episodic character of the whole.

The play opens with a lamentation by Aurelio, a
captive, over his fate, the worst feature of which seems
to be that he is pursued by the love of Zara, a Moorish
beauty, whose slave he has become. Zara enters with
her servant Fatima, and both try their wiles on the
troubled Aurelio. He remains obdurate, and the servant resolves to attempt some more effective expedient to
induce his affection; Aurelio invokes divine aid in order
that he may remain loyal to the tenets of his faith. A
number of passages leave the impression that Cervantes
desired to give voice to his very devout religious feeling
and to his abhorrence of the creed of Islam. He who
issues from captivity with an unsullied record, morally
and religiously, is his thought, makes himself worthy of
the noblest crown of victory. Then follows the discussion of two slaves who rehearse their capture and hard

lot, the speech of one of them being identical with a portion of the letter which Cervantes had sent to the King's Secretary, Mateo Vázquez. Some of the most touching scenes in the play have no connection with the plot. One presents a slave market with two Moorish merchants eager to buy, and a crier who has for sale a family consisting of father, mother, two small boys, and a babe. Parents and children are rudely parted; there is no more moving picture in all Cervantes than that of the separation in which the mother, full of gentleness and piety, counsels her little boys to remain true to their faith and to depend on the help of Christ. Another captive, Sylvia, has been purchased by Izuf, the husband of Zara, and presented to her as a servant. Sylvia turns out to be the promised bride of Aurelio, and to give the situation an absurd balance, the master falls in love with the new slave girl as the mistress had fallen in love with Aurelio. In the meantime Fatima makes use of a traditional incantation derived from classic sources or their imitators; having raised a demon she exacts from him a promise of assistance, which appears in the personifications of Necessity and Opportunity. A scene in which one of the slaves attempts to flee to Oran has already been spoken of in connection with Cervantes' own plots to escape from captivity. Necessity and Opportunity now try to convince Aurelio of the error of his ways, by painting to him the advantages to be derived from yielding to Zara's passion; but he has seen Sylvia again, and no arguments are of avail. The Dey of Algiers pres-

ently appears on the scene, and after purchasing from
Izuf, for one thousand ducats, the two lovers, Aurelio
and Sylvia, he grants them their liberty in return for
a promise that they send him from Spain twice the
amount he has just paid. At the same moment the arrival of the noted redemptionist, Juan Gil, is announced,
and the play closes with the general rejoicing of all the
slaves, and a devout paean of thanks to the Virgin for
her motherly clemency.

The ardent religious feeling of the play, so thoroughly
Spanish in character, is enhanced by a fervent patriotic
tone which must have awakened a sincere response among
the spectators at the theatre. Thus, the Dey of Algiers,
enraged at the daring deeds of fugitive slaves, exclaims:

I know not to what race these captive Spanish dogs belong.
I learn of a fugitive: it is a Spaniard; of one who makes light
of his shackles: a Spaniard; of one who robs and ruins us, or
commits a thousand other wrongs: a Spaniard; surely Heaven
imbues their breast with an indomitable, impetuous courage,
ready for good or evil. A special virtue have I noted in them:
they keep their word without treason, an opinion confirmed by
the faith which many noble Spaniards have kept with me.

In the *Numantia* Cervantes reached his loftiest patriotic note, and it is likely that the inspiring passages
which embody the noble spirit of Spanish valor, of the
willing immolation of the individual to the state, have
won for this particular play its warmest praise. The
Numantians are presented as typical Spaniards, and

the siege and destruction of the ancient Iberian city at
the hands of the Romans is intended to depict Spanish
courage and ready self-sacrifice in the face of an enemy.
Cervantes probably took his material directly from national chronicles, but committed the mistake of preserving the ample canvas of his prose sources. His chief
dramatic personages thus become the inhabitants of a
whole city, and the individual characters are overwhelmed by the mass spirit of the action. The manuscripts in which the play has survived reveal a far more
acceptable condition of the text than was the case with
Pictures of Algiers. It may, therefore, he assumed that
the drama was more fortunate in meeting with universal
approval in its day and so was preserved in a form
nearer its original conception. The list of personages
prompts the question how the play could have been put
on the boards in the days of the author with any artistic
success; for at that time the stage machinery and the
setting were still of a primitive character. It included
not only all the inhabitants of the city of Numantia,
but the Roman army; not only mortals of every kind
or occupation, priest, magician, ambassador, general and
the like, but examples of those personifications on the
introduction of which Cervantes later dwelt with pride:
War, Famine, Disease, Spain, the River Duero, a Demon,
a Dead Body, Fame and others. From the stage directions we may infer that all this array caused the property man no little worry. Near the opening scene we
read, "Let as many soldiers as possible enter at this

point, armed after the ancient fashion, that is, without firearms.'' Spain enters as a ''maiden crowned with towers and bearing a castle in her hand.'' The Duero and his tributaries are represented by boys who come in ''dressed as rivers,'' which must have taxed the imagination of the stage manager as it does the reader. Another annotation says ''in this scene all who are taking part in the play must come out dressed as Numantians.'' The stage directions of Cervantes always have something naïve or primitive about them. Thus in a later play, *The Prisons of Algiers,* he says, ''These parts may be taken by two or three small boys even if they have to be gathered off the streets.''

The *Numantia* is divided into four acts, which consist, like *Pictures of Algiers,* of isolated episodes rather than a well constructed plot. The Roman general Scipio, angered at the failure of his great army to subdue a handful of citizens, determines to make a final effort by starving the city into submission. An offer of peace on the part of the Numantians is rejected, and the Romans prepare for the final assault. Spain and the River Duero thereupon appear and the impending tragic fate of the city is revealed in their dialogue, with its compensation, which is to be the future greatness of Spain. In the second act the Numantian elders sit in council and discuss the state of the city and such hopes as remain of saving it. They decide to suggest to the Romans the ordeal of the single combat as a means of saving Numantia from her doom. They also make sacrifices to

Jupiter, but the ceremony is desecrated by a devil who plays havoc with the burnt offering, scatters the fire and then disappears. The magician, Marquino, then has recourse to witchcraft in order to bring back the soul, and with it the breath of life, to a dead body, hoping thus to learn the fate of the city. The words of the soul, temporarily revived, corroborate the unfavorable prophecy of the River Duero, but in a more enigmatic form; they promise that the Romans will be the life as well as the death of Numantia, that the Numantians will be destroyed, but that the Romans will never triumph, the hidden meaning no doubt being that the inhabitants will reap immortality for having immolated themselves rather than surrender to the enemy. In the third act Scipio scornfully rejects the proposal of a single combat, and we thereupon witness scenes of privation and agony within the city, the anguish of mothers and children, the helplessness of the men, the slow but irresistible approach of their impending fate. All this is deeply pathetic rather than dramatic, but there are some passages of tragic depth and genuine inspiration which still affect every reader. The heroic determination which animates this people to resistance, however hopeless, the devotion which is voiced in the comfort and aid they give one another, the lofty pride which prevents every citizen without exception from bowing the neck under the Roman yoke, are the utterances not only of a genuine Spanish soul, but rise out of a deep understanding of humanity. It is, therefore, unlikely that any contemporary playwright could have given these sentiments as noble and convincing a tone as Cervantes. A single example of the heroism depicted will illustrate the character of the whole play. Morandro, lover of Lira, a beautiful girl, meets her and learns from her that both her mother and brother have succumbed to hunger, that only her youth and vigor have sustained her, and that he cannot hope to see her alive much longer. In his anguish over her fate, the young man determines to approach the camp of the Romans and procure some of the bread of the enemy. He succeeds in his quest, but having been wounded in the attempt, he has barely enough strength left to return to Lira, to whom he gives the bread he has won, and then falls dead. The end of the city now approaches, on horror's head horrors accumulate, Famine and Disease stalk through the streets, husbands slay their wives and children, and those who are not killed in battle stab themselves to avoid being taken. A youth, the last living personage, still in possession of the keys of the city, has mounted a tower of the wall. There Scipio sees him and urges him to surrender in return for wealth and liberty. But the youth is now the sole heir of the heroism of Numantia, and after taunting Scipio for his failure to reduce the citizens, he hurls himself from the tower. The Romans enter the city to find only heaps of corpses and desolation everywhere; no living person has survived to be borne in triumph through the streets of Rome. The play closes with a speech by Fame, extolling the glory of Numantia.

Indeed the whole drama leaves the impression that it consists only of the personification of lofty ideas, the chief of which is patriotism.

If we consider these two plays in relation with the dramatic art of other playwrights of Cervantes' first period—the only mode of reaching a just estimate of them—we shall find that they are among the very worthiest in spite of their manifest technical imperfections. They are marked, as we saw, the one by a devout and sincere religious feeling, the other by a love of country unequalled by any of Cervantes' contemporaries. No other playwright has given voice to the heroic spirit of the Spanish people in an equally lofty utterance. They manifest, furthermore, a compelling creative talent striving to find expression and groping for an adequate form. The poetic and dramatic defects of these plays might have been modified, had Cervantes' first efforts felt the guiding influence of the more perfect art, of the more convincing models of the early seventeenth century. As it was, Cervantes had remained one of a brotherhood of writers whose natural gifts were insufficient to change the accepted formula of the drama. Not until the varied and genuine endowment of a Lope de Vega made "the new art" irresistible in its spontaneity and vitality could artistic progress be effected; but when Cervantes was again actuated to try his hand at the writing of plays many years had elapsed, and by the peculiar turn which his matured genius had taken he found himself out of sympathy with the popular taste. *Pictures of Algiers* and the *Numantia* were thus dictated largely by the manner of his early contemporaries, whose conception and method Cervantes was unable to alter radically. The examples which he had before him were apparently convincing, for these two plays are closely related to them in their manner of metrical expression, in their language as well as those essentials of dramatic feeling and technique by which a playwright stands or falls. But it is impossible to read *Pictures of Algiers* and the *Numantia* without recognizing that behind them stands a great personality, a spirit already capable of expressing wide human sympathy, a potential esthetic gift enclosed in a crude form. The versification of both plays is exceedingly uneven, frequently lacking flexibility and smoothness. Notably the rhymes are often monotonous and deliberate. The most inspired passages, however, display a real gift for eloquent and lofty rhetoric especially suited to the peculiar sentiments of these plays.

When, in the first part of *Don Quixote*, Cervantes expressed disapproval of the new character of the drama, his unhappy mood found relief in an appeal to the more satisfactory nature of the stage as it was when he was first actively interested in it. In those days, he tells us, referring to the eighties of the sixteenth century, the drama had not yet been perverted:

I have sometimes endeavored to convince managers that they are mistaken in the notion they have adopted, and that they would attract more people, and get more credit, by producing plays in accordance with the rules of art, than by absurd ones, but they are so thoroughly wedded to their own opinion that no argument or evidence can wean them from it.

I remember saying one day to one of these obstinate fellows: "Tell me, do you not recollect that a few years ago, there were three tragedies acted in Spain, written by a famous poet of these kingdoms, which were such that they filled all who heard them with admiration, delight, and interest, the ignorant as well as the wise, the masses as well as the higher orders, and brought in more money to the performers, these three alone, than thirty of the best that have been since produced?"

"No doubt," replied the manager in question, "you mean the *Isabella,* the *Phyllis,* and the *Alexandra.*"

"Those are the plays I mean," said I; "and see if they did not observe the principles of art, and if, by observing them, they failed to show their superiority and please all the world; so that the fault does not lie with the public that insists upon nonsense, but with those who don't know how to produce anything else. . . . [Ch. 48.]

The plays mentioned by Cervantes were composed by a younger writer, Lupercio Leonardo de Argensola, a poet and historian of repute. The *Phyllis* has been lost, and, judging by the name, may have been some pastoral tragedy. The other two, *Alexandra* and *Isabella,* are inferior to Cervantes' own work in every respect save in occasional verses, the best of which give some evidence of Argensola's genuine poetic gifts. It is incredible that they ever enjoyed the popularity which Cervantes ascribes to them, unless we are to understand by his praise that the dramas of Argensola represent a

wholly new effort, an ampler tragic canvas than had
been attempted by any other dramatist. The plays reveal all the technical crudeness of an innovation, and
the youth of the author who presented them in 1585, in
his twenty-sixth year, may be sufficient to account for
his artless conception of what is genuinely tragic. In a
prologue to *Alexandra,* pronounced by Tragedy, the author tells the public naïvely enough to expect "nothing
but tears, deaths, wars, envy, inclemency and cruelty."
The action of both plays is very deliberate; the long
metrical forms, which are characteristic also of the first
period of Cervantes, retard the forward motion and
become monotonous and heavy. The externals of personification, augury, ghosts and the like may have made
a novel impression, but in the subsequent history of the
theatre this immature mixture of passion, bombast and
rhetoric was swept off the stage and there is only Cervantes' praise left to puzzle us. In the midst of all the
violence and bloodshed, the only character which re-
tains any interest for us is that of Isabella, a noble
Christian maiden who dwells in Saragossa during the
medieval period of Moorish domination and becomes a
victim of her purity and faith. Perhaps Cervantes, who
in his reference to Argensola was recalling things long
past, was deceived by his memory, and had in mind such
isolated traits as this. When he speaks of the wisdom
of following the rules of art, we are led to infer from
other phrases in *Don Quixote,* that he meant allegiance
to the traditional classic unities of time, place and ac-

tion. In that case his plea needs a very generous interpretation, for his own plays can hardly be said to adhere to these tenets, notably in place and action; we are thus obliged to conclude that in practice he was unable to stem the current of his times and to embody in his own dramatic efforts purely academic principles.

As a matter of fact Cervantes was not endowed with the true playwright's vision, which would have revealed to him that he was struggling with the unnatural formula of an art about to be transformed out of its imperfect stage, that in its rapid development the Spanish drama was beginning to look forward, and that in the advent of Lope de Vega all subsequent creations of a dramatic character were to receive a new poetic voice and the breath of life. How Cervantes received these changes we shall see when we examine the second period of his dramatic productivity. In the *Postscript* of his *Journey to Parnassus* he tells us how he one day met on the streets of Madrid a young fop, one Pancracio de Roncesvalles, wealthy, and, as it turns out, given to writing bad verse; the following dialogue ensues:

Miguel. What kind of poetry do you most affect, the lyric, the heroic, or the comic?

Pancracio. I am apt at all styles, but that which engages me most is the comic.

Miguel. Your worship, then, must have written some comedies?

Pancracio. Many, but only one of them has been put upon the stage.

Miguel. Was it well received?

Pancracio. By the vulgar, no.

Miguel. And by the enlightened?

Pancracio. As little.

Miguel. And the reason?

Pancracio. The reason was, that they blamed it for being long-winded in its speeches, not too pure in its verses, and altogether void of invention.

"These are blemishes," I replied, "that would have damned the comedies of a Plautus."

"And the worst of it is," he rejoined, "that they left themselves no means of judging it, for they hooted it off the stage before it was half finished. The manager reserved it for another day, but it was no use, for scarcely five persons came."

"Believe me," I said to him, "that comedies have their times as beautiful women have; and chance as well as wit plays a part in hitting these precisely. I have seen a comedy pelted in Madrid, which was crowned in Toledo. Let not your worship, then, be discouraged by the first failure, but proceed to compose others; for when you least dream of it you may succeed with one which will bring you in both credit and coin."

"Of the coin I make no account," he replied, "but fame I would prize, be it much or little. For it is a thing of exquisite delight and no less importance, to see crowds of people issuing from the comedy, all in fine humor, and the poet who wrote it standing at the door of the theatre, receiving congratulations from all around."

The dramas of the eighties were by no means all as bad as that of Pancracio, but a sound estimate of them can hope to place them only at the threshold of Spain's great age. They are characterized on the whole by absence of genuine psychological presentation of the relations of men and women, by a poetic expression which still betrays the uncertain hand of one feeling his way over an untried course, by bald externals, by crude impulses and primitive emotions, by the savage force of hatred and revenge, and the constant resolve to murder somebody. All these traits constitute a formula that may shock an audience, but they do not awaken that finer response which only elevated spiritual tragedy can arouse. The chief claim which Cervantes has to praise above his early contemporaries is his finer touch, his unconscious striving toward an esthetic achievement which he was destined to reach only in another form of immortal creation. His early dramas are, therefore, indispensable in any complete study of the noble structure which he ultimately reared.

It is possible that Cervantes might have remained in Madrid in spite of his very moderate success on the stage, and continued his aspirations to fame in this field, had it not been for those "other occupations," the need of bread, which forced him to lay aside his pen. In the *Postscript* to the *Journey to Parnassus,* he says: "When a poet is poor, half of his divine fruits and fancies miscarry by reason of his anxious care to win his daily bread." This he now had to do. In what condition he left his mother and sisters we do not know; it seems that they were as usual in the hands of Providence. His wife, we must assume, remained with her own fam-

ily at Esquivias when Cervantes began a new career of
checkered duties and employments in Seville in the
spring or summer of 1587. The next fifteen years, during which he is lost to literature except for a few occasional pieces, do not make pleasant rehearsal.   Yet
underneath their prosaic and often pathetic history lies
concealed the most important and influential epoch in the
growth of his genius. At the capital Cervantes had, no
doubt, been in touch with the world of letters; its many
gifted authors and poets were for the most part known
to him. He was by the character of what his pen had
produced one of them, by his acceptance of current
standards in the various types of literary expression
he had remained a simple member of an extensive circle
of writers. Henceforth he was to move by himself, un-
influenced by models, unhampered by conservative points
of view; and his genius, entrusted to the moulding of
a great world of facts, grew mature along new lines.
His mind could now conceive more fitly an original art
of prose fiction related to real life and imbued with warm
blood, individuality and humanity. His years of sol-
diering and of slavery had given him the ability of
assimilating the impressions left by a most variegated
career; they had taught him the value of stoicism, which,
although it never reached the conscious expression of
an extensive philosophy, was still the vast and solid
foundation upon which he reared his edifice of tolerant
interpretation of the vagaries and follies of mankind.
Only because of his contact with the actualities of his
wanderings could his art become impregnated with the

infinite phases of human activities. It was what he saw and could analyze that gave him a new psychology of fiction and that gift of revealing and explaining the motives behind the thoughts and actions of his innumerable characters.

Cervantes' first employment was that of commissary of the government, a post in which he was responsible to a high civilian official in charge of supplying the King's army and navy, together with peninsular as well as outlying garrisons, with wheat, barley, oil and other local products. By royal command issued at Seville, orders were sent to various townships in Andalusia, requesting the local authorities to accumulate and store such quantities as the purveyor general saw fit to demand. The carrying out of these requests was put into the hands of delegated commissaries, such as Cervantes, whose task was made difficult by the arbitrary nature of a procedure of which they were generally innocent, but for which they were held responsible; they were present and accessible and the communal opposition needed some head upon which to visit its wrath. Orders to bring in supplies were thus obeyed either with ill-will or disregarded, and when the commissary arrived to take over his requisitions, he often found that all the work of sequestration remained to be done. The steps required were vexatious, but undoubtedly brought Cervantes into touch with every conceivable type of man and woman in town or village. He lodged at the inns; he had to consult magistrates, aldermen, district judges and notaries; he heard, whether he would or not, the complaints of those whose products had been seized; he inspected and appraised the crops; and not infrequently, when the populace resorted to violent opposition and even rioting, the commissary was obliged to call in the help of the constable, not only for the protection of his person, but to further the carrying out of the King's orders. The archives which deal with these prosaic events often reveal scenes of this character and there can be no doubt that Cervantes witnessed his full share of them. Records of his peregrinations through Andalusia, of his enforced visits to a score of towns have survived, and if it were not for the fruits of the experiences which he derived from them, they would hardly be worthy of more than a passing reference in his biography. His salary was normal, as such things went in those days, varying from ten to sixteen reals a day (equivalent approximately to $4 and $6.50 today), and would, no doubt, have been sufficient for his maintenance, if he had received it with some regularity. But frequently at the end of a long period of service covering many months, his pay was still in arrears, and nothing but a miracle could make the bureaucratic machinery of the government move a little faster. This defect of procrastination on the part of the authorities was well known to the communities whose products were sequestrated; they dreaded the orders of the purveyor general because the fruits of their labors were taken from them in return for payment which arrived long after the transaction and sometimes not at all. Indeed, the opportunities for leakages were many through lawsuits, false weights and the recriminations ensuing therefrom, and, above all, through the dishonesty of an occasional official or commissary who had ample occasion to pocket a little of the vast sum which went through his hands. The annoyances of this business were bound to throw their shadow over Cervantes, and his records are filled with the difficulties and misfortunes which pursued him. He was by no means a skilled man in handling involved accounts of purchase and sale, yet the evidence is convincing that he was honest and impartial, and that many of the straits in which he became involved were due to these qualities. An example may suffice. Upon one occasion, in the town of Écija, by requisitioning cereals and bread belonging to the Dean and Chapter of Seville, he promptly brought down upon his head the anger and excommunication of that religious body. This was a serious matter and obliged Cervantes to procure at once the restoration of his rights to participate in the privileges of his church, for without them he was an outcast.

When Cervantes first went to Andalusia as commissary in 1587, he was employed in gathering provisions for Philip II's great fleet, at some evil hour called "the Invincible Armada," and intended to crush the power of that enemy of the Faith, Queen Elizabeth of England. The event, no doubt, awakened in Cervantes numerous memories of fighting under the great Álvaro de Bazán, the Marqués de Santa Cruz, who was again to lead this imposing force to victory. Cervantes celebrated the project in an *Ode to the Armada,* and though it is apparent that his inspiration was due to hearsay, to the rumors of great preparations which his laborious tasks did not permit him to share, his verses betray the patriotic fervor of which he had upon other occasions given proof. But the ill-starred campaign against England was beset by every misfortune and planned with every conceivable blunder that could insure its failure. At the outset it was deprived of all cohesion and leadership by the death of its admiral, Álvaro de Bazán. The equipment was defective, and the provisions proved stale or inadequate. The enthusiasm and valor of the Spanish soldiery were as great as ever, but with an utter lack of organization they were of no avail. When, therefore, in the Biblical words used jeeringly by Francis Bacon, ''the Armada came out against us one way and fled before us seven ways,'' Cervantes penned another ode on the fleet's discomfiture, urging the heroic sons of Spain to make another and greater effort against the heretic,

> Hateful to Heaven and on earth detestable,
> For then inevitable must be his fall,
> When proud and vain has been his rise.

These odes, an occasional complimentary sonnet inscribed to a friend, and a ballad or two, would seem to indicate that Cervantes was still in touch with the world of letters. There can be no question that his occupation was irksome to him, yet no better prospects opened to his view. Thus much we may infer from a memorial to the King drawn up in May, 1590, already mentioned above (p. 59), in which he gave an account of his military services and begged to be considered as a candidate for one of four positions available in the Indies, "an accountantship in the new kingdom of Granada, the governorship of the Province of Soconusco in Guatemala, the office of Purser for the galleys at Cartagena, or that of chief magistrate of the city of La Paz." His request was refused, and the fate which saved him from letters when his slave days came to an end, this time prevented his choice of a bureaucratic career. It is not easy to believe that this would still have been compatible with the literary achievement which awaited him.

Cervantes' harrowing tasks thus continued to engross him, and although he disappears from sight now and then, we learn from various documents that neither his financial condition nor his future seemed any brighter. Worst of all, his heart was no doubt constantly elsewhere, in Madrid or in Seville, where there were theatres, and where literary fame and perhaps money could be earned. This hope may have been at the bottom of an interesting contract which Cervantes signed in September, 1592, with an impresario, Rodrigo Osorio, to furnish him with six plays, the plots and titles of which were to be left to the author; they were to be delivered one by one, "written with the proper clearness." We may assume that the "clearness" demanded refers to the handwriting and not to the plot. Other conditions of the transaction awaken an amused speculation to-day. They are that each play was to be put on the stage within twenty days after it had been delivered, and if it turned out to be one of the best ever represented in public, the author was to receive for each one fifty ducats, to be paid within eight days; even if the plays were not put on in the specified time, the author assumed that the impresario was pleased with them none the less and would pay the said fifty ducats. But the most striking feature of the contract is Cervantes' assurance of success, although he closes the agreement with a slight inconsistency by stating that if any of the plays did not turn out to be one of the best ever seen in Spain the impresario could keep his money. It is not likely that the public was ever granted an opportunity of giving its verdict on the compositions in question. We have no evidence that they were ever written, or ever begun. Nor have we any means of relating them to subsequent productions for the stage.

Within a few weeks after this transaction Cervantes found himself in grave difficulties over an illegal seizure of wheat, the price of which he was condemned to pay. The possibility of prolonged incarceration hung over him, but he was able to obtain his release on bail. Thus his financial annoyances continued, for he was ground between two mill-stones, a clumsy system of government, and the hostility or procrastination of the townships with which he dealt. Their culmination came in 1595. He had been commissioned to collect from the district of Granada some taxes which were overdue. Having thus gathered a considerable sum of the government's money, he entrusted it to a banker of Seville, a certain Portuguese Simón Freire, and received from him a bill of exchange payable at Madrid. When Cervantes presented his check to Freire's correspondents, they refused to honor his claim, as the Sevillan banker had failed in the meantime and sent no funds. This appears to have been the unhappy termination of his employment in government commissions. The sum was subsequently recovered by the Treasury, but Cervantes still had other accounts to settle. Whether his books were in a confused condition, whether all of his statements had not been received, or whether miscalculations were made in the government offices is not clear; the latter is very likely to have been the case. At all events, as late as 1597 his accounts covering a portion of the year 1594 were examined and showed a deficit of about 2,300 reals (equivalent to $900— $1,000 today). Before this difficulty was adjusted, Cervantes had been sentenced to jail in Seville, where he seems to have remained from September to December of 1597. He was again freed after securing the necessary bail, but the affair hung over his head for a number of years thereafter. There is no clear evidence for believing that he was again imprisoned by the government in 1602, as has been inferred from certain documents of that date; his debt was small according to his own claim, and the government may have recognized not only that he had no money from which to obtain payment, but that the confusion in the books could not be attributed to him. Whatever the facts may be, Cervantes does not seem to have paid any attention to the government's repeated summons to appear and settle his accounts.

The incident of his imprisonment has the peculiar interest that it is generally associated with the inception of *Don Quixote*. In the *Preface* Cervantes thus addresses the reader:

"Without my swearing it thou mayst believe me that I would this book, as it is the child of my brain, were the fairest, gayest, and cleverest that could be imagined. But I could not contravene the law of Nature that everything therein should beget its like. What, then, could this sterile, ill-tilled wit of mine beget but the story of a dry, shriveled, whimsical offspring, full of thoughts of all sorts and such as never came into any other imagination—just what might be begotten in a prison, where every misery is lodged and every doleful sound makes its dwelling?"

The interpretation of this passage to the effect that Cervantes wrote or began his masterpiece in prison seems forced and unnatural. No author, however ingenuous he may be, is going to put on record the ignominious fact that he spent a period of his life in jail, and least of all in a work of the character of *Don Quixote*, intended for a wide public. Even if it were possible to give the passage the meaning that *Don Quixote* was planned in jail —because a man under such circumstances has a great deal of leisure at his disposal—the wording of the phrase would not justify such a conclusion. It is far more likely that we are dealing with a purely literary figure. Be all this as it may, the shadow of these incarcerations has hung over Cervantes and his great work more than is justifiable. Viewed against the background of his extraordinary career, they are insignificant and worthy only of the briefest consideration.

After the unfortunate affair with the Portuguese banker, Cervantes' occupation is uncertain. His chief place of residence still appears to have been Seville, and we may infer that he undertook any private commission entrusted to him, to keep body and soul together. He was poorer than ever, and may have felt that the great emporium, Seville, the heart of Spain's trade with the Indies, was the most favorable ground for his business ventures. What other reasons prevented him from joining his wife or sisters it is hard to say. His mother had died in 1593, and in 1599 his daughter, Isabel de Saavedra had been received into the household of his sister Magdalena. His wife, we must assume, was cared for in Esquivias. Unquestionably his literary ambitions were reviving, but we have no reliable information which associates his name with the numerous poets and artists residing in Seville. In May, 1595, he won a prize consisting of three silver spoons for a poem commemorating the canonization of San Jacinto, which he contributed to a competition instituted at Saragossa. In 1596 he wrote a famous sonnet satirizing the inept Duke of

Medina Sidonia for achieving the relief of Cadiz after it had been plundered and evacuated by the English under the Earl of Essex. The sonnet closes with the following lines:

> The sky grew dark; a rumbling seized the ground,
> Which threatened total ruin as it shook;
> And into Cadiz, with a prudence fine,
> Soon as the Earl had left it safe and sound,
> In triumph marched Medina's mighty Duke!

Finally, in 1598, Cervantes wrote what must be considered his most successful poem—an irregular sonnet—for it won universal renown throughout Spain. It was occasioned by a catafalque which formed part of the funeral exequies in memory of Philip II, and is characterized by spontaneity and rare satirical wit. It has been admirably translated by Gibson. The poet represents himself as entering the cathedral, and remaining dumbfounded by what he saw:

> I vow to God such grandeur stuns my brain!
>   I'd give a crown its wonders to detail;
>   For such a grand machine on such a scale
> Beggars description, makes invention vain.
> Now, by the living Christ, each piece, 'tis plain,
>   Is worth a million! Pity it should fail
>   To last an age! Hail, grand Sevilla, hail,
> In wit and wealth a second Rome again!
> I'd wager that the soul of the deceased,

On such a sight as this to gloat and gaze,
  Hath left its joys eternal in the skies.
A listening puppy answered: "I at least,
  Sir soldier, doubt not what your honor says,
  Who dares to think the opposite—he lies!"
      On this, to my surprise,
The stripling stinted, fumbled with his blade,
Looked sideways, vanished, and no more was said.

For the long stretch of almost four years, from the summer of 1600 to the spring of 1604, no facts have been discovered which throw any light on Cervantes' whereabouts, and we are, therefore, ignorant of the occupation by which he gained his bread. The absence of any information makes it probable that he was no longer in Seville, and the most natural assumption is that he had returned to his wife. Since her most likely residence was at Esquivias, Cervantes may well have settled down there and occupied himself with some local business connected with her small estate. He was now approaching old age and must have been more and more eager to devote his time to his pen. Another circumstance may be taken into consideration. From 1601 to 1606 Valladolid was the capital of the kingdom; the court was invariably a center of attraction not only for place hunters in need of their daily bread, but for men of letters, who generally moved in the wake of some aristocratic Maecenas. At some date of this period during which Cervantes disappears from view he may well have determined once more to try his fortune at the capital. But Valladolid seems a less likely residence for him than Esquivias, the silence of all archives regarding him leads to the natural inference that he had withdrawn into a secluded existence.

One thing is certain, he was at work on *Don Quixote*. The foundation for the book had been thoroughly laid. In the storehouse of his mind an infinite number of pictures had been accumulated; the vast array of human characters who had passed before him, the images of towns and cities, the manifold impressions of his military campaigns, his captivity, his subsequent wanderings, constituted a wealth of material upon which he was to draw unceasingly for his work. Such a wellspring could never dry up or lose its freshness and vitality. The only question remaining for him would be how to mingle the romance and color of life with its bald facts and maintain at the same time a fine balance, a convincing simplicity, a largeness of view. The result seems to have been achieved with little effort, almost unconsciously; for he needed no other instrument than his peculiar endowment, his wide vision, his sane interpretation of human life, his power of invention and his incomparable narrative gift. The multiform externals of his career, his struggles and sufferings, were the secure base upon which his work rested; nature and fortune contributed their share to the ultimate character of his art. For the events of his life had as a background a favored portion of the globe, the Mediterranean, Italy, Algiers, Andalusia, names which awaken pictures of nature at her best, together with a wide range of human activities in all the arts of war and peace. In Spain, especially in Andalusia, the genius of Cervantes could mature and acquire a fund of constant inspiration from the very character of the land and its people, from their wit and gift of human intercourse, their sanity, their imagination. The spiritual harvest of his career thus required no refinement through the agency of academic studies, no solidifying through the admixture of accepted systems of thought, no completion through routine training. In itself it was amply sufficient to inspire a new literary art, and to give the world one of its masterpieces in fiction. When we meet Cervantes again at Valladolid in 1604, the manuscript of *Don Quixote* was ready for press.

CHAPTER VI

THE RELATION OF CERVANTES TO THE CULTURE OF THE RENASCENCE AND THE FICTION OF THE SIXTEENTH CENTURY

T was the outward course of events of Cervantes' life that moulded his career and gave to his chief pages so much of their enduring charm. His relation to the intellectual life of his times on the eve of his great production will now occupy our attention, and we shall examine his share in what was read and thought, in so far as this helped to shape the character of his work and influence its ultimate achievement. When Cervantes tells his readers how he came upon the story of *Don Quixote* (I, 9) in a bundle of discarded pamphlets on a public square of Toledo, he adds that he was impelled to examine them because of his "fondness of reading even the very scraps of paper in the streets." By this statement he reveals in a most interesting fashion his own habit of mind, his love of books, which is corroborated by all that he has written. But in spite of the evidence that he was a wide reader there appears to have been nothing systematic in his method: he read whenever he had the leisure for it, and as is the case so often with self-taught men of genius, the impression made by books was very profound and lasting.

We have also seen, that whatever relation he may have had with academic halls must have been before his twenty-first year, during the early period of his life of which we have no documentary evidence. His works would unquestionably show traces of a university career if he had had one; not a single one of his contemporaries who is known to have attended the College of Salamanca or that of Alcalá, fails to make evident the results of such training. But in the mental attitude of Cervantes, in his conception of life and his interpretation of men's thoughts and actions, there is a singular aloofness from the intellectual forces of his times. He assimilated random thoughts and betrays here and there the influence of master works of his age. But he can be identified with no current of ideas, no specific philosophy, no scientific system or movement. His mind was not speculative and his attitude toward the political and religious tenets of those days was as uncritical as that of any man of the people. It is only when he deals with the social side, with daily life and its realities that his intellect becomes singularly keen. Few men had travelled more extensively in their youth than he, or seen more of different countries and civilizations; and yet questions regarding the earth, the history and character of its inhabitants, natural phenomena of sea and sky, constituted no problems for him. So far as may be gleaned from his casual references to anything that fell outside of his own vision, that stood apart from what he had lived and experienced, he was willing to accept without question the assertions of the writers whom chance brought to his attention. Stories from chronicles, miscellanies, books of travel, even when they approached the absurd, were woven into some of his narratives. But this is only the case when his imagination, his inventive faculty, carries him from the known into the unknown, only when he leaves the delineation of an inn, a country feast, an adventure upon Spanish highways for the description of customs in Greenland or the northern seas of which he had not the faintest knowledge.

Cervantes' life coincides with the flowering period of Spain's contribution to Renascence culture. The sixteenth century is noteworthy because of its many eminent scholars and humanists, some of whom achieved prominence as interpreters of classical literature; others were unsurpassed as exponents of the most peculiar and best of Spanish thought. An illuminating test ought therefore to be possible of Cervantes' knowledge of the classics and his reflection of the ideas and philosophy of the ancients. Such a study, however, is, if not negative, not fruitful in ample results. It would be unjustifiable pedantry to deny him any acquaintance with the world of Greece and Rome because he is prone to indulge in casual and superficial citations of brief Latin phrases, of mere classical names or apothegms, which can have no significance to academic specialists in ancient literature and culture. He could well be a child of Renascence culture and give evidence of its finest aspects without betraying at every turn signs of humanistic learning. The world of classic thought was mastered by the usual curriculum of study extending over a number of years. Cervantes had no such training, nor would its ordinary fruits have found a place in his genial portraiture of the world of his own day. It is, therefore, no discredit to him that he does not compare with some of his great contemporaries in knowledge of the classics. He stands quite alone, and it need not concern his admirers that such men as Quevedo, Lope de Vega, Luis de León and Ercilla often reveal how profoundly they were affected by Greek or Latin studies. On the other hand, whether we have in mind the Odes of Horace, the poetry of Virgil, the philosophy of the Stoic Seneca, thoughts from Plato and Aristotle, or some manifestation of that Renascence of the classics which dominated the schools and universities during the youth of Cervantes, the author of *Don Quixote* and the *Novels* betrays nowhere that he had ever given the ancients prolonged and sympathetic study.

Some enthusiastic admirers of Cervantes have gone so far as to attribute to him the mastery of all human knowledge. This is due not only to the vast conception of the world which he has created for his characters, but to a naïve concession to learning and the scholastic point of view which now and then crops out in him. This would seem to be an incongruous feature of his work if it were not the natural result of his aloofness from pedantry and academic ways of thought. However inconsistent it may seem, men of intellect who have not received the so-called benefits of a university career are frequently filled with regret at having been thus shut out. A tacit recognition that they have missed these privileges and pleasures is revealed in their respect for the prestige and authority of famous writers and books. There is something of this in the attitude of Cervantes toward humanistic learning and the academic traditions. But the defects occasioned by this feature are negligible and are offset by his constant return to a wholesome and ever fresh point of view. He ridicules the manner of those contemporary authors who strewed classical phrases over their pages and otherwise paraded their pedantry by citing the sources on the margins. Some at whom he mocked had even gone so far as to add an index of all the names quoted, that the reader might see at a glance the extent of their learning. In the prologue to *Don Quixote* he tells us:

As to references in the margin to the books and authors from whom you take the aphorisms and sayings you put into your story, it is only a question of fitting in nicely any sentences or scraps of Latin you may happen to have by heart, or at any rate that will not give you too much trouble to look up; thus when you speak of freedom and captivity, insert

Non bene pro toto libertas venditur auro;

and then refer in the margin to Horace, or whoever said it; or if you allude to the power of death, come in with——

Pallida mors aequo pulsat pede pauperum tabernas,
Regumque turres.

If it be friendship and the love God bids us bear to our enemy, go at once to the Holy Scriptures, which you can do with a very small amount of search, and quote no less than the words of God himself: *Ego autem dico vobis: diligite inimicos vestros.* If you speak of evil thoughts, turn to the Gospel: *De corde exeunt cogitationes malae.* If of the fickleness of friends, there is Cato, who will give you his distich:

Donec eris felix multos numerabis amicos,
Tempora si fuerint nubila, solus eris.

With these and such like bits of Latin they will take you for a grammarian at all events, and that nowadays is no small honor and profit.

And in the *Colloquy of the Dogs* Cervantes' satire takes on a more humorous turn:

Berganza. There are some Spaniards who in their conversation utter from time to time some short and compendious Latin sentences, giving those who do not understand their phrases to suppose that they are great Latinists, although they are scarcely able to decline a noun or conjugate a verb.

Cipión. For less evil do I hold this than what those who really know Latin are apt to do; for some of them, speaking to a shoemaker or a tailor, are so ill-advised that they pour out Latin like water.

Berganza. From this we can infer that he who speaks Latin in the presence of one who is ignorant of it, sins as much as he who employs Latin phrases, although ignorant of them.

Cipión. Again, another thing you can observe is, that there are some who by being Latinists are not saved from being asses.

Berganza. But who doubts it? The reason is clear; for as in the time of the Romans all used to talk Latin as their mother tongue, there would be some foolish fellow among them whom talking Latin would not prevent from being a fool.

Cipión. For knowing how to be silent in Spanish and talk in Latin there is need of judgment, brother Berganza.

Berganza. Yes, there is, since a silly remark can be made in Latin as well as in Spanish, and I have seen stupid professional men and tiresome grammarians and Spanish speakers lard their words with bits of Latin, which can with much ease weary the world not once, but many times.

During the sixteenth century the widespread interest which was taken in Greek and Latin writers prompted the translation into Spanish of a number of great works. The immediate result of this popularization was a very general acquaintance with the history and letters of Greece and Rome, and an assimilation by Spanish literature of their matter and form. Homer's *Odyssey,* Musaeus' *Hero and Leander,* Virgil's *Aeneid* and Ovid's *Metamorphoses,* presented in the language of contemporary fiction or poetry, took their places by the side of romances of adventure or tales of love and martial deeds. Not a few translations in the field of history, philosophy and verse, were accompanied by bulky annotations which included a vast amount of miscellaneous and unrelated information, and attempted to interpret the ancient world to Renascence readers. Numerous collections of apothegms and anecdotes forthwith culled the best thoughts and incidents from all these; it is, therefore, not surprising to find that on the stage, in lyric verse and narrative prose of every kind, classic instances are repeated, and that references to the characters and episodes of ancient legend and mythology acquire the nature of commonplace. This casual infiltration is, no doubt, far removed from the scientific study of the classics characteristic of academic centers, but it was sufficient to give even casual readers of contemporary letters some knowledge of antiquity.

Cervantes has made clear his interest in certain classic authors, whom he could learn to know and love from such secondary sources; he indicates by direct confession or manifest imitation to what extent he is indebted to them. His gift of assimilation stood him in good stead in storing up congenial material, and his fancy wove into its own creations the choicest portions of his random reading. Thus the influence of various prose books, notably such stories as Heliodorus' *Theagenes and Chariclea,* Achilles Tatius' *Clitophon and Leucippe,* which was retold in a Spanish version, *Clareo and Florisea,* by Núñez de Reinoso, and Apuleius' *Golden Ass,* or the satirical *Dialogues* of Lucian, is apparent from time to time on his pages.

The conclusion imposes itself, that even if Cervantes' writings betray no profound acquaintance with ancient literature and culture, his genius was, nevertheless, stamped by the choicest spirit of the Renascence, its formal charm in art and letters. He could have absorbed this not only in the atmosphere of the great Italian cities in which he sojourned, and where were exposed to view the noblest forms of architecture and statuary; but in Madrid, Seville and other Spanish communities where contact with intellectual and artistic activities would reveal to him the rarest aspects of contemporary civilization, he must have found renewed inspiration. The essence of antiquity, reborn and remoulded in multiform beauty, was to become a part of his creation. It finds expression in the harmony of his style, the balance and self-restraint of his art, the serenity and repose of his mind, in the sound and genial interpretations of human society. His philosophy of stoic self-denial and disregard of unimportant pleasures was surely derived from Renascence culture; but it is fused with a humorous presentation of our foibles and weaknesses; it is through the agency of this sane philosophy that his pictures of cold facts and harsh realities are relieved and made reassuring by the sweeter moral victories of virtue, faith, and idealism.

Contemporary lyric and dramatic poetry never ceased to influence the growth of Cervantes' art, but it deserves less place in a consideration of his mind on the eve of the appearance of his great prose works than those narrative forms of literary expression which are more closely related to his own. He occasionally reflected in his style the peculiar charm of a borrowed poetic phrase, and the

dialogue of master delineators of the common people,
such as Lope de Rueda, father of the Spanish stage
(p. 134), may be traced in some of Cervantes' best
pages. But his chief works, *Don Quixote* and the *Novels,*
are normally related above all to contemporary fiction
in its manifold forms. Whether this relation is as intimate as could be assumed from the usual continuity of
fiction remains to be examined.

The library of Don Quixote, which is carefully scrutinized in the sixth chapter of the first part, in order that
all books which have unhinged the mind of the hero
may be burned, is as noteworthy for the works which it
did not contain as for those which it did and which, for
the greater part, are condemned to the flames. The
chivalrous, pure and unworldly character of Don Quixote
could have nothing in common with degrading passions
and realities, and it is therefore not strange that he did
not possess either the *Celestina* or the *Lazarillo de Tormes.* We had occasion to see how at the time when
Cervantes was writing his *Galatea* the realism of these
books could not yet have appealed to him. But during
the years which intervened between his return from captivity and the inception of *Don Quixote* the psychological excellence of those two creations, in their genre the
foremost in the world's literature, must have become
more and more evident. At all events, such influence as
may be ascribed to them must be placed in the period
during which Cervantes' great realistic formula was
maturing. It will be worth while to examine them and

discover what qualities in each could appeal to him.

In the preliminary verse of *Don Quixote*, Cervantes says of the *Celestina*, "It is a book in my opinion divine, if it made the human element less plain." This characterizes the work fittingly and reveals what features Cervantes would instinctively discard, and which he would make his own. The tragic story of Calisto and Melibea, written toward the end of the fifteenth century and in part, at least, by one Fernando de Rojas, is a romance in dialogue. In the course of the century which followed its publication it acquired fame throughout Europe. It was translated into numerous languages and as late as 1631 an English version by Mabbe saw the light. The plot is slight and is given by the author in the following résumé:

Calisto was of noble lineage, of clear intellect, of gentle disposition, of nice manners and endowed with many charms, but of moderate means. He was captivated by love for Melibea, a young maiden, generous, of lofty extraction, exalted by her prosperous state, for she was the only heir of her father Pleberio, and dearly beloved by her mother Alisa. Through the importunity of Calisto her purity was overcome, owing chiefly to the intervention of Celestina, a wicked and shrewd old woman, and of two of Calisto's servants who had been corrupted by her wiles. As a result the lovers and those who served them came to a bitter and ill-starred end.

This story is thrown on a large canvas, and the drawing of its characters, its minutely painted scenes, its life-like dialogue, reveal an unequalled master in psychological delineation for those times. The original version was written in sixteen acts and would readily be classed as a great tragedy, were it not for its large number of scenic subdivisions and the consequent lack of a well-knit and concentrated action. The genius of the author, not unlike that of Cervantes, shows itself in his skilful choice of personages, his rare gift of penetrating into their souls, his richness and variety of popular phrase. The description of all the primitive passions, the unveiled presentation of vice and crime, manifest an endowment for realistic portraiture which unquestionably occasioned the stricture set down by Cervantes, but this is all the more astounding when the finer qualities of the book are considered. The delicacy which the author shows in depicting the young maiden Melibea in her home, occupied by her domestic tasks and accompanied by her parents and servants, is as attractive as the effrontery and licentiousness of his minutely drawn scenes of low life are repellent. But the good and evil of the picture were alike indispensable features of the author's conception. This was no other than an exuberant painting of a very complete social picture, ranging from the sombre and intricate life of the underworld, the activities of street and market-place with their color and turmoil, to the interior of the dignified and decent home of Melibea's parents. The author handles with equal dexterity the intrigues and shameful plottings of Celestina's low circle of associates, which terminate in murder and on the gallows, and the moving story of Calisto's and Melibea's passion and sin, which are expiated by their untimely and violent death.

The dominant notes of passion and sin are precisely those with which the genius of Cervantes could have no sympathy. Hatred, revenge, violence, the carrying out of base impulses and the satisfaction of low desires constitute the elements of a type of fiction which has nothing in common with Cervantes' conception of the novel. Traits of depraved human nature occur in his portraiture, but he instinctively refines by the touch of his art what nature herself leaves repulsive. The base, the intrinsically hideous traits of human life, bald pictures of the materialistic instincts which drag the soul in the dust, had no share in the lofty conception of his esthetic formula. We shall see, especially in his *Novels,* how Cervantes introduces aspects of sin and moral corruption, but always with a noble restraint in sentiment and style, with a sense of delicacy absolutely unknown before his own day. Indeed, it must be admitted that in the presentation of themes of love, especially the intricate psychology of the heart of woman and of her moral relations with man, Cervantes seems loath to accept wholeheartedly the procedures of realism. In the introduction of amorous episodes, in the expression of gentle emotions and soft sentiments his art attempted nothing new, but had recourse, as a rule, to the old-fashioned method and even to the diction of the sentimental, unpsychological love story which preceded him. There can be no question that his robust nature, his normal dislike of mawkish emotion, his delicate irony and sense of the ridiculous, made impossible the creation of scenes of love on the same high level with the rest of his canvas of human life. Cervantes almost invariably avoids serious dialogues in such cases and resorts to narrative. The nearest approach to what may be called a love story can be found in such novels as *The Gypsy Girl* and *The Illustrious Kitchen-maid*. These tales acquired in his hands an enduring charm chiefly because the career of hero and heroine becomes fused with a score of related occurrences of equal importance to the narrative. The analysis of gentle feelings unquestionably interfered with the progress of his pictures, and it is for this reason that his presentation of human life has retained its pristine freshness in everything except his stories of love; if these have grown pale, it is due to his acceptance of a process that was not wholly his, a concession to current tastes which had not outgrown the sentimental and unreal methods of an inferior art.

The *Celestina*, however, has other positive qualities which were of influence on Cervantes and may be traced in his final achievement. On the eve of Spain's "Golden Age" of letters few authors were as deeply imbued as Rojas with the spirit of humanism. His intense interest in the living speech and thoughts of his characters, as well as his resourcefulness in expression, his eloquence, his moralizing, his classical diction, his ample vocabulary, his erudition, are the fruits of the best culture of his day and permitted him to give to his portraitures the depth, the realism and sincerity for which they are justly famous. There can be no doubt that all this left a deep impression on the thought and art of Cervantes. Nor could he fail to be influenced by certain outward traits of Rojas' technique, namely, the purely structural features of his dialogue. A scene from the *Celestina* containing the author's chief note of an intense interest in life may serve as an example of the material which would stimulate the growth of Cervantes' style in dialogue and narrative, and influence certain phases of his thought, notably as a humanist or satirist.

Celestina, the astute old woman of the play, who has acquired a reputation for her adroitness in bringing lovers together, has been persuaded by Calisto, the young hero, to visit the home of Melibea. She is to spy out some opportunity of conversing with the young girl alone, in order to interest her in his suit. The old woman is admitted into Melibea's house by a servant under the pretext that she has some newly spun yarn for sale. Alisa, Melibea's mother, bids her come up, and Celestina enters with a modest and sanctimonious air:

Celestina. Madam, the grace of God be with you and your noble daughter. My afflictions and diseases have prevented me from visiting your house, as I ought to have done, but God knows the honesty of my intentions. . . . To my other misfortunes lack of money is now added and I have no other remedy than selling some yarn. Your servant tells me you have need of it. Although poor, I am not dependent on charity, so here it is if you can use it.

Alisa. You fill me with pity and I would gladly relieve your needs. . . . If your yarn is as you say it will be well paid.

Celestina. As I say? May all my days and my old age be as fit. It is as thin as the hair on the head, even and strong as the strings of a guitar, white as a snow-flake, prepared, spun and reeled entirely by these fingers. Here it is in skeins; only yesterday I got three copper pieces for the ounce as I live.

Alisa. Daughter Melibea, do you see to this honest woman for I am already late in visiting my sister. I have not seen her since yesterday, although she sent her page for me. She is much worse.

Celestina (*to herself*). In this illness the Devil shows his hand, giving me the opportunity I require.

Celestina is now left alone with Melibea and begins her insidious conversation with homely wisdom and counsel:

Celestina. I could desire no better company. May God give you joy of your youth and flowering days, for it is the time when most pleasures and the greatest joys may be attained. On my faith, old age is merely an inn for diseases, an abode for meditation, the friend of ill-humor and ceaseless anguish; it is an incurable wound, it means regret for the past, pain in the present, and worry for the future; it is the neighbor of Death, a hut ill-thatched into which the rains enter, a willow crook which bends with only a slight burden.

Melibea. Why do you speak so ill of what all the world desires so eagerly to reach?

Celestina. It desires a great evil and much toil. Men desire to attain it because by arriving at old age they have lived, and living is sweet, and only by living we grow old. Thus the boy desires to be a youth and the youth an old man and the old still older with all the accompanying afflictions: all just to live. For as the saying goes, "let the hen live even if it be with the pip." But who may tell you, lady, of the havoc of old age, of the inconveniences, the hardships, the cares and ills, the cold and heat, the discontent and regrets, of that wrinkling of the face, the fading of the hair's color, the imperfect hearing, the failing sight with the eyes grown dim, the sunken mouth, the loss of the teeth and the uncertain gait? And if poverty be added, all other hardships become silent; for then indeed the worst surfeit is that of hunger.

Melibea. I realize that each one speaks of the church fair according to his experiences in it; the rich no doubt sing another song.

Celestina. My daughter, on every journey there's a stretch of bad road. The rich attain happiness and peace by other and secret channels covered over as they are by flattery. . . .

Melibea. Then you regret your youth? Would you return to it?

Celestina. Mad is the traveller, lady, who, weary of the hardships of the day, wishes to begin his journey over again, for he returns but to the same spot. It is better to possess the things that are disagreeable than to expect them, for you are then nearer their end. There is nothing sweeter or more welcome to the tired traveller than the Inn. Therefore, even if youth is joyful, the truly old do not desire it; because he who is without reason or sense loves nothing so much as the thing he lost.

Melibea. If only to live longer, it is good to desire it, as I said. [Act IV.]

This is the essence of humanism worthy of note; for the purely urban realism of the *Celestina* would be of slight importance to the growth of Cervantes' art had it not been for certain features of Rojas' technique, for his multifarious speech and homely wisdom.

Far less great as a creation, but no less striking for its originality is the anonymous rogue story of *Lazarillo de Tormes,* the biography of a knavish lad, composed about the middle of the sixteenth century. It has been denied that the picaresque type to which this tale belongs exerted any influence on the esthetic formula of Cervantes. As was the case with the *Celestina* there are in the *Lazarillo* certain aspects with which Cervantes probably had no sympathy. Its bald style is at times stripped of every vestige of beauty, its syntax is crude, its vocabulary compared with that of other great books of the Renascence is slight. Above all the cynicism of its philosophy, the disregard which it displays for our finer instincts, the one-sidedness of its presentation of human society, are far removed from Cervantes' finely balanced conception of fiction as an image of life. But the *Lazarillo* is a brief little work, hardly more in extent than one of Cervantes' novels, and it would be unreasonable to attribute to it more influence than it could possibly have. Yet considering its size and scope the importance of the *Lazarillo* cannot be overrated. As a realistic adventure story it pointed a new way, and its intimate relation with life, so rare in Spanish fiction

which preceded Cervantes, is precisely the element
which associates it with his own formula of the novel.
Manifestly Cervantes surpassed the *Lazarillo* even in all
its positive qualities, but the perfection of his own art,
nevertheless, permits us to look back sympathetically
on the modest little work with which it is bound to be
related in the history of realism. The gift of wit and
satire displayed by the author of the *Lazarillo* is striking, its note of ridicule and burlesque has been the model
for all subsequent rogue stories; but it is best connected with specific traits in the style of Cervantes,
notably of some of his novels, such as *Rinconete and
Cortadillo*, his *Colloquy of the Dogs, The Jealous
Estremaduran, The Illustrious Kitchen-maid*, by the
firmness of outline which it gives to its episodes and
characters. The author never wastes any words, he is
parsimonious in any expression of sentiment, yet by a
few strokes of his pen he places before us the essentials
of his portraiture. In this very trait Cervantes became
unsurpassed, and he may well have recalled the excellence, in this particular, of the chief of Spanish rogue
stories.

Lazarillo's first master is a blind old man, and the
history of their relations was probably inspired by an
oral tradition already popular long before the little
book was composed:

About this time a blind man came to lodge at the inn, and
thinking that I should do very well to lead him about, asked

my mother to part with me for that purpose. My mother recommended me strongly, stating that I was the son of an excellent man who died in battle against the enemies of our faith, and "I trust in God," added she, "that he will never make a worse man than was his father." She confided me to his care as an orphan boy, and entreated him to use me with kindness. The old man promised to receive me, not as a servant, but as a son; and thus I commenced service with my aged master. . . .

We left Salamanca, and, having arrived at the bridge, my master directed my attention to an animal carved in stone in the form of a bull, and desired me to take him near it. When I had placed him close to it he said, "Lázaro, if you put your ear close to this bull, you will hear an extraordinary noise within." In the simplicity of my heart, believing it to be as he said, I put my ear to the stone, when the old man gave my head such a violent thump against it, that I was almost bereft of sense, and for three days after I did not lose the pain I suffered from the blow. My old master laughed heartily at the joke: "You rogue," said he, "you ought to know that a blind man's boy should have more cunning than the very devil himself."

It seemed to me as though that moment had awakened me from the simplicity of childhood, and I said to myself, "the old man says truly. I am now alone, and if I do not keep a sharp lookout for myself, I shall find none to assist me." We commenced our journey, and in a very few days I began to reap the benefit of my master's instruction. As he found me an apt scholar he was much pleased, and would say, "I have no silver or gold to give you; but, what is far better, *I can impart to you the result of my experience*, which will always enable you to live; for though God has created me blind, yet he has endowed me with faculties which have served me well in the course of my life." And I verily believe that, since God created the world he never formed a human being with wits more acute than those of my blind old master. He was as keen as an eagle in his own calling. He knew upwards of a hundred prayers by heart. His tone of voice was pleasing, and though low, was distinct enough to be heard all over the church where he usually recited them. His countenance was humble and devout; and his deportment when he recited his prayers was free from affectation and distortion of visage, which so many are apt to practice.

We have here the important feature of the emphasis which the author lays on human experience; we are repeatedly impressed by an attempt to show how these personages live. Firmness of detail, noticeable in the clear outline of the chief portraitures, preciseness in the delineation, are no less striking in the picture of another master of Lazarillo, this time a priest. The absence of any reverence for the servant of the church, or any depth of religious feeling, makes it probable that the satire was composed by a heterodox Spaniard, not in sympathy with the personage he depicts:

There is an old proverb which speaks of getting out of the frying-pan into the fire, which was indeed my unhappy case in this exchange of masters. The old blind man, selfish as he was, seemed an Alexander the Great in point of munificence, on comparison with this priest, who was without exception the most niggardly of all miserable wretches I have ever met with. It seemed as though the meanness of the whole world was gathered together in his despicable person. It would be hard to say whether he inherited this disposition or whether he had adopted it with his cassock and gown. He had a large old chest, well secured by a lock, the key of which he always carried about him tied to a part of his clothing. When the charity bread came from the church he would with his own hands deposit it in the chest, and then carefully turn the key.

Throughout the whole house there was nothing to eat. Even the sight of such things as we see in other houses, such as smoked bacon, cheese or bread, would have done my heart good, although I might have been forbidden to taste them. The only eatable we had was a string of onions, and these were locked up in a garret. Every fourth day I was allowed *one;* and when I asked for the key to take it, if any one chanced to be present, he would make a serious matter of it, saying, as he gave me the key, "Take it and return quickly; and don't look for tit-bits all the time;" speaking as though all the sweets of Valencia were there. . . .

When we were at mass, no money came to the plate at the offering that he did not observe. He had one eye on the people and the other on my fingers. His eyes danced about the money-box as though they were quicksilver. When offerings were given he kept an account, and when it was finished, that instant he would take the plate from my hands and put it on the altar. I was not able to rob him of a single copper in all the time I lived with him, or rather all the time I starved with him. I never fetched him any wine from the tavern, but the little that was left at church he locked up in his chest, and he would make that serve all the week. In order to excuse all this covetousness he said to me, "You see, my boy, that priests ought to be very abstemious in their food. For my part, I think it a great scandal to indulge in viands and wine as many do." But the curmudgeon lied most grossly, for at convents or at funerals, when we went to pray, he would eat like a wolf and drink like a fish; and now I speak of funerals, God forgive me, I was never an enemy to the human race but at that unhappy period of my life, and the reason was solely that on those occasions I ate well and was satisfied.

The number of characters thus delineated does not exceed half a dozen, but their remarkable individuality must have been striking at a time when fiction still presented shadowy figures, men and women who were characterized by stereotyped qualities and animated by traditional literary sentiments. In the *Lazarillo* the foremost place must be given to the portrait of the gentleman in waiting, not only because of his life-like drawing, but because as a satire on the *hidalgo* class—the idle gentleman pursued by poverty yet upheld by his pride —he is related to the great creation, Don Quixote. And in these two types are expressed the chief differences between the realism of their two creators. Lazarillo's new master is a penurious, hollow sham, a bald and cynical burlesque of many a contemporary *hidalgo*. Everything connected with him is empty, his house, his larder, his purse, his head, and his heart. There is no sentiment wasted on him except that of false pride and overweening honor. But Cervantes, while satirizing the type of gentleman who is poor and of no particular service to the state, never for a moment allows the reader to lose sight of his dominating qualities of virtue, of simplicity of life, and of high ideals. Don Quixote is the soul of the type; Lazarillo's master is the mere shell.

The clock had struck one, when we arrived at a house before which my master stopped; and throwing his cloak open, he drew from his sleeve a key with which he opened the door. I followed him into the house, the entrance of which was extremely dark and dismal, so much so, as to create a sensation of fear in the mind of a stranger; and when within I found it contained a small courtyard and tolerably-sized chambers. The moment we entered he took off his cloak, and enquiring whether I had clean hands, assisted me to fold it, and then, carefully wiping the dust from a seat, laid it thereon. He next seated himself beside it and began to ask me a variety of questions, as to who I was, where I came from, and how I came to that city; to all of which I gave a more particular account than exactly suited me at that time, for I thought it would have been much more to the purpose had he desired me to set the table and serve up the soup, than ask me the questions he then did. . . .

My master went to bed, putting his clothes under his head, instead of a pillow, and ordered me to seek my rest at his feet; which I accordingly did, though the situation precluded all hope of sleep. The canes of which the bedstead was composed, and my bones which were equally prominent, were throughout the night engaged in a continual and most unpleasant intimacy; for considering my illness and the privations which I had endured, to say nothing of my present starving condition, I do not believe I had a single pound of flesh on my whole body. Throughout that day I had eaten nothing but a crust of bread, and was actually mad with hunger, which is in itself a bitter enemy to repose. . . .

As the morning appeared we arose, and I set about cleaning my master's clothes and putting them in order; I helped him to dress very much to his satisfaction. . . .

He then sheathed his sword and girded it round him, and with an easy, gentlemanlike carriage, bearing himself erect and throwing the corner of his cloak over his shoulder, or under his arm, placing his right hand on his side he sallied forth, saying: "Lázaro, see to the house while I go to hear mass, and make the bed during my absence; the vessel for water wants filling, which you can do at the river that runs close by; but take care to lock the door when you go, lest we should be robbed, and put the key on this hinge in case I return before you that I may let myself in."

He then walked up the street with such an air of gentility that. a stranger would have taken him for a near relation of the Count of Claros or, at least, for his *valet de chambre*.

"Blessed be the Lord!" said I, "who, if he inflicts misfortunes, gives us the means of bearing them. Now who on meeting my master would dream but that he had supped well and slept well; and although early in the morning, that he had also breakfasted well? There are many secrets, my good master, that you know and that all the world is ignorant of. Who would not be deceived by that smiling face and that fine cloak? Who would believe that such a fine gentleman had passed the whole of yesterday without any other food than a morsel of bread which his boy had carried in his breast for a day and a night? To-day washing his hands and face and for want of a towel obliged to dry them with the lining of his garments—no one would ever suspect such things from the appearance before them. Alas! how many are there in this world who voluntarily suffer more for their false idea of honor than they would undergo for their hopes of an hereafter!"

As a story of adventure *Lazarillo de Tormes* saw the light at a time when another type of adventure tale was at its highest vogue, the romance of chivalry. Yet how could two types of fiction be more distinct or farther removed one from the other! The *Lazarillo* is succinct, unadorned, cold, real, tangible in its presentation of scenes or of men; the romance of chivalry, prolix, flowery, sentimental, remote and fantastic; the first psychologically a noteworthy experiment, the other an expression of utter disregard for any relations between fiction and real life. The popularity of the romance of chivalry may, however, be justified partly by the nature of Spanish culture and, partly, by the mental attitude of the individual Spaniard. The civilization of Spain during the Renascence is remarkable for its many sides, its variety, its power of assimilating in art, in science and in letters the best of the age. But the political instability combined with social unrest did not permit all these manifestations of refinement to become perfected and crystallized with equal vigor or with the same fulness of achievement throughout. In the arts painting, sculpture, wood-carving, architectural ornamentation, passed through an organic growth to a genuine fulfilment; many of the crafts, such as silk-weaving and the making of rare cloths, have left unique treasures. Humanistic studies, philosophical works which fused the best of ancient and Christian idealism, have taken their place among the noblest fruits of the Spanish intellect. Lyric poetry and the drama were destined to become unsurpassed in amplitude and variety of expression. But the novel, in the finished form which it acquired in the hands of Cervantes, did not develop in the same way along a straightforward course from specific beginnings to a rounded whole; the seed, flower and fruit of its history can with difficulty be presented as a connected sequence. This constitutes, in a sense, a rare condition of things for the magical appearance of Cervantes' masterpieces. His *Don Quixote* is so immeasurably superior to anything that precedes it and so complete, that it becomes puzzling to associate it organically with the history of fiction of the sixteenth century. It is no satisfactory solution to call it the last and the best of all tales of knight-errantry; it cannot be the crown of that which it refutes; it stands alone in unique splendor. Itself the most lasting of Spanish works of fiction, it is, nevertheless, most intimately related to the least enduring type which preceded it, the romance of chivalry. This self-contradiction is logically followed through in the whole work, as may be evident when we examine the story of *Don Quixote*. The history of Cervantes' other master work, his *Novels*, is practically identical with that of *Don Quixote*. Cervantes himself asserts that he was the first in Spain to write novels, and by this statement makes patent the aloofness of his own creation.

But the trend of Spanish culture would explain the popularity of these monstrous tales of chivalry and the relatively slow and sporadic growth of realism in fiction very imperfectly, if we did not consider also the mental attitude of those who sincerely enjoyed such books. An illuminating explanation of their devotion has been sought in the intense individualism of the Spanish character. Personal excellence, the achievements of bravery, skill and intelligence, were popular themes; the spirit of daring and conquest animated the Spaniard of the sixteenth century, and the reading of fantastic adventures would readily nurture and sustain such a conception of individual worth. The lies and absurdities of fiction were not viewed critically so long as the narrative was attractive and told of warriors and battle, or an occasional amorous interlude.

The romance of chivalry was not a Spanish creation; its cradle was medieval France; in Spain it became popular, but never of the people; it enjoyed a very pronounced vogue among various classes of readers without reflecting in any sense the life of the Spanish nation. Such books as the *Amadis of Gaul,* we are told, were enjoyed by the Emperor Charles V, who ordered them to be read to him during his siestas; we may surmise, however, that *Amadis of Gaul* made him forget the weight of an empire chiefly by its power of inducing opportune slumber. Still, such readings were but the continuation of an ancient custom, and kings and courtiers had stories read to them as in former times the poems of the minstrels had been recited or sung. Santa Teresa tells us in her frank and naïve autobiography that among her chief sins of youth was the reading of romances of chivalry:

> It seems to me that much harm began to come to me from a thing I shall now tell. I often think how ill those parents act who do not try to have their children always see things of virtue of all kinds. . . . My mother was fond of books of chivalry, and as much pleasure did she get from this pastime as I¹ did evil; nor was her labor lost, for our eagerness to read them grew; perchance she did it so as not to think of her many worries and to keep her children occupied lest they waste their time on other things. My father was so greatly troubled over this that we had to be careful not to let him see it. Thus I began to acquire the habit of reading these books . . . and I saw nothing wrong in wasting many hours of the day and night in this vain practice without the knowledge of my father. To such an extreme did I lose myself in the habit that if I did not have a new book of chivalry I was very unhappy. [Chap. 2.]

Men of letters before and after Santa Teresa's day regretted their folly in reading tales of knight-errantry; churchmen preached against them, and the great writer, Luis de León, epitomizes their point of view when he says: "If men were moved by the spirit of God they would, first, and before all things, condemn the *Celestina* and books of chivalry and the other thousand tales and works full of vanity and indecencies with which the souls of men are continually poisoned." A sane and speculative mind such as that of the famous humanist, Juan de Valdés, expressed his profound remorse for having admired them, and he added the illuminating confession that he had read them *all*. A law of 1553 prohibited printing and selling them in the Indies, and in 1555 a petition of the Cortes that all such books be burned was earnestly considered.

The Spanish romances of chivalry awaken interest today solely through the name of Cervantes. To judge by his unusual acquaintance with them, a fact made evident throughout the narrative of *Don Quixote,* Cervantes had spent no little time in reading these strange tales. Whether this experience falls chiefly into the years of his youth, when their vogue was greatest and a new romance in folio saw the light almost every year, or whether he glanced over the latest lucubrations as they appeared in after years, is not easy to affirm. But it is possible to infer from his knowledge as well as his mature opinion not only that he had been, at some time or other, an appreciative reader of this literature, but that he scanned with mingled interest and disgust the publications which continued to see the light. Unfortunately the scornful estimate which he set down in his old age is all that we have, yet there is nothing illogical in the belief that he too in his boyhood days may have harbored a secret admiration for Amadis and his clan. Perhaps this inference is corroborated by the faint praise which he bestows upon *Amadis of Gaul* by calling it "unique in its line."

The criticism of the books of chivalry voiced by Cervantes is all-important to any real understanding of the conception and development of the history of *Don Quixote;* it will always remain the final word to be said about them. The use which he made of their structure and material is especially interesting because the weft of the great picture of life embodied in *Don Quixote* is woven upon a background of imitation or burlesque of those same tales. They alone of contemporary fiction were ample enough to serve Cervantes' purpose; their generous canvas is not limited to a city, all highways are open to knights-errant, the frontiers of nations seem to disappear, the bottomless seas and the expanse of the air are their domain. In their imaginary world the conception of time and space is lost under the influence of the magical and supernatural which disregard all physical laws.

In the forty-seventh chapter of the first part of *Don Quixote* Cervantes begins a very illuminating argument on the romances of chivalry by means of a detailed presentation of their characteristics; he throws light not only upon the strange vogue of these books during the sixteenth century, but also upon his own narrative art. When Don Quixote is returning to his village from his second quest of adventures, the strange obsession of the good knight is touched upon by those who are accompanying him:

The canon and his servants were surprised anew when they heard Don Quixote's story, and when it was finished he said, "To tell the truth, Sir Curate, I, for my part, consider what they call books of chivalry to be mischievous to the state. Though led by idle and false taste I have read the beginnings of almost all that have been printed, I never could manage to read any one of them from beginning to end; for it seems to me they are all more or less the same thing, and one has nothing more in it than another. In my opinion, this sort of writing and composition is of the same species as the fables they call Milesian, nonsensical tales that aim solely at giving amusement and not instruction, exactly the opposite of the apologue-fables which amuse and instruct at the same time. Although it may be the chief object of such books to amuse, I do not know how they can succeed when they are so full of such monstrous nonsense. For the enjoyment the mind feels must come from the beauty and harmony which it perceives or contemplates in the things that the eye or the imagination brings before it. Nothing that has any ugliness or disproportion about it can give any pleasure." [I, 47.]

No statement made by Cervantes is a fuller analysis than this of his own esthetic formula, of the beauty and harmony of his style and of the balance of his artistic conception. Thus the chief darts of his satire would be first directed against all that is ugly, grotesque and unclean. To any sane judgment the exaggerations and absurdities of these romances must be apparent:

What beauty or what proportion of the parts to the whole, or of the whole to the parts, can there be in a book or fable where a lad of sixteen cuts down a giant as tall as a tower and makes two halves of him as if he were an almond cake? When they want to give us a picture of a battle, after having told us that there are a million combatants on the side of the enemy, let the hero of the book be opposed to them, and we have perforce to believe, whether we like it or not, that the said knight wins the victory by the single might of his strong arm. What shall we say of the facility with which a born queen or empress will give herself over into the arms of some unknown wandering knight? What mind that is not wholly barbarous and uncultured, can find pleasure in reading of how a great tower full of knights sails away across the sea like a ship with a fair wind, and will be to-night in Lombardy and to-morrow morning in the land of Prester John of the Indies, or some other that Ptolemy never described nor Marco Polo saw? . . .

How can there be any human understanding that can persuade itself there ever was all that infinity of Amadises in the world, or all that multitude of, famous knights, all those emperors of Trebizond, all those Felixmartes of Hircania, all those palfreys, damsels-errant, serpents, monsters, giants, marvellous adventures and enchantments of every kind, battles and prodigious encounters, splendid costumes, love-sick princesses, squires made counts, droll dwarfs, love letters, billings and cooings, swashbuckler women, and, in a word, all that nonsense the books of chivalry contain? For myself, I can only say, that when I read them, so long as I do not stop to think that they are all lies and frivolity, they give me a certain amount of pleasure; but when I come to consider what they are, I fling the very best of them at the wall, and would fling it into the fire if there were one at hand. They richly deserve such punishment as cheats and imposters out of the range of ordinary toleration, and as founders of new sects and modes of life, and teachers that lead the ignorant public to believe and accept as truth all the folly that they contain. [I, 47.]

It is evident from many passages in the fiction of Cervantes that he kept in mind the intimate relation which must be established between the reader and his book, the response which must be awakened in him by the characters and episodes of the narrative. With the exception of the *Celestina* and its immediate descendants which belong rather to the history of dramatic dialogue than of the novel, there was as yet in Cervantes' day no conception of fiction based, according to our modern phraseology, on psychological accuracy, on incisive and truthful delineation of the minds and hearts of men and women. Nor is there ever in any of the slight and casual phrases of Cervantes which may be called self-revealing, any conscious expression of such a conception. The great realism of Cervantes was an achievement with regard to which he himself had no well-rounded critical point of view. At least he never reasons at length about it, except in so far as he champions solely that which is possible or probable in fiction as against the false and the unreal:

If I am told that the authors of books of this kind write them as fiction, and therefore are not bound to regard niceties of truth, I would reply that fiction is all the better the more it looks like truth, and gives the more pleasure the more probability and possibility there is about it. Plots in fiction should be wedded to the understanding of the reader, and be constructed in such a way that, reconciling impossibilities, smoothing over difficulties, keeping the mind on the alert, they may surprise, interest, divert, and entertain, so that wonder and delight joined may keep pace one with the other. All this he will fail to effect who shuns verisimilitude and truth to nature, wherein lies the perfection of writing. [I, 47.]

From this statement it is evident that Cervantes laid the greatest stress on the reader's enjoyment, which is to be derived only from what seems to be true. This precept, however, was vaguely conceived and set down without any attempt at self-analysis, a quality never embodied in the sane and genial art of Cervantes. He himself does not seem to have been conscious of the real artistic scope of his achievement, for in his old age he gave the widest interpretation to the idea of "what was possible and probable" in fiction by creating one of his least convincing works, the *Persiles and Sigismunda*. The quarrel which Cervantes had with the books of chivalry was identical with that of Charles V's law-givers, who in 1555 desired to see these creations banished from a well-ordered republic because they were lying and immoral.

I have never yet seen any book of chivalry that puts together a connected plot complete in all its members, so that the middle agrees with the beginning, and the end with the beginning and middle. On the contrary, they construct them with such a multitude of members that it seems as though they meant to produce a chimera or monster rather than a well-proportioned figure. Besides all this they are harsh in their style, incredible in their achievements, licentious in their amours, uncouth in their courtly speeches, prolix in their battles, silly in their argu-

ments, absurd in their travels, and, in short, wanting in everything like intelligent art. For this reason, they deserve to be
banished from the Christian commonwealth as a worthless
breed. [I, 47.]

How was the attitude of the incurable devotees to be
changed, how could the public be educated up to a finer
and saner point of view? If the efforts of council chamber and pulpit had failed to curb the perverted taste
of the public, perhaps a burlesque would help to accomplish their purpose. Time and the progress of civilization were already effectively undermining the growth
of these tales; consequently this idea of Cervantes was
the only practical one: to hold up to ridicule a literary
monstrosity. Thereafter no one who had been amused
by reading the narratives of Don Quixote's adventures
could again turn to the stories of chivalry with genuine
pleasure.

An excellent review of some of the publications with
which Cervantes was acquainted is given in the list of
romances which Don Quixote possessed and which was
examined, as we saw above, in the sixth chapter of the
first part of his history. All kinds are represented, the
better ones, such as *Amadis of Gaul,* the prototype of
all the others, *Palmerin of England* and *Tirante* being
saved from condemnation; but many of the most fantastic and absurd, such as the numerous descendants of
Amadis, besides *Olivante de Laura, The Knight Platir,
The Knight of the Cross,* and *The Mirror of Chivalry* (a

Carolingian romance), are condemned to be burned as dangerous or immoral.

The last original romance of chivalry, *Poliscence de Beocia,* by Juan de Silva, was published in 1602, and during the years which immediately followed the appearance of *Don Quixote* only an insignificant number of the older ones were reprinted. In September, 1604, the first part of Cervantes' masterpiece was licensed for the press at Valladolid, and it was issued at Madrid early in 1605; during the author's life it was reprinted various times in Spain, Portugal, Italy and the Low Countries. Thus we may assume that the public greeted *Don Quixote* with favor, and that the romances of chivalry received their last mortal blow in accordance with the modest purpose of its author. Of its full meaning and of its triumphal career in subsequent years it is now time to speak.

CHAPTER VII

"THE RESOURCEFUL KNIGHT, DON QUIXOTE DE LA MANCHA" (PART I)

N his preface to *Don Quixote* Cervantes puts into the mouth of a friend the following advice:

Since this book of yours aims at nothing more than to destroy the authority and influence which books of chivalry have in the world, there is no need for you to go a-begging for aphorisms from philosophers, precepts from Holy Scripture, fables from poets, speeches from orators, or miracles from saints. Take care only that your style and diction run musically, pleasantly and plainly, with clear, proper, and well-placed words, setting forth your purpose to the best of your power and as well as possible, and putting your ideas intelligently, without confusion or obscurity. Strive, too, that in reading your story the melancholy may be moved to laughter, and the merry made merrier still; that the simple shall not be wearied, that the judicious shall admire the invention, that the grave shall not despise it, nor the wise fail to praise it. Finally, keep your aim fixed on the destruction of that ill-founded edifice of the books of chivalry, hated by some and praised by many more; for if you succeed in this you will have achieved no small success.

A preface which attempts to explain an author's reason for writing his book is, as a rule, unsatisfactory, and in the case of *Don Quixote* the alleged object would, of course, fail to include the whole scope of the work. There can be no question that Cervantes was successful in the two main purposes which he mentions, that of pleasing every kind of reader, and that of being instrumental in hastening the downfall of the romances of chivalry. Yet if this had been the measure of his achievement *Don Quixote* would not now rank as anything more than a literary curiosity of his age. However, before Cervantes had completed the second part of his work he was aware that the original conception had gone much farther, that generations or nations which had never read a romance of chivalry would derive pleasure and profit out of reading this story of his own invention. The purpose of his book as originally conceived and as expressed in his preface was no doubt completely satisfied by the opening chapters of the history of *Don Quixote*. To burlesque the stories of knights-errant little more was necessary than the presentation of a single protagonist, a knight in search of adventures:

> A worthy man,
> That fro the tyme that he first bigan
> To ryden out, he loved chivalrye,
> Trouthe and honour, freedom and curteisye.

Cervantes begins, after the manner of a truly great narrator, with the simplest outline, and through a career of impressive experiences develops step by step, half unconsciously, the noble soul of his hero. At the outset hardly more than the externals of this rare personage are presented to us. His surroundings, his daily food, details of his dress and personal appearance, as well as his unique idiosyncrasy, are described with a firmness of outline that had, as we have seen, few precedents:

In a village of La Mancha, the name of which I have no desire to call to mind, there lived not long since one of those gentlemen that keep a lance in the lance-rack, an old buckler, a lean hack, and a greyhound for coursing. A stew of rather more beef than mutton, a meat-salad on most nights, an omelet of brains on Saturdays, lentils on Fridays, and a pigeon or so extra on Sundays, made away with three-quarters of his income. The rest of it went in a doublet of fine cloth and velvet breeches and shoes to match for holidays, while on week-days he made a brave figure in his best homespun. . . . The age of this gentleman of ours was bordering on fifty; he was of a hardy habit, spare, gaunt-featured, a very early riser and a great sportsman. . . .

You must know, then, that the above-named gentleman whenever he was at leisure (which was mostly all the year round) gave himself up to reading books of chivalry with such ardor and avidity, that he almost entirely neglected the pursuit of his field sports, and even the management of his property. To such a pitch did his eagerness and infatuation go that he sold many an acre of tillage land to buy books of chivalry to read, and brought home as many of them as he could get. . . . In short he became so absorbed in his books, that he spent his nights from sunset to sunrise, and his days from dawn to dark, poring over them; and what with little sleep and much reading his brains got so dry that he lost his wits. His fancy grew full of what he used to read, enchantments, quarrels, battles, challenges, wounds, wooings, loves, agonies and all sorts of impossible nonsense. It so possessed his mind that the whole fabric of invention and fancy he read of was true, that to him no history of the world had more reality in it. [I, 1.]

Thus the original outline of the character of Don Quixote embraces only the picture of a crack-brained knight who has become unbalanced by too much reading of such fiction, and his logical field for adventure becomes the great highway of Spain:

In short, his wits being quite gone, he hit upon the strangest notion that ever madman in this world hit upon, and that was, that he fancied it was right and requisite, as well for the support of his own honor as for the service of his country, that he should make a knight-errant of himself, roaming the world over in full armor and on horseback in quest of adventures. He would put in practice himself all that he had read of as being the usual practices of knights-errant: righting every kind of wrong, and exposing himself to peril and danger from which, in the issue, he was to reap eternal renown and fame. [I, 1.]

In this, his idealism, his spirit of service and sacrifice

are already evident, but wholly in the garb of burlesque.

Don Quixote now takes the next step: he cleans and repairs his rusty and old-fashioned armor as best he can, he goes to make ready his bony and worn steed, he invents a fair lady worthy of his high emprise. These he baptizes with dignified and high-sounding names, calling his lady "Dulcinea del Toboso," his hack "Rocinante," and his own name, Alonso Quixano, he exchanges for "Don Quixote de la Mancha." In all this he would not be unworthy of the great knight Amadis himself. After these preparations he is ready to set forth on the road as a world-reformer. To complete the picture of his madness Cervantes makes him select the hottest day of July for his first venture, with a baked, treeless plain as his background, and starts him off on his strange and immortal career. But the first drawback to his situation immediately becomes clear: he has no one to talk with but himself, and this feature alone may have been the determining factor in bringing him back to his village after a very brief absence and letting him sally forth anew under completely changed circumstances.

Don Quixote's first experience at a roadside inn, which he promptly takes for a castle, is a clever burlesque of typical scenes from the romances of chivalry; the innkeeper becomes a warden, women at the door are princesses, a swineherd becomes the customary dwarf—and thus his illusion is complete. "Still it dis-

tressed him to think he had not been dubbed a knight,
for it was plain to him that he could not lawfully
engage in any adventure without receiving the order of
knighthood.'' This process involved the ritual of keeping vigil over his arms, for which Cervantes could have
found models in many a story dealing with the history
of young knights about to undertake momentous adventures. The innkeeper, a rogue and an Andalusian,
a mixture which generally makes a rare combination of
wit and shrewdness, accedes to the wishes of his guest
that he perform the ceremony of dubbing him a knight.
Don Quixote thereupon watches his arms near a water-
ing-trough in the yard, where he comes to blows with
some muleteers who desecrate the ceremony by touching them. The ritual of arming him, of girding on his
sword and putting on his spurs is finally completed,
and Don Quixote is allowed to proceed on his way.

Two brief adventures close the story of his first sally:
one with a farmer whom he catches chastising a delin-
quent shepherd lad, and another with a caravan of
Toledan merchants on their way to the south. The
latter are commanded to admit the superior beauty of
Dulcinea, Empress of La Mancha, whereupon one of
the merchants replies:

"Sir Knight, I entreat your worship in the name of this present company of princes, that, to save us from charging our
consciences with the confession of a thing we have never seen
or heard of, and one moreover so much to the prejudice of the

Empresses and Queens of the Alcarria and Estremadura, your worship will be pleased to show us some portrait of this lady, although it be no bigger than a grain of wheat. For by the thread one gets at the ball, and in this way we shall be satisfied and easy, and you will be content and pleased. Nay, I believe we are already so far agreed with you that even though her portrait should show her blind of one eye, and distilling vermillion and sulphur from the other, we would, nevertheless, to gratify your worship, say all in her favor that you desire." [I, 4.]

Don Quixote is about to punish such blasphemy, when Rocinante stumbles and falls, and her rider, once upon the ground, is unable to rise because of the weight of his armor. In this defenceless position Don Quixote's lance is broken to pieces by one of the drivers, who also administers to him a sound drubbing and leaves the hero stunned and defeated upon the road.

Finding, then, that in fact he could not move, he bethought himself of having recourse to his usual remedy, which was to think of some passage in his books, and his craze brought to his mind that about Baldwin and the Marquis of Mantua, when Carloto left him wounded on the mountain-side, a story which the children have by heart, and the young men do not forget, and the old folk repeat and even believe; and for all that not a whit truer than the miracles of Mahomet. This seemed to him to fit exactly the case in which he found himself; so, making a show of severe suffering, he began to roll on the ground and with feeble breath repeat the very words which the wounded knight of the wood is said to have uttered:

"Where art thou, lady mine, that thou
    My sorrow dost not rue?
Thou canst not know it, lady mine,
    Or else thou art untrue."

And so he went on with the ballad as far as the lines:

"O noble Marquis of Mantua,
    My uncle and liege lord!"   [I, 5.]

When he had reached this line a farmer from his
native village happens to pass by. This rustic, who is
driving an ass to the mill, the fallen hero at once mis-
takes for some character from his beloved romances
and ballads, supposing that he has been sent either to
rescue or to take him prisoner. Remonstrances on the
part of the newcomer are of no avail; he thereupon
places Don Quixote on his own beast, gathers up the
arms and the fragments of his lance, which he binds
upon Rocinante's back; and thus he conducts the knight
back to his village, a bruised and discomfited personage.
On his arrival Don Quixote begs to be carried to his
bed and calls for the wise enchantress, Urganda, to
heal him of his grievous wounds.

It has seemed worth while to give the essentials of
the first sally, in order to demonstrate that it is still
throughout a burlesque, that the madness of Don
Quixote is carefully sustained from beginning to end.
The logical inference, however, is that Cervantes had

become aware that his simple conception was by no means commensurate with the vast possibilities of his tale. Don Quixote manifestly needed a foil by way of contrast in the personage of a constant companion with whom to discourse about the ways and occurrences of this world. Only by such an addition was Cervantes able to introduce some of those portions of his work which have since become imperishable literature: his unsurpassed dialogues, his humor, his comprehensive grasp of Castilian speech. Cervantes was now to find his great vehicle of self-expression; henceforth the reader would get something better than mere burlesque, and the author could set down every variety of language and sentiment, grave or gay, cultured or rustic, noble or commonplace. He could make more ample use of all he had seen and experienced; in the future his canvas would reflect life itself far more than parody the books which the demented knight had too assiduously read.

At this stage, in a whole chapter (ch. 6), which he inserts between the first and second sallies of his hero, Cervantes gives a detailed discussion of the library which had worked such havoc with the hidalgo's mind. If we except a few titles related to pastoral literature, to lyric and epic verse, the bulk of his collection is made up of romances of chivalry. Hardly more than a purely literary interest attaches to the discussion of these books. In fact, it is their actual association with Don Quixote, on the one hand, and the opinion which his creator held of them, on the other, that give the chapter its unique value. Still, it may be questioned whether the course of the narrative required this extensive digression. The brief and succinct statement made at the very outset regarding the pernicious influence of these romances on Don Quixote's mind was sufficient, and it remains more effective than the lengthy rehearsal of his entire library. The scene, however, in which the contents are analyzed and condemned to the flames forms an episode that, taken by itself, is of value to the history of Spanish fiction. It is also enhanced by the inimitable touches of the author's wit, notably when the disconcerted owner of the library is persuaded that it was destroyed by a hostile magician. In this last feature Cervantes imitates the romances of chivalry, since all great knights have supernatural enemies. But they may also be aided by friendly sages, who record their deeds. This last device Cervantes presently develops in another imitation. In the ninth chapter we learn that the history of Don Quixote was originally composed by an Arabic historian, and translated for Cervantes into its Castilian form by a Morisco. This feigned authorship is often referred to in the course of the narrative.

The preparations for the second sally are esthetically and spiritually more comprehensive; outside of the confines of Don Quixote's little village looms the great world of realities; the knight of La Mancha is now to carry his idealism abroad, to develop and make known his higher self, to interpret to the reader the moving-picture of humanity. In order that he may effectively do so Cervantes places by the knight's side what is perhaps his own greatest creation, the squire Sancho Panza. The character of the rustic Sancho is simplicity itself, in so far as he epitomizes the average mind or·disposition of the villager; he cannot read or write and his experience has been confined to life behind the plough or among the beasts of the field. He is endowed with the shrewdness and the homely common sense derived from routine hardships and unremitting daily toil for bread. The first delineation of Sancho is limited, as was the case with Don Quixote, to a few essential traits:

Meanwhile Don Quixote worked upon a farm laborer, a neighbor of his, an honest man, if indeed that title can be given to him who is poor, but with very little wit in his pate. In a word, he so talked him over, and with such persuasions and promises, that the poor clown made up his mind to sally forth with him and serve him as squire. Don Quixote, among other things, told him that he ought to be ready to go with him gladly, because at any moment an adventure might occur that might win an island in the twinkling of an eye and leave him governor of it. On these and the like promises Sancho Panza left wife and children, and engaged himself as squire to his neighbor.

[I, 7.]

Lured, therefore, by promises which he undoubtedly does not grasp, but which seem to imply social and financial betterment for himself and family, Sancho accepts

Don Quixote's offer and becomes one in an immortal partnership. His outfit is completed by the addition of his faithful companion, the ass, Dapple, constituting a worthy balance for Rocinante and completing the newly formed fellowship. As was to be expected from one so deeply versed in the etiquette of chivalry, Don Quixote was at first perplexed over the impropriety of setting forth with a squire mounted in this undignified fashion:

About the ass, Don Quixote hesitated a little, trying whether he could call to mind any knight-errant taking with him a squire mounted on ass-back, but no instance occurred to his memory. For all that, he determined to take him, intending to furnish him with a more honorable mount when a chance of it presented itself, by appropriating the horse of the first discourteous knight he encountered. Himself he provided with shirts and such other things as he could, according to the advice the innkeeper had given him. All this having been settled and done, without taking leave, Sancho Panza of his wife and children, or Don Quixote of his housekeeper and niece, they sallied forth from the village one night unseen by anybody, and made such good way in the course of it that by daylight they held themselves safe from discovery, even should search be made for them. [i, 7.]

Don Quixote and Sancho have now been launched together in the world, all highways are theirs, and in the character of Don Quixote alone they carry the essentials which will enable them to come victorious out of any adventure that may arise. The bonds and laws of actual society no longer exist, the limitations imposed by narrow conceptions and perverted customs are definitely thrust aside; henceforth all decisions on good and evil, on right and wrong, are to be made by the visionary hero. For, as Don Quixote himself says: ''Knights-errant are independent of all jurisdiction, their law is their sword, their charter their prowess, and their edicts their will.'' But as life invariably restores a balance between extremes, so the idealism of the new knight unwittingly finds a corrective lens in the squire who is destitute of any imagination or vision. This contrast is wrought out, as we shall see, in numberless details, and related, as only a man of Cervantes' experience could contrive, to every adventure, to every activity of men and women, in short, to his presentation and interpretation of humanity. The contrast is naturally bound to endure through their entire association, because of the irreconcilable contradiction which exists not only between the two minds of Don Quixote and Sancho, but, by the essence of life itself, between our body and spirit, our demerits and virtues, our illusions and achievements.

It would be futile to attempt more than a brief résumé of the types of adventures with which our two protagonists now meet. Many events in *Don Quixote* are widely known among readers of all nations, even among those who have never penetrated into the history or scope of the entire book. Some of its episodes acquired the character of universal folklore and not a few became a kind of literary tradition, wholly apart from the rest of the story, immediately after its first appearance. This was the case with such adventures as the combat with the windmills, which Don Quixote took for giants, the battle with the two flocks of sheep which he held to be mighty armies, the conquest of a barber's basin which could be nothing else than the enchanted helmet of Mambrino, a Moorish king in Boiardo's *Orlando,* or that of the confusion and turmoil of a certain inn which had all the appearance of being an enchanted castle. In these particular adventures it was undoubtedly the delightful burlesque which first attracted the reader, and which has maintained their popularity through the centuries. It would be vain to argue with the average person that there is something deeper to each scene, and Cervantes himself would have been contented with the superficial judgment of the vast body of his readers: that the pleasure and entertainment derived from perusing *Don Quixote* are its chief claims to immortality. And this is true enough: for the humor and wit of the book will constitute its eternally youthful qualities; they above all others have appealed alike to old and young. The verdict of the ages cannot be gainsaid; but to the student of Cervantes' achievement falls the ampler task of fortifying the public's unreasoning approval of his salient merits by a more detailed discussion of the full meaning of his creation. Though the traditional popularity of the burlesque in *Don Quixote* is a most valuable asset to begin with, the pages which derive their reason for existence from the books of chivalry would fall very short of giving a sound estimate of Cervantes' work.

Behind the infinite variety of adventures experienced by Don Quixote and Sancho there is, of course, the unparalleled inventive gift of their creator, his style, his narrative processes, his play of fancy, in short, his art. These are all apparent in the elaboration of adventures, which by themselves would have retained hardly more than a purely literary interest; they are expressed in the skillful application of the outcome which, whether it be disastrous or successful, is the result of the mistaken inferences of the master, who refuses to make use of his corrective lens, Sancho Panza.

Let us take as an example the adventure with the two flocks of sheep and note the steps by which Cervantes produces a well-rounded whole out of the episode and its ensuing commentary. Don Quixote has observed the clouds of dust raised by the approaching herds and proceeds to give his ignorant squire an elaborately eloquent account of the two armies about to approach, and of the histories of the peoples which they represent:

What a number of countries and nations he named, giving to each its proper attributes with marvellous readiness, brimful and saturated with what he had read in his lying books! Sancho Panza hung upon his words without speaking, and from time to time turned to try if he could see the knights and giants his master was describing, and as he could not make out one of them he said to him, "Señor, devil take it, if there is a sign of any man you talk of, knight or giant, in the whole business. Maybe it's all enchantment, like the phantoms last night."

"How can you say that!" answered Don Quixote; "do you not hear the neighing of the steeds, the blare of the trumpets, the roll of the drums?"

"I hear nothing but a great bleating of ewes and sheep," said Sancho; which was true, for by this time the two flocks had come close.

"The fear you are in, Sancho," said Don Quixote, "prevents you from seeing or hearing correctly, for one of the effects of fear is to derange the senses and make things appear different from what they are; if you are in such fear, withdraw to one side and leave me to myself, for alone I suffice to bring victory to that side to which I shall give my aid;" and so saying he gave Rocinante the spur, and putting the lance in rest, shot down the slope like a thunderbolt. Sancho shouted after him, crying, "Come back, Señor Don Quixote; I vow to God they are sheep and ewes you are charging! Come back! Unlucky the father that begot me! What madness is this?" [1, 18.]

The adventure of course ends in disaster for the misguided knight, and when the dust is once more laid and a profound disillusionment on the part of Don Quixote might well be expected, his ignominious defeat is wholly wiped out and annulled by his unconquerable spirit:

Sancho ran to get something from his saddle-bags wherewith to relieve his master, but not finding them, he well nigh lost his senses and cursed himself anew, and in his heart resolved to quit his master and return home, even though he forfeited the wages of his service and all hopes of the government of the promised island.

Don Quixote now rose, and putting his left hand to his mouth to keep his teeth from falling out altogether, with the other he laid hold of the bridle of Rocinante, who had never stirred from his master's side, so loyal and well-behaved was he, and betook himself to where the squire stood leaning over his ass with his hand to his cheek, like one in deep dejection. Seeing him in this mood, looking so sad, Don Quixote said to him, "Bear in mind, Sancho, that one man is no more than another, unless he does more than another. All these tempests that fall upon us are signs that fair weather is coming shortly, and that things will go well with us, for it is impossible for good or evil to last forever. Hence it follows that the evil having lasted long, the good must be now nigh at hand; so you must not distress yourself at the misfortunes which happen to me, since you have no share in them."

"How have I not?" replied Sancho; "was he whom they tossed in a blanket yesterday perchance any other than my father's son? And the saddle-bags that are missing to-day with all my treasures, did they belong to any other but myself?"

"What! are the saddle-bags missing, Sancho?" said Don Quixote.

"Yes, they are," answered Sancho.

"In that case we have nothing to eat to-day," replied Don Quixote.

"It would be so," answered Sancho, "if there were none of the herbs your worship says you know in these meadows, those with which knights-errant as unlucky as your worship are wont to supply such shortcomings."

"For all that," answered Don Quixote, "I would rather have just now a quarter of bread, or a loaf and a couple of sardines than all the herbs described by Dioscorides, even with Doctor Laguna's notes. Nevertheless, Sancho the Good, mount your beast and come along with me, for God, who provides for all things, will not fail us—more especially when we are so active in his service as we are—since he fails not the midges of the air, nor the grubs of the earth nor the tadpoles of the water, and is so merciful that he maketh his sun to rise on the evil and on the good, and sendeth rain on the just and on the unjust."

"Your worship would have made a better preacher than knight-errant," said Sancho. [I, 18.]

The average reader has no doubt always taken delight in the burlesque of this ridiculous battle, but the culti-vated mind will also enjoy its interpretation as long as books are read. No better example could be found of the skill with which Cervantes appeals to a universal human sympathy, to the need of spiritual courage and resiliency to offset defeat and overthrow.

It was evidently part of Cervantes' program of ad-ventures to let an occasional conquest or victory alter-nate with the discomfiture "to which knight-errantry is by its nature inured." By this process the narrative acquires infinite variety and gives both Sancho and Don Quixote opportunity for many-sided self-expression; it brings knight and squire into touch with every unex-pected development of facts, and relates their fantastic quest to the tangible things of life in town or upon the highway. However perplexing may be to them the out-ward aspect of these victories, and however little they may seem to harmonize with the nonsensical laws made

by men, no doubt crosses the mind of Don Quixote to
lessen his achievement, or to make his deeds less worthy
of eternal memory. Thus, after the terrific single combat between ''the gallant Biscayan and the valiant
Manchegan'' in the ninth chapter, from which Don
Quixote emerges victorious, Sancho's gratification is not
unmixed, for the Holy Brotherhood whose business is
to preserve peace on the highways may yet have a word
to say. But Don Quixote has no recollection of any
episode in which the police interfered with a knight-
errant; he is aware only of the glory of his triumph and
tries to reassure his timorous squire:

"You need have no uneasiness, my friend," said Don Quixote,
"for I will deliver you out of the hands of the Chaldeans, much
more out of those of the Brotherhood. But tell me, as you live,
have you seen a more valiant knight than I in all the known
world? Have you read in history of any who has or had finer
mettle in attack, more spirit in maintaining it, more dexterity in
wounding or skill in overthrowing?"

"The truth is," answered Sancho, "that I have never read any
history, for I can neither read nor write, but what I will venture
to bet is that a more daring master than your worship I have
never served in all the days of my life, and God grant that this
daring be not paid for where I have said; what I beg of your
worship is to dress your wound, for a great deal of blood flows
from that ear, and I have here some lint and a little white oint-
ment in the saddle-bags."

"All that might be well dispensed with," said Don Quixote,
"if I had remembered to make a vial of the balsam of

Fierabras, for time and medicine are saved by one single drop."

"What vial and what balsam is that?" said Sancho Panza.

"It is a balsam," answered Don Quixote, "the receipt for which I have in my memory, with which one need have no fear of death, or dread dying of any wound. . . . You shall give me to drink but two drops of this balsam, and you shall see me become sounder than an apple."

"If that be so," said Panza, "I renounce henceforth the government of the promised island, and desire nothing more in payment of my many and faithful services than that your worship give me the prescription for this supreme liquor, for I am persuaded it will be worth more than two reals an ounce anywhere, and I want no more, to pass the rest of my life in ease and honor. But it remains to be told if it costs much to make it." [I, 10.]

Thus, by living in hopes of sure profit, Sancho is becoming more convinced of the genuineness of his new mission. Moreover, now and then a victory brings to him an immediate substantial gain, and, as a result, the flexible moral code of knight-errantry seems ever more attractive. This is especially brought out in the delightful conquest of the helmet of Mambrino, mentioned a moment ago. No episode in the story of Don Quixote's adventures more skillfully fuses the fancied images in the master's brain with the facts of the world as they are seen by the squire; the issue and the commentary on the battle give in an unsurpassed way the contrast between the two protagonists and their two points of view.

Don Quixote sees approaching "one who wears on his head the helmet of Mambrino," but Sancho is filled with the gravest misgiving, as he has reason to be at the opening of every new adventure, and he tells his master that he is mistaken:

"How can I be mistaken in what I say, unbelieving traitor?" returned Don Quixote; "tell me, do you not see yonder knight coming towards us on a dapple-gray steed, who has upon his head a helmet of gold?"

"What I see and make out," answered Sancho, "is only a man on a gray ass like my own, who wears something that shines on his head."

"Well, that is the helmet of Mambrino," said Don Quixote; "stand to one side and leave me alone with him; you shall see how without saying a word to save time, I shall bring this adventure to an issue and possess myself of the helmet I have so longed for."

"I will take care to stand aside," said Sancho. . . .

The fact of the matter as regards the helmet, steed, and knight that Don Quixote saw, was this. In that neighborhood there were two villages, one of them so small that it had neither apothecary's shop nor barber, which the other which was close to it had, so the barber of the larger served the smaller. In it there was a sick man who required to be bled and another man who wanted to be shaved, and on this errand the barber was going, carrying with him a brass basin. But as luck would have it, as he was on the way it began to rain, and not to spoil his hat, which probably was a new one, he put the basin on his head, and being clean, it glittered at half a league's distance. He rode upon a gray ass, as Sancho said, and this was what made it seem to Don Quixote to be a dapple-gray steed and a knight and a golden helmet. . . .

The barber, who without any expectation or apprehension of an attack saw this apparition coming down upon him, had no other way of saving himself from the stroke of the lance but to let himself fall off his ass. No sooner had he touched the ground than he sprang up more nimbly than a deer and sped away across the plain faster than the wind, leaving the basin on the ground. . . .

Don Quixote told Sancho to pick up the helmet, and he taking it in his hands, said, "By heaven, the basin is a good one, and worth a real of eight if it is worth a maravedi," and handed it to his master, who immediately put it on his head, turning it round, now this way now that, in search of the visor. Not finding it he said, "Clearly the pagan to whose measure this famous head-piece was first forged must have had a very large head; but the worst of it is half of it is wanting."

When Sancho heard him call the basin a head-piece he was unable to restrain his laughter, but remembering his master's wrath he checked himself in the midst of it.

"What are you laughing at, Sancho?" said Don Quixote.

"I am laughing," said he, "to think of the great head the pagan must have had who owned this helmet, for it looks exactly like a regular barber's basin."

"Do you know what I suspect, Sancho?" said Don Quixote; "that this wonderful piece of this enchanted helmet must by some strange accident have come into the hands of some one who was unable to recognize or realize its value, and who, not knowing what he did, and seeing it to be of the purest gold, must have melted down one-half for the sake of what it might be worth, and of the other made this, which is, as you say, like a barber's basin. But be it as it may, to me who recognize it, its transformation makes no difference." [I, 21.]

The amusing difference of opinion between the knight and his squire is so impressively presented that no reader can fail to become greatly absorbed in the enchanted piece of metal and its subsequent history. But the victory could not leave Sancho without his due share, and its benefits become manifest in the windfall derived from his master's achievement. Sancho's eye falls upon the mount which the barber abandoned in his flight:

"Will your worship tell me what are we to do with this dapple-gray steed that looks like a gray ass, which that Martino whom your worship overthrew has left deserted here? From the way he took to his heels and bolted, he is not likely ever to come back for it. By my beard, but the gray beast is a good one."

"I have never been in the habit," said Don Quixote, "of taking spoil of those whom I vanquish, nor is it the practice of chivalry to take away their horses and let them go on foot, unless, indeed, it be that the victor have lost his own in the combat. ..."

"God knows I should like to take it," returned Sancho, "or at least to change it for my own, which does not seem to me as good a one. *Verily the laws of chivalry are strict, since they cannot be stretched to let one ass be exchanged for another.* I should like to know if I might at least change trappings."

"On that head I am not quite certain," answered Don Quixote, "and the matter being doubtful, pending better information, I say you may change them, if you have urgent need of them." [I, 21.]

From the elucidation of this triumph it is apparent

that Sancho has been won over to the life of knight-errantry, for he expresses a desire to see an event so worthy as that in which a new pack-saddle has been acquired for Dapple fitly recorded. Cervantes reintroduces the helmet of Mambrino towards the close of the first part, in that admirable scene at the inn in the course of which bedlam is stirred up over an argument whether the barber's basin is truly the famous helmet in question, and whether Sancho's new pack-saddle is a riding-saddle. The whole chapter (45) reveals Cervantes' consummate skill in working up a farcical episode to a climax and restoring a perfectly normal situation at the close.

It may be presumed that the best portions of Don Quixote's history, notably in this first part, are those in which Cervantes emphasizes the characters, the points of view, the moral attitudes of the two protagonists towards all they see and experience. In this lies the inexhaustible well-spring of Cervantes' humor, which no change of time or custom has permitted to grow stale. It can be best illustrated by a few notable examples. Don Quixote has just come out of a battle victorious, but with one ear badly used, and hunger as well as physical discomfort begin to show themselves in spite of his disdain for the vexations of body and stomach. He turns to his squire for a remedy:

"See if you have anything for us to eat in those saddle-bags, because we must presently go in quest of some castle where we may lodge to-night and make the balsam I told you of, for I swear to you by heaven, this ear is giving me great pain."

"I have here an onion and a little cheese and a few scraps of bread," said Sancho, "but they are not victuals fit for a valiant knight."

"How little you know about it," answered Don Quixote. "I would have you know, Sancho, that it is the glory of knights-errant to go without eating for a month, and even when they do eat, that it should be of what comes first to hand. This would have been clear to you if you had read as many histories as I have. . . . Although it is plain that knights-errant could not do without eating and performing all the other natural functions, because, in fact, they were men like ourselves, it is plain too that, wandering as they did the greater part of their lives through woods and wilds and without a cook, their most usual fare would be rustic viands such as those you now offer me; so do not seek to make a new world or pervert knight-errantry."

"Pardon me, your worship," said Sancho, "for, as I cannot read or write, I neither know nor comprehend the rules of the profession of chivalry. Henceforward I will stock the saddle-bags with every kind of dry fruit for your worship as you are a knight; and for myself, because I am not one, I will furnish them with poultry and other things more substantial." [I, 10.]

This contrast in the characters of Don Quixote and Sancho is brought out at every turn with a variety that keeps pace with the many different adventures which mark their careers. On one occasion both have been much belabored by some Galician carriers who did not comprehend the mission of a knight-errant. Sancho

takes the occasion of this defeat to express his natural
pacifism, not unmixed with a touch of cowardice, which
generally shows itself when the valor of the master has
led them to the brink of disaster:

"Sir, I am a man of peace, meek and quiet, and I can put up
with any affront because I have a wife and children to support
and bring up. So let it be likewise a hint to your worship as it
cannot be a mandate, that on no account will I draw a sword
either against clown or against knight, and that here before
God I forgive all the insults that may have been offered me or
may be offered me, whether they have been, are, or shall be
offered me by high or low, rich or poor, noble or commoner,
not excepting any rank or condition whatsoever." [I, 15.]

The irreconcilable points of view of master and servant
are made manifest most clearly in the occasional discussions of the purpose of their lives. In them we have
subtly displayed the fundamental contrast of the romance, the difference between the illusory victories of
life and the realities of defeat, yet not without a hint
of the balance between the two issues which characterizes
the average life of man and woman. An unsuccessful
day now and then betrays the genuine Sancho:

"The best and wisest thing, according to my small wits, would
be for us to return home, now that it is harvest-time, and attend
to our business, and give over wandering from Zeca to Mecca
and from pillar to post, as the saying is."

"How little you know about chivalry, Sancho," replied Don
Quixote; "hold your peace and have patience. The day will

come when you will see with your own eyes what an honorable
thing it is to wander in the pursuit of this calling. Tell me,
what greater pleasure can there be in the world, or what delight
can equal that of winning a battle, and triumphing over one's
enemy? None, beyond all doubt."

"Very likely," answered Sancho, "although I know nothing
about it. All I know is that since we have been knights-errant,
. . . we have never won any battle except the one with the Biscayan, and even out of that your worship came with half an
ear and half a helmet the less. From that until now it has all
been cudgelings and more cudgelings, cuffs and more cuffs, I
getting the blanket-tossing to boot, and falling in with enchanted
persons on whom I cannot avenge myself so as to know what
the delight, as your worship calls it, of conquering an enemy is
like." [I, 18.]

Thus, if it be possible to summarize the impressions
of Cervantes' vast material for comedy, it may be said
that the humor of *Don Quixote* consists chiefly in un-
foreseen situations which arise from the violent con-
trasts and incongruities inherent in the main theme: a
medieval knight who sets out to seek adventures in an
unromantic, modern world. We see in their turn the
ideal offset by the real, the poetic by the prosaic, the
sane by the absurd, and over the whole hovers the un-
practical spirit of the dreamer who tries in vain to
reconcile them. The very first contrast lies between the
hero's lofty purpose to stem the tide of wickedness and
the meagreness of his resources, which are only a miserable lance, the fragment of a helmet, and rusty, poorly

patched armor. Another incongruity lies in the scene
of action in which those noble aims are to be realized,
namely, the vast desert-plain of La Mancha. Into this
waste the hero rides out when the summer sun makes
the highways untenable, and the wanderer who ventures forth can find shelter only in an occasional inn
or under a parched tree. Finally there is the contrast
on which are based so many humorous situations and
episodes, that of the two inseparable protagonists themselves. The humor of their position lies in the different
manner in which each comments on the result of the
master's rashness. While the clod gives vent to his
disappointment or irritation in a mild "I told you so,"
the visionary quickly rises above all his reverses and
defies the very teachings of experience. The equanimity
with which Don Quixote bears all the ills that befall
him, is what Sancho cannot comprehend. Sancho is
constantly torn by conflicting feelings: on the one hand,
he has a firm trust in his master's goodness, out of which
he imagines some benefits may be reaped; and, on the
other, he has an equally firm conviction that his master
is a consummate madman and may at the very next
adventure prove his squire's irreparable ruin. Owing
to Don Quixote's repeated promises to win both riches
and authority for him, the hopes of realizing such advancement keep Sancho resolutely at the knight's side.
Though doubts and scruples at times assail him about
the condition of his master's mental equipment, he does
not hesitate to apostrophize him as "the cream, the

skimming and the flower of knight-errantry," or to praise his valor extravagantly in the presence of others. At the ebb-tide of his confidence in the outcome of his idle wandering, when both are lost in the wilds of the Sierra Morena, they stumble on a wallet filled with some gold pieces. These Don Quixote generously hands over to Sancho, and so the latter's service becomes for a time, at least, something better than an unprofitable stretch of fasting varied only by a series of drubbings. But the spirit of such an episode serves especially to bring out the contrast between the unselfish nature of the old-fashioned hidalgo, who seeks only rewards of a spiritual nature in return for his sacrifices, and that of his modern, unromantic squire, who prefers any palpable material profit, whether it be for his pocket or his belly.

Owing to the variety of Don Quixote's adventures, the canvas of the romance is one of the largest in the history of fiction. It represents the world of Spain, and the delineation of its infinite types is sufficient to afford a comprehensive review of its people. *Don Quixote* presents parched plains or wooded landscapes; fields and mountains as well as villages and highways have their share in the drawing. As the numberless caravan of its personages passes before our view, we can discover in firm outline individuals of every class and type. How many there are that seem alive! The shepherds who tend their flocks and are now shown in their habit as they lived, the innkeeper who is almost as mad a devotee of romances of chivalry as the hero, the funeral procession which is proceeding from one town to another, the galley slaves, of whom each one is carefully portrayed, the guests of the inn at which Don Quixote takes the sudden confusion to be a reproduction of the discord of Agramante's camp, made famous by Ariosto—these persons and scenes known to old and young in Spain, are a part of the moving panorama of *Don Quixote*.

A large portion of the first part of *Don Quixote* is, however, conceived in a serious vein. As the book grew without any definite plan, it may have occurred to the author to vary the adventures of Don Quixote and Sancho by introducing a number of formal elements: these are either complete short stories, wholly, or, in part, unrelated to the main narrative, or they are single episodes and passages which likewise have no direct bearing on the career of his two protagonists, or, at least, give a place of secondary importance to Cervantes' original purpose of writing only burlesque. These features, which may be called sober both in their style and content, are for the most part skilfully interwoven with the adventures of Don Quixote, and, with few exceptions, afford a welcome alternative to the comic scenes. Some of them have been criticised, but they were, on the whole, prompted by Cervantes' sense of harmony, by his desire not to overdo the scenes of humor and parody. Whatever may be their technical defects as unsuitable additions to the main story, they contain the noblest examples of Cervantes' prose and represent the highest level reached by the Castilian language in an age which for many reasons has been worthily styled the golden century.

The purely literary element of the first part of *Don Quixote* is readily distinguished. It consists first of speeches or discourses on subjects related more or less intimately to Don Quixote, to his reading, his profession, his philosophy of life. As a confession of faith these now and then acquire a profound additional interest by revealing traits of Cervantes' own mind, the fruits of his experiences, together with details of an autobiographical character. Excerpts from them have frequently found a foremost place in Spanish prose anthologies, and many a school child can recite passages from the description of the golden age of the world, or from the no less well-known discourse on the relative merits of careers of arms and of letters. Portions of a discourse on the romances of chivalry, put into the mouth of the Canon, have already been quoted, and an important exposition of contemporary dramatic art will be discussed later. It may not come amiss to quote briefly from Don Quixote's speech on arms and letters a portion in which Cervantes discloses his opinions of the military career, and adds touches from his own experience:

As we began in the student's case with poverty and its accompaniments, let us see now if the soldier is richer, and we shall find that in poverty itself there is no one poorer; for he is dependent on his miserable pay, which comes late or never,

or else on what he can plunder, seriously imperilling his life
and conscience. Sometimes his nakedness will be so great that
a slashed doublet serves him for uniform and shirt, and in the
depth of winter he has to defend himself against the inclemency
of the weather in the open field with nothing better than the
breath of his mouth, which, I need not say, coming from an
empty place, must come out cold, contrary to the laws of nature.
To be sure, he looks forward to the approach of night to make
up for all these discomforts on the bed that awaits him, which,
unless by some fault of his, never sins by being over narrow.
He can easily measure out on the ground as many feet as he
likes, and roll himself about in it to his heart's content without
any fear of the sheets slipping away from him. Then, after
all this, suppose the day and hour for taking his degree in his
calling to have come; suppose the day of battle to have arrived,
when they invest him with the doctor's cap made of lint, to
mend some bullet-hole, perhaps, that has gone through his tem-
ples, or left him with a crippled arm or leg. Or, if this does
not happen, and merciful Heaven watches over him and keeps
him safe and sound, it may be he will be in the same poverty
he was in before, and he must go through more engagements
and more battles, and come victorious out of all before he
betters himself; but miracles of that sort are seldom seen. For,
tell me, sirs, if you have ever reflected upon it, by how much
do those who have gained by war fall short of the number of
those who have perished in it? No doubt you will reply that
there can be no comparison, that the dead cannot be numbered,
while the living who have been rewarded may be summed up
with three fingers. [I, 38.]

The second kind of serious literary element consists
of novelistic incidents, or short stories. Mention has

been made of descriptions of the life of shepherds. In
this Cervantes reverted to his first literary devotion,
and not without retaining some of the artificiality of the
pastoral novel. In his story of the shepherdess, Marcela,
and her ill-fated lover, the youth, Grisóstomo (chapter
12 and following), much of the bucolic vein, notably its
cultivated style, has been preserved, but two important
distinctions make evident the transformation of Cervantes' art. He abandons any extensive expression in
verse, and he makes a conscientious effort not to mar
the realistic atmosphere of his setting. The sentimental
death of Grisóstomo is thus an improvement over similar
pathetic incidents of the pastoral novel. The most
prominent piece of traditional artifice in the episode is
the long discourse of Marcela who appears unexpectedly
at the burial of Grisóstomo and explains to her astonished listeners the reason for her indifference to the
dead man and her innocence in his death. This unnatural situation is saved by Don Quixote, who immediately
decides to exercise one of the chief functions of his calling, that of succoring a distressed damsel.

The most successful introduction of a pastoral episode
is that which may be found near the end of the first
part of Don Quixote's history. It is one of the last
adventures before his return to his native village. A
certain goatherd in search of one of his herd comes
across the knight's party while they are camped upon
the grass partaking of a meal. As is usual in the case
of these interruptions the goatherd, who is really a lad

of good family, uses the occasion, made to his hand, to
tell the story of his life. Sancho, however, is at the
moment in quest of something more substantial than a
story and remarks:

"I withdraw my stakes from this game and will retreat with
this meat-pie to the brook there, where I mean to victual myself
for three days. For I have heard my lord, Don Quixote, say
that a knight-errant's squire should eat until he can hold no
more, whenever he has the chance, because it often happens to
them to get by accident into a wood so thick that they cannot
find a way out of it for six days. If the man is not well filled
or his saddle-bags well stored, there he may stay, as very often
he does, turned into a dried mummy."

"You are in the right of it, Sancho," said Don Quixote; "go
where you will and eat all you can, for I have had enough, and
only want to give my mind its refreshment by listening to this
good fellow's story." [I, 50.]

The tale which the goatherd now tells is admirable
in style, but its contents conform to the sentimental
manner of the love and adventure tale of the Renascence.
In this Cervantes made a distinct concession to the taste
of his readers; and although he has succeeded by the
beauty of his diction in raising the narrative far above
anything attempted in the short story in his times, its
romantic elements have not the lasting vitality of his
realism. It is again the turn which events take which
saves the situation. Don Quixote, impressed by the sad
fate of the heroine in the goatherd's tale, would have

volunteered at once to rescue her from the convent in which she is confined, were it not for a prior engagement which restrains him:

The goatherd eyed him, and, noticing Don Quixote's sorry appearance and looks, he was filled with wonder, and asked the barber, who was next him, "Señor, who is this man who makes such a figure and talks in such a strain?"

"Who should it be," said the barber, "but the famous Don Quixote of La Mancha, the undoer of injustice, the righter of wrongs, the protector of damsels, the terror of giants, and the winner of battles?"

"That," said the goatherd, "sounds like what one reads in the books of the knights-errant, who did all that you say this man does; though it is my belief that either you are joking, or else this gentleman has empty lodgings in his head."

"You are a great scoundrel," said Don Quixote, "and it is you who are empty and a fool. . . ."

The idyllic scene thus ends in another comic upheaval, and in his unequal combat with the goatherd Don Quixote once more becomes acquainted with the drubbings to which knight-errantry is heir.

Far more extensive than the use of the pastoral vein is that of the sentimental love story. By contrast with the humor and wit of the history of *Don Quixote* this admixture constitutes the chief serious portion of an otherwise comic romance, and it therefore becomes necessary to examine the manner in which Cervantes introduces it. When Don Quixote has freed the chain of

criminals whom he met upon the highway on the ground
that they were being conducted to the galleys against
their will, Sancho, with his mind as usual on the facts
of the situation, warns his master that knights-errant
have not the value of two coppers with the Holy Brotherhood; that he and his master will presently hear their
arrows whistling about their ears, that to retire from
danger is not to flee, and that, "it is the part of wise
men to preserve themselves today for tomorrow." Don
Quixote agrees to take this advice for once and with-
draws out of reach of the fury which Sancho dreads.
They make for the heart of the Sierra Morena, among
the crags and deep forests of which Sancho will feel
secure from pursuit. Here, too, Don Quixote can carry
out a desire which he has always harbored, to do penance in solitude in honor of his disdainful lady Dulcinea,
as did Amadis of Gaul on the Peña Pobre for the sake
of his obdurate Oriana.

Into this burlesque Cervantes interweaves the double
love story of Cardenio and Luscinda, Fernando and
Dorotea. The beginnings are made known by means
of narratives; the development and conclusion form a
part of the career of Don Quixote and Sancho. The
plot is somewhat intricate for this reason, but has been
skillfully handled. Cardenio, in love with the fair Luscinda, makes known his affection to his intimate friend,
Fernando, who promises to aid him in his suit. Fernando, a young nobleman of lofty station, plays the
part of a double traitor; he not only attempts to win

Luscinda away from Cardenio, but at the same time breaks an earlier engagement of his own in the form of a promise of marriage given to Dorotea. Luscinda, urged by her parents to accept Fernando, is led by him to the altar against her will, and Cardenio, who does not tarry long enough to learn that the unhappy marriage ceremony has been broken off before its consummation, becomes subject to fits of madness, in the course of which he flees to the wilds of the Sierra Morena. There he is sustained by merciful shepherds who take pity on his wretched state. In the forest he meets Don Quixote, and during a lucid interval tells his sad story, but not without some comic interruptions on the part of the equally mad knight.

Dorotea, abandoned by Fernando, and in despair over his broken promise, also flees to the Sierra Morena disguised as a boy. Here, by chance, she meets the barber and the curate of Don Quixote's village, who have come in search of the wandering knight and squire, and she narrates to them her history up to the time of her flight into the mountains. We thus find Cardenio and Dorotea, two important personages of the love story, the barber, the curate, Don Quixote and Sancho united in the Sierra Morena. Cervantes now saw himself confronted with the problem of inducing Don Quixote to leave his abode of penance and to return home. This is accomplished by having Dorotea feign that she is a distressed princess, who has come all the way from Guinea to seek redress for an injury done her by a malevolent giant.

All embark now together on the new enterprise, and their first sojourn is made at a hostelry where the history of the four lovers is satisfactorily concluded. Luscinda, who has been abducted from a convent by Fernando, is, through the power of coincidence which rules these stories, brought to the same inn where the threads of her confused history are unravelled: Fernando agrees to take back Dorotea, and Cardenio wins Luscinda. The happy outcome makes all those present shed so many tears "that one would have supposed a heavy calamity had fallen upon them."

The traditional elements of this plot are numerous and its inherited traits of old-fashioned story-telling are among the least felicitous additions to the series of Don Quixote's adventures. There can be no question that Cervantes has displayed his usual ingenuity in making this romantic tale an inseparable part of his great book. But its demerits are strangely out of keeping with his own conception of realism, with "the probability of those occurrences" which may be admitted in fiction. The madness of Cardenio, his flight, as well as that of Dorotea, into the forest, their meeting and the manner of their redemption are all possible, separately conceived, but highly improbable as a related course of events. The character of the abhorrent Fernando is thoroughly unconvincing. The manner in which his prompt change of heart wins the immediate forgiveness of all and brings about the solution of all difficulties constitutes a weak and unsatisfactory close. The char-

acter of Dorotea, her wit and resourcefulness, are among
the redeeming features of the story and make her the
only living personality of its plot. It is, therefore, repellent from a purely artistic point of view to think
that her mere reunion with such a villain as Fernando
should compensate her for the wrongs he had done her.
But according to the intrinsic character of the older
love and adventure story, a study of the nature of
woman had for the most part remained in embryo. She
is generally represented devoid of any will of her own,
she yields to man's passion because nature created her
frail, and her unique quality, that of great beauty,
naturally becomes subservient to the higher mental and
spiritual qualities of man. In the charming character
of Dorotea, Cervantes mounts above this unpsychological
tradition, and consequently the characters of the others,
especially that of her repulsive lover and of the lacrimose
Luscinda, seem unnatural amid their realistic surroundings. It may be that Cervantes himself was slightly
troubled over the course of his invention, for he introduces a justification of his procedure in the middle of
his narrative:

Happy and fortunate were the times when that most daring
knight Don Quixote of La Mancha was sent into the world;
for by reason of his having formed a resolution so honorable as
that of seeking to revive and restore to the world the long-lost
and almost defunct order of knight-errantry, we now enjoy in
this age of ours, *so poor in light entertainment,* not only the

charm of his veracious history, but also of the tales and episodes contained in it, which are, *in a measure,* no less pleasing, ingenious, and truthful, than the history itself. [I, 28.]

The tale of *Ill-advised Curiosity,* which is also introduced, constitutes another addition of secondary importance. Cervantes recognized later that, wholly apart from the interest which may attach to the story, the manner of its introduction was an inartistic mistake. Shortly after arriving at the hostelry, Don Quixote and his party get into an amusing argument with the innkeeper, who is as great a devotee of books of chivalry as the knight and possesses a number of them. His firm belief in the truth of their contents forms a delightful pendant to the madness of Don Quixote, for he remarks that he would rather have a child of his burnt than see one of these books destroyed. He brings them out to show to his guests, and among them is discovered the manuscript of a novel, entitled *Ill-advised Curiosity.* The curate is persuaded to read it to the assembled listeners, and we thus have no organic reason for its incorporation into *Don Quixote.* Cervantes admitted this in the second part of his book, for he recognizes the justice of contemporary criticism, which had already pointed out that the narrative was an insertion wholly out of place.

In previous chapters a story entitled *The Captive* has been mentioned, because its autobiographical details are of the greatest value and interest to every reader of

Cervantes. While Don Quixote and his friends are foregathered at the inn where all the characters of the double love story have met, their conversation is interrupted by the arrival of a traveller whose appearance might well have been copied from that of Cervantes himself, for we are told that he was "a man of a robust and well-proportioned frame, in age a little over forty, rather swarthy in complexion, with long mustaches and a full beard, and, in short, his appearance was such that if he had been well dressed he would have been taken for a person of quality and good birth." In due time the Captive tells his experiences, and although it may be said that even this tale is an unrelated addition to the history of *Don Quixote*, it has the justification, at least, of fitting into the atmosphere of an inn where travellers of every description were wont to tarry and exchange the stories of their adventures. And we have every reason to be grateful for the illuminating pictures which it contains of the career of Cervantes himself.

It would take us too far afield to rehearse all the resources of the author's inventive gift in making of the inn a moving picture of boundless variety, with episodes both serious and gay. The highest achievement of the first part is reached here in the diversification of the dialogue and of the scenes, in the richness of vocabulary and homely, current phrase, in the mastery of description as well as of movement, in the course of which all the interwoven threads of his variegated story are unravelled smoothly and without effort. The guests at the inn gradually disperse, and the solution of Don Quixote's return is admirably handled. A number of his companions, whose ringleaders we may assume are the barber and curate, devise a plan by which the credulous knight is completely deceived. They hire an ox-cart to carry him to his village, and having constructed "a kind of cage with wooden bars," they seize Don Quixote while asleep, and shut him up within it. Under the conviction that he has been overcome by phantoms of the castle in which he is lodging and imprisoned by the power of enchantment, Don Quixote submits to being carried off against his will. Some of the incidents which occur during his return have already been mentioned (pp. 197, 236), and it remains to refer briefly to the first sketch of a character introduced at his home-coming, namely the wife of Sancho Panza. The part which she plays in his subsequent history is one of Cervantes' happiest inspirations. The meeting of the wandering squire and his spouse is depicted as follows:

At the news of Don Quixote's arrival Sancho Panza's wife came running, for she by this time knew that her husband had gone away with him as his squire, and on seeing Sancho, the first thing she asked him was if the ass was well. Sancho replied that he was, and better than his master.

"Thanks be to God," said she, "for being so good; but now tell me, my friend, what have you made by your squirings? What gown have you brought me back? What shoes for your children?"

"I bring nothing of the sort, wife," said Sancho; ". . . be content for the present; for if it please God that we should again go on our travels in search of adventures, you will soon see me a count, or governor of an island, and that not one of those everyday ones, but the best that is to be had."

"Heaven grant it, husband," said she, "for, indeed, we have need of it. But tell me, what's this about islands, for I don't understand it."

"Honey is not for the mouth of the ass," returned Sancho; "all in good time you shall see, wife, nay, you will be surprised to hear yourself called 'your ladyship' by all your vassals." [I, 52.]

Don Quixote in the meantime is taken into his house and put to bed, while his niece and housekeeper "renewed their maledictions upon the books of chivalry, and implored Heaven to plunge the authors of such lies and nonsense into the bottomless pit." The possibility of a third sally is hinted at, but no definite indication that Cervantes had determined upon writing a second part is given.

The defects of this masterpiece need not be pointed out at length. They are inherent in the character of its narrative, in the simple beginning without a definite plan, and in the scope which it assumed during its unlimited growth. Cervantes was the first to admit the demerits of its unrelated features, and only trivial or academic criticism will point out an occasional oversight by the author. Near the beginning of the second part Cervantes devotes considerable space to an analysis of the first; and, as his own words are always the most illuminating, it will be worth while to quote some portions of his self-criticism; Sancho reports to his master that he has just heard that their history is already abroad in books:

"The author of our history," said Don Quixote, "must be some sage enchanter; for to such nothing that they choose to write about is hidden." . . . If, however, it were the fact that such a history were in existence it must necessarily, being the story of a knight-errant, be grandiloquent, lofty, imposing, ample and true. With this he consoled himself somewhat, though it made him uncomfortable to think that the author was a Moor, . . . and that he might have dealt with his love affairs in some indecorous fashion, which might tend to the discredit and prejudice of his lady, Dulcinea. [II, 2, 3.]

The student Sansón Carrasco—called by his academic title, the bachelor—one of the new and most successful creations of the second part, as we shall see, now enters, and treating Don Quixote like a famous knight, he kneels before him and kisses his hand:

Don Quixote made him rise, and said, "So then, it is true that there is a history of me, and that it was a Moor and a sage who wrote it?"

"So true is it, señor," said Sansón, "that my belief is that there are more than twelve thousand volumes of the said history in print this very day, . . . and I am persuaded there will not be a country or language in which there will not be a translation of it."

"One of the things," observed Don Quixote, "that ought to give most pleasure to a virtuous and eminent man is to find himself in his lifetime in print, familiar in peoples' mouths with a good name. I say with a good name, for if it be the opposite, then there is no death to be compared with it."

". . . There are those," replied the bachelor, "who have read the history and say they would have been glad if the author had left out some of the countless cudgelings that were inflicted on Señor Don Quixote in various encounters."

"That's where the truth of the history comes in," said Sancho. [II, 3.]

The first part is finally characterized as follows:

It is so plain that there is nothing in it to puzzle over; the children turn its leaves, the young people read it, the grown-up understand it, the old folk praise it. In a word, it is so thumbed and read and got by heart by people of all sorts, that the instant they see any lean hack, they say, "There goes Rocinante." . . . In short, the said history is the most delightful and least injurious entertainment that has been hitherto seen, for there is not to be found in the whole of it even the semblance of an immodest word. . . . [II, 3.]

Cervantes furthermore admits the inexplicable error of the first edition in connection with the history of Dapple. In the course of the narrative the reader hears that the ass has disappeared without being told how, and a little later Sancho is seen mounted once more upon his faithful companion. Again there is no explanation of his return. As a matter of fact this is but one of the many demerits of the first edition. Owing to the careless way in which it was printed its typographical errors are numerous; whole phrases seem to have dropped out, in which omission portions of the story of Dapple may well have been included. The punctuation is of the crudest, and the problems which arise in the determination of a pure text are numberless. As a piece of defective book-making the first edition, the only authoritative one, of the first part of *Don Quixote*, is worthy to be placed by the side of the first folio of Shakespeare. For this reason Cervantes divined correctly what would be the fate of his work when he hints that it would require a commentary to make certain things clear to the modern reader. And indeed, among great books, none has received more detailed attention from scholars the world over.

Yet every new study has set upon a firmer foundation the originality, the broad humanity of Cervantes' masterpiece. Its fame has steadily grown, and each fresh word of praise has, without a discordant voice, but served to present a truer measure of its vast purport. In the case of many an eminent literary work the personality of the author has faded from its pages, but Cervantes is ever present by the side of his book; and although civilization, and with it our customs, may change radically, the essentials of his creation will endure, because they have become an inalienable portion of human thought, and represent an unassailable interpretation of human society.

CHAPTER VIII

"THE RESOURCEFUL KNIGHT DON QUIXOTE DE LA MANCHA" (PART II)

EN years elapsed between the publication of the two parts of Cervantes' masterpiece, and the intimate connection between them will justify the discussion of the sequel before the intervening facts of his life between 1605 and 1616 are considered. The composition of the second part presumably occupied most of this decade: there are indications that Cervantes was again at work on the romance in 1606 or 1607, and the dedication of the completed work to the Count of Lemos is dated the last of October, 1615. The final approval was signed November 5, and the title page bears the imprint 1615, but the book could hardly have been in general circulation before the new year. In the fourth chapter Don Quixote questions the young student, Carrasco, about some details regarding the first part of his story, and he adds:

"Does the author promise a second part at all?"

"He does promise one," replied Sansón; "but he says he has not found it, nor does he know who has it; and we cannot say whether it will appear or not. So, on that head, as some say that no second part has ever been good, and others that enough has been already written about Don Quixote, it is thought there will be no second part. Yet some, who are jovial rather than saturnine, say, 'Let us have more quixotic deeds, let Don Quixote charge and Sancho talk, and no matter how it may turn out, we shall be satisfied with that.' "

"And what does the author mean to do?" said Don Quixote.

"Why," replied Sansón, "as soon as he has found the history which he is now searching for with extraordinary diligence, he will at once give it to the press." [II, 4.]

If Cervantes had any misgivings about the relative merits of the two parts of his story, the verdict of posterity would have reassured him. While there are many critics who have maintained that the first part is unsurpassed, an equal number has been of the opinion that the second part in every way equals, or even excels the first. Without going into this question, we shall see that the two parts are very distinct in character, that Cervantes not only made concessions to the critics of the first part, but followed the advice in the quotation just given. Henceforth it was to be truly a history of Don Quixote and Sancho Panza with as few unrelated additions as possible. But Cervantes at times continues to be perplexed over the limitations which this resolve imposed upon his narrative: and he takes issue with himself for beginning "a story so dry and of so little variety as this of Don Quixote, for he found himself forced to speak perpetually of him and Sancho, without venturing to indulge in digressions and episodes more serious and more interesting.'' As a result, therefore, of this principle of restriction in the material the two protagonists of the story are never lost from view; even when they do not appear on the scene together their separation is brief, and we are always conscious of their indissoluble partnership. Thus, when Sancho is sent away to take over the governorship of the ''island'' which was so often promised to him—in accordance with the custom of victorious knights who create their squires governors or kings of conquered territory—he is followed by the solicitous interest of Don Quixote, who starts him off with wise counsel and keeps in touch with him by writing him a letter filled with paternal devotion.

This concentration upon two individuals was bound to make both characters widely different from the Don Quixote and Sancho Panza whom we have met in the first part. During the first and second sallies, which constitute the earlier history of the hero, episodes and action predominate. Don Quixote's hallucinations about the calling of a knight-errant form the basic idea to which most prominence is given, the broader humor and the more farcical scenes and burlesques are completely in accord with such an attitude of mind. In the sequel, however, his madness is, if not always secondary to the sober and noble traits of his character, at least so greatly refined and restrained as to make logical the development of his saner nature. It is the same with Sancho, who when he first begins his quest of adventures is merely a peasant and swineherd, much bewildered at seeing himself taken out of his realistic world and plunged into an imaginary life of romance, to save abducted damsels, to fight giants or whole armies, and house with an empty stomach in enchanted castles. In living with these creations Cervantes moulded them step by step into something far more comprehensive, and, as a consequence, mere adventures were replaced more and more by delineation of character. The development of the individualities of Don Quixote and Sancho Panza had another striking advantage in that it reflected itself in the drawing of other characters whom Cervantes introduced in the third sally. Here numerous types and individuals have sprung into being, so firmly and minutely drawn that they move before the reader with no less vitality than the knight and squire themselves.

In amplifying the character of Don Quixote Cervantes was able to bring him into closer relation with the life he himself knew, to make him not only a dreamer with incorrect inferences about everything he saw, but a clear-headed reasoner on the character of human society. The intermittent sanity of the knight justified placing in his mouth a careful discussion of various subjects, morality or matters of the nature of social problems, together with contemporary aspects of government and the proper organization of communities of man. Cervantes presents this development in Don Quixote gradually, with a skill which permits the assumption

that he was consciously leading him away from that
earliest conception of a caricature to the most subtle
shaping of a spiritual personality. In the first part
Don Quixote does not feel that he must explain or
apologize for the nature of his calling; in the second
part he seems to realize that the self-imposed task of
reforming a perverted world may not be understood by
everybody, and so, upon one occasion he expatiates upon
his point of view to a new acquaintance, Don Diego de
Miranda, an admirable gentleman and a sane contrast
to Don Quixote. After the knight has reached ''the
furthest and the highest point of his unexampled courage,'' in an amusing combat with a lion, which is witnessed by the dumbfounded Don Diego, he feels obliged
to enlighten him as follows:

"No doubt, Señor Don Diego de Miranda, you set me down
in your mind as a fool and a madman, and it would be no
wonder if you did, for my deeds do not argue anything else.
But, for all that, I would have you take notice that I am neither
so mad nor so foolish as I must have seemed to you. A gallant
knight shows to advantage bringing his lance to bear adroitly
upon a fierce bull under the eyes of his sovereign, in the midst
of a spacious plaza; a knight shows to advantage arrayed in
glittering armor pacing the lists before the ladies in some
joyous tournament, and all those knights show to advantage
that entertain, divert, and, if we may say so, honor the courts
of their princes by warlike exercises, or what resemble them.
But to greater advantage than all these does a knight-errant
show when he traverses deserts, solitudes, cross-roads, forests,

and mountains, in quest of perilous adventures, bent on bringing them to a happy and successful issue, all to win a glorious and lasting renown.   To greater advantage, I maintain, does the knight-errant show bringing aid to some widow in some lonely waste, than the court knight dallying with some city damsel. All knights have their own special parts to play; let the courtier devote himself to the ladies, let him add lustre to his sovereign's court by his liveries, let him entertain poor gentlemen with the sumptuous fare of his table, let him arrange joustings, marshal tournaments, and prove himself noble, generous, and magnificent, and above all a good Christian, and so doing he will fulfill the duties which are especially his; but let the knight-errant explore the corners of the earth and penetrate the most intricate labyrinths, at each step let him attempt impossibilities, on desolate heaths let him endure the burning rays of the midsummer sun, and the bitter inclemency of the winter winds and frosts; let no lions daunt him, no monsters terrify him, no dragons make him quail; for to seek the latter, to attack the former, and to vanquish all, are in truth his main duties.   I, then, as it has fallen to my lot to be a member of knight-errantry, cannot avoid attempting all that to me seems to come within the sphere of my duties; thus it was my bounden duty to attack those lions that I just now attacked, although I knew it to be the height of rashness; for I know well what valor is, that it is a virtue which occupies a place between two vicious extremes, cowardice and temerity; but it will be a lesser evil for him who is valiant to rise until he reaches the point of rashness, than to sink until he reaches the point of cowardice; for, as it is easier for the prodigal than for the miser to become generous, so it is easier for a rash man to prove truly valiant than for a coward to rise to true valor; and, believe me, Señor Don Diego, in attempting adventures it is better to lose by a card too many than by a card too few; for, to hear it said, 'such a knight is rash and daring,' sounds better than 'such a knight is timid and cowardly.'"

"I protest, Señor Don Quixote," said Don Diego, "everything you have said and done is proved correct by the test of reason itself; and I believe, if the laws and ordinances of knight-errantry should be lost, they might be found in your worship's breast as their own proper archive and repository." [II, 17.]

We have here an admirable example of the mixture of nonsense and sanity in a character who is still living in the atmosphere of a world created by lying books and false inferences; but he is no longer unrelated to aspects of the society in which he lives, for he can point out its salient characteristics in an illuminating manner. Even nobler and more spiritual is the apology which Don Quixote makes to his hosts, the Duke and Duchess who have received "the famous Knight of the Rueful Countenance" under their hospitable roof:

"Is it, haply, an idle occupation, or is the time ill spent that is consumed in roaming the world in quest, not of its enjoyments, but of those arduous toils whereby the good mount upwards to the abodes of everlasting life? If gentlemen, great lords, nobles, men of high birth, were to rate me as a fool I should take it as an irreparable insult; but I care not a farthing if clerks who have never entered upon or trod the paths of chivalry should think me foolish. Knight I am, and knight I will die, if such be the pleasure of the Most High. Some take the broad road of overweening ambition; others that of mean and servile flattery; still others that of deceitful hypocrisy, and some that of true religion. But I, led by my star, follow the narrow path of knight-errantry, and in pursuit of that calling I despise wealth, but not honor. I have redressed injuries, righted wrongs, punished insolences, vanquished giants, and crushed monsters. I am in love, for no other reason than that it is incumbent on knights-errant to be so; but though I am, I am no carnal-minded lover, but one of the chaste, platonic sort. My intentions are always directed to worthy ends, to do good to all and evil to none." [II, 32.]

The amount of madness which remains in Don Quixote is therefore just enough to disconcert his listeners and add to the description of his deeds and character an amused interest; his positive qualities on the other hand, expressed in his lofty idealism and virtue, make him worthy of the enduring fame and honor which are the sole objects of his sufferings and of his quests.

It would have been fatal to the inner regeneration of Don Quixote to retain the primitive portraiture of Sancho, and Cervantes, with his usual sense of balance, has known how to bring about a corresponding refinement in the character and mental equipment of the servant. The squire's discretion and polish awaken astonishment not unmixed with gratification, especially in Don Quixote, who has raised him out of his lowly estate and exalted him to a place of distinction. But here, too, Cervantes does not let the reader forget that Sancho, in any garb or under any circumstances, is the same shrewd, matter-of-fact peasant's son. He may have increased his fund of wisdom of life and acquired an inexhaustible stock of proverbs and pointed sayings, his judgment may have been greatly sharpened, and he may have assumed a large measure of intellectual independence. But he is still the clod whose spiritual uplift has not yet included self-denial, or disdain for appetizing food. Because of these deficiencies the contrast between master and servant is still very marked, and Cervantes manages to bring this out from time to time in delightful, unobtrusive touches. On the eve of the wedding feast of the wealthy Camacho, into which the adventures of Don Quixote and Sancho are most happily woven, as we shall see presently, we find our two heroes beginning a new day in a characteristic fashion:

Scarce had the fair Aurora given bright Phœbus time to dry the liquid pearls upon her golden locks with the heat of his fervent rays, when Don Quixote, shaking off sloth from his limbs, sprang to his feet and called to his squire Sancho, who was still snoring. Seeing this, Don Quixote, ere he roused him, thus addressed him: "Happy are you, above all the dwellers on the face of the earth, who, without envying or being envied, sleep with tranquil mind. . . . Ambition breaks not your rest, nor does this world's empty pomp disturb you, for the utmost reach of your anxiety is to provide for your ass, since upon my shoulders you have laid the support of yourself. . . . The servant sleeps and the master lies awake thinking how he is to feed him, advance him and reward him. The distress of seeing the sky turn brazen and withhold its needful moisture from the earth is not felt by the servant but by the master, who in time of scarcity and famine must support him that has served him in times of plenty and abundance."

To all this Sancho made no reply, because he was asleep, nor would he have wakened up so soon as he did had not Don Quixote brought him to his senses with the butt of his lance. He awoke at last drowsy and lazy, and casting his eyes about in every direction, observed, "There comes, if I don't mistake, from the quarter of that arcade a steam and a smell a great deal more like fried rashers of bacon than sedge and thyme." [II, 20.]

In the first part the wit and intelligence of Sancho are more imitative than in the second; he takes his cue for much that he says from the speech and even the vocabulary of his master. Being new to the business of knight-errantry, he is engrossed chiefly by his adventures or misadventures, in short, by the need of adapting himself to his new calling. In the second part he has taken the measure of his master's profession and become acquainted with all of his qualities. After many bruises and drubbings his intelligence has awakened, and he shows judgment as well as independence in his point of view. It is fair to assert that in the development of Sancho's mind and character, far more than in the delineation of Don Quixote, Cervantes gave expression to a type of wisdom and eloquence and to a shrewd analysis of life which constitute the essence of his humanism. In the second part Sancho has, therefore, become a philosophical squire; new situations awaken in him a train of ideas, and although his master is frequently irritated by the growing flood of his words, the animadversions of the squire are generally to the point. Undoubtedly, one of the chief attractions which the quest of adventures now has for him, is the opportunity to converse to his heart's desire. In connection with the wedding of Camacho, who is noted in the community for his great opulence, Sancho learns that the bride has a rejected suitor, one Basilio, who is well known and popular because of his dexterity at games and his personal attractions; but he is as poor as Camacho is rich. This situation is discussed by Sancho:

"It is my opinion a poor man should be content with what he can get, and not go looking for dainties at the bottom of the sea. I will bet an arm that Camacho could bury Basilio in reals; and if that be so, as no doubt it is, what a fool the bride, Quiteria, would be to refuse the fine dresses and jewels Camacho must have given her and will give her, and take Basilio's bar-throwing and sword-play. . . . On a good foundation you can raise a good building, and the best foundation and ground-work in the world is money."

"For God's sake, Sancho," said Don Quixote here, "stop that harangue; it is my belief, if you were allowed to continue all that you begin every instant, you would have no time left for eating or sleeping; you would spend it all in talking."

"If your worship had a good memory," replied Sancho, "you would remember the articles of our agreement before we started from home this last time; one of them was that I was to say all I liked, so long as it was not against my neighbor or your worship's authority; and so far, it seems to me, I have not broken the said article."

"I remember no such article, Sancho," said Don Quixote. [II, 20.]

A little later, Sancho again asserts that in any choice between the two suitors, Camacho is the man for him; his idealistic master, who thinks the poor Basilio the worthier person, chides him:

"It is easy to see that you are a clown, Sancho," said Don Quixote, "and one of the sort that cry, 'Long life to the conqueror.'"

"I don't know of what sort I am," returned Sancho, "but I know very well I'll never get such elegant skimmings off Basilio's pots as these I have got off Camacho's;" and he showed him a bucketful of geese and hens, and seizing one began to eat with great gaiety and appetite, saying, "a fig for the accomplishments of Basilio! As much as you have, so much are you worth, and as much as you are worth so much do you have. As a grandmother of mine used to say, there are only two families in the world, the Haves and the Haven'ts, and she stuck to the Haves. To this day, Señor Don Quixote, people would sooner feel the pulse of 'Have,' than of 'Know'; an ass covered with gold looks better than a horse with a pack-saddle. . . ."

"Have you finished your harangue, Sancho?" said Don Quixote.

"Of course I have finished it," replied Sancho, "because I see your worship takes offence at it; but if it were not for that, there was work enough cut out for three days."

"God grant I may see you dumb before I die, Sancho," said Don Quixote.

"At the rate we are going," said Sancho, "I'll be chewing clay before your worship dies; and then, maybe, I'll be so dumb I'll not say a word until the end of the world or, at least, until the day of judgment."

"Even should that happen, O Sancho," said Don Quixote, "your silence will never come up to all you have talked, are talking and will talk in all your life; moreover, it naturally stands to reason, that my death will come before yours. So I never expect to see you dumb, not even when you are drinking or sleeping, and that is the utmost I can say."

"In good faith, señor," replied Sancho, "there is no trusting that fleshless one, I mean Death, who devours the lamb as soon as the sheep, and, as I have heard our curate say, treads with equal foot upon the lofty towers of kings and the lowly huts of the poor. That lady is more mighty than dainty, she is no way squeamish, she devours all and is ready for all, and fills her saddle-bags with people of all sorts, ages and ranks. She is no reaper that sleeps out the noontide; at all times she is reaping and cutting down, as well the dry grass as the green. . . ."

"Say no more, Sancho," said Don Quixote at this; "don't try to better it and risk a fall; for in truth what you have said about Death in your rustic phrase is what a good preacher might have said. . . ." [II, 20.]

The entire passage with all its wisdom and humor deserves to be quoted in full. Its eloquence and its shrewd moralizing no less than its vitality and wide application recall some of the humanistic qualities which were pointed out in the *Celestina*. They were a notable manifestation of the Renascence, and the peculiar skill with which Cervantes has developed them constitutes one of the charms of the sequel of his masterpiece. An added touch of wit may be found in the growing liberties which Sancho takes with Don Quixote; his impertinence is an evidence of his newly acquired mental independence, yet only in extreme cases does it draw the wrath of the noble knight. Under these new circumstances of their relations, of their greater devotion to one another, which are but the natural result of their common victories and reverses, each has formed a well-rounded opinion of the other. When knight and squire reach the palace of the Duke and Duchess who entertain them, they find ample opportunity to converse, and each unburdens his soul to the hosts. Don Quixote thus describes Sancho:

"I would have your graces understand that Sancho Panza is one of the drollest squires that ever served knight-errant; sometimes he utters such shrewd absurdities that it is an amusement to try and make out whether he is simple or sharp; he has mischievous tricks that stamp him rogue, and blundering ways, that prove him a booby; he doubts everything and believes everything; when I fancy he is on the point of coming down headlong from sheer stupidity, he comes out with something shrewd that sends him up to the skies. After all, I would not exchange him for another squire, though I were given a city to boot, and, therefore, I am in doubt whether it will be well to send him to the government your generosity has bestowed upon him. I perceive in him a certain aptitude for the work of governing, so that, with a little trimming of his understanding, he would manage any government as easily as the king does his taxes; and, moreover, we know already by ample experience that it does not require much cleverness or much learning to be a governor, for there are a hundred round about us that

scarcely know how to read, and govern like a gerfalcon. . . ."
[II, 32.]

Sancho, for his part, has had frequent occasions, no
doubt, to feel apologetic about his master's actions, but
never until now has he had such an opportunity to give
vent to his feelings. The Duchess especially is greatly
amused by him and desires to hear him talk, and Sancho
displays before her the pearls of his thoughts, his opinions of everything and of everybody, his plans and
ambitions, and all interlarded with a wealth of proverbs.
The Duchess questions him about the wisdom of serving
a mad knight; a voice tells her, she says:

"'If Don Quixote be mad, crazy, and cracked, and Sancho
Panza his squire knows it, and, notwithstanding, serves and
follows him, and goes trusting to his empty promises, there
can be no doubt he must be still madder and sillier than his
master; and, that being so, it will be cast in your teeth, señora
duchess, if you give the said Sancho an island to govern; for
how will he who knows not how to govern himself know how
to govern others?'"

"By heaven, señora," said Sancho, "that doubt comes natural;
but your grace may bid it speak out plain, and say what it
likes; for I know it says true; and that if I were wise I should
have left my master long ago; but this was my fate, this was
my bad luck; I can't help it, I must follow him; we're from the
same village, I have eaten his bread, I'm fond of him, he is
free-handed, he gave me his ass-colts, and above all I'm faithful; so it's quite impossible for anything to separate us, except
the pickaxe and shovel. And if your haughtiness does not like

to give me the government you promised, God made me without
it, and maybe your not giving it to me will be all the better
for my conscience, for fool as I am, I know the proverb, 'To
her hurt the ant got wings,' and it may be that Sancho the
squire will get to heaven sooner than Sancho the governor.
'They make as good bread here as in France,' and 'By night all
cats are gray,' and 'A hard enough case his, who hasn't breakfasted by two in the afternoon,' and 'There's no stomach a hand's
breadth bigger than another,' and the same can be filled 'with
straw or hay,' as the saying is, and 'The little birds of the
field have God for their purveyor and caterer,' 'Four yards
of Cuenca frieze keep one warmer than four of Segovia broad-
cloth,' and 'When we quit this world and are put underground
the prince travels by as narrow a path as the journeyman,' and
'The Pope's body does not take up more feet of earth than the
sacristan's,' for all that one is higher than the other; for when
we go to our graves we all pack ourselves up and make ourselves small, or rather they pack us up and make us small in
spite of us, and then—good-night to us. And I say once more,
if your ladyship does not like to give me the island because I'm
a fool, I, like a wise man, will take care to give myself no
trouble about it. . . ."   [II, 33.]

In this inexhaustible well-spring of homely wit and
philosophy, in the heaping up of popular phrases, the
dialogue of Cervantes likewise reveals a certain relationship to that of the *Celestina*. The vast distinction lies
in his perfected style and diction. Only rarely has Cervantes overshot the mark in allowing Sancho to make
use of words or sentences which under no circumstances
could sound natural in his mouth, as when, on one occa-

sion (ch. 8) he speaks of the "prerogatives possessed by the bodies and relics of Saints," and again when (ch. 40) he protests against the unfairness of the chroniclers of knights' deeds who "write curtly, 'Don Paralipomenon of the Three Stars accomplished the adventure of the six monsters' without mentioning such a person as his squire, who was there all the time, just as if there were no such being." All this is explained by the fact that Sancho has taken on an unusual polish through constant contact with the well read Don Quixote.

Thus the newly acquired trait of intelligent talkativeness displayed by Sancho enabled Cervantes to give unrestricted expression to his own great gift, perhaps his very greatest, that of his dialogue. It was through this instrument that it became possible to discuss and analyze the widest range of subjects, and place before the mental eye of the reader a truthful and detailed image of contemporary society. One more example will be worth while. After Don Quixote and Sancho have met upon the highway a company of actors travelling in a cart from one village to another, our heroes are led to expatiate upon the business of actors and the moral aspect of plays in general. Don Quixote, voicing the enthusiasm of Cervantes himself, extols players, "who place before us at every step a mirror in which we may see vividly displayed what goes on in human life," and then he continues:

"Have you not seen a play acted in which kings, emperors,

popes, knights, ladies, and divers other personages were introduced? One plays the ruffian, another the knave, this one the
merchant, that the soldier, one the sharp-witted fool, another
the foolish lover; and when the play is over, and they have
put off the dresses they wore in it, all the actors become equal."

"Yes, I have seen that," said Sancho.

"Well, then," said Don Quixote, "the same thing happens in
the comedy and life of this world, where some play emperors,
others popes, and, in short, all the characters that can be
brought into a play; but when it is over, that is to say when life
ends, death strips them all of the garments that distinguish
one from the other, and all are equal in the grave."

"A fine comparison," said Sancho; "though not so new but
that I have heard it many and many a time, as well as that other
one of the game of chess; how, so long as the game lasts, each
piece has its own particular office, and when the game is finished
they are all mixed, jumbled up and shaken together, and stowed
away in a bag, which is much like ending life in the grave."

"You are growing less simple and more shrewd every day,
Sancho," said Don Quixote.

"Yes," said Sancho; "it must be that some of your worship's
discretion sticks to me. . . ."   [II, 12.]

In addition to the development of the dialogue in the
second part, the delineation of specific personages who
are added to the canvas received the greatest care.
There is, first, the pendant to Sancho, his wife, Teresa
Panza, who is drawn in the same delightful vein which
characterizes her husband. Teresa represents the essence
of sanity; she is a counterbalance for her talkative husband whose ambition to become a governor and to rise

in the world has gone to his head. Teresa does not appear frequently in the book, but in a scene or two Cervantes has portrayed her character sufficiently so as to make her quite as tangible a figure as Sancho. These two are fully worthy of one another, they are versed in the same popular phrases and proverbs, and by the interpretation of their own world they remain whole-hearted children of the soil, untutored peasant folk who use the wits nature has given them. The main difference between them, however, so humorously brought out by Cervantes, is the new point of view Sancho has acquired in his wanderings, that the lowly condition from which both have sprung is no longer good enough for a man of his prospects. Teresa, who has little regard for knight-errantry, knows how small those prospects are, and tries to oppose her husband's notions by common sense. One day after an interview with his master, Don Quixote, Sancho comes to tell Teresa that he has determined to set out once more in quest of adventures. The following dialogue between the two ensues:

"I know well enough, husband," said Teresa, "that squires-errant don't eat their bread for nothing, and so I will be always praying to Our Lord to deliver you speedily from all that hard fortune."

"I can tell you, wife," said Sancho, "if I did not expect to see myself governor of an island before long, I should drop down dead on the spot."

"Very well then, husband," said Teresa, "let the hen live though it be with the pip. Live, and let the devil take all the governments in the world; you came out of your mother's womb without a government, you have lived until now without a government, and when it's God's will you will go, or be carried to your grave, without a government. How many are there in the world who live without a government, and continue to live all the same, and are reckoned in the number of people! The best sauce in the world is hunger, and as the poor are never without that, they always eat with a relish." [II, 5.]

But Teresa is manifestly made of the same clay as Sancho, and the prospect of advancement, however faint, is not without its lure. So she qualifies her objections to her husband's project:

"But mind, Sancho, if by good luck you should find yourself with some government, don't forget me and your children. Remember that Sanchico is now full fifteen, and it is right he should go to school, if his uncle the abbot has a mind to have him trained for the church. Consider, too, that your daughter, Mari-Sancha, will not die of grief if we marry her; for I have my suspicions that she is as eager to get a husband as you to get a government. . . ." [II, 5.]

The rest of this amusing discussion about the kind of man the daughter is to marry is one of the most famous passages of *Don Quixote*, and has already been referred to briefly (p. 29). It was extensively imitated by later writers, especially outside of Spain. It may suffice to speak here of the indebtedness of Molière, who in his *Bourgeois Gentilhomme* has put the essence of the discussion between Sancho and Teresa into the dialogue between M. Jourdain and his wife, who, like Teresa, is greatly worried about her husband's ambitions for her daughter.*

In the second part of *Don Quixote* Cervantes employs various methods of delineation, either, as in the case of Sancho Panza and of his wife, by conversation—a process of self-revelation in which Cervantes is supreme master—or by direct description, in which the appearance and character of the personages are drawn, sometimes objectively, in the words of the author, sometimes in those of the personages themselves. An excellent example of Cervantes' gift of direct portraiture may be found in the young student, Sansón Carrasco—generally called by his academic title, the bachelor—a fellow-townsman of Don Quixote, who plays an important part in two adventures by engaging the knight in single battle. Carrasco is briefly but clearly drawn when he first appears before the reader:

The bachelor, though he was called Samson, was of no great bodily size, but he was a very great wag. He was of a sallow complexion, but very sharp-witted, somewhere about four and

---

* There is very slight evidence, however, that Molière used Cervantes' text; he probably took his material entirely from earlier French plays based on the story of *Don Quixote,* and composed by Guérin de Bouscal in the thirties of the seventeenth century.

twenty years of age, with a round face, a flat nose, and a large
mouth, all indications of a mischievous disposition and a love
of fun and jokes. Of this he gave a sample as soon as he saw
Don Quixote, by falling on his knees before him and saying,
"Let me kiss your mightiness's hand. . . ." [II, 3.]

After the knight has set out for the third time in
quest of adventures, Sansón and his two friends, the
barber and the curate, put their heads together to devise
some means "to induce Don Quixote to stay at home in
peace and quiet without worrying himself with his ill-
starred adventures." They decide that Sansón is to
sally forth in the disguise of a knight-errant and having done battle with Don Quixote and vanquished him,
the defeated knight would be at the mercy of the victor.
Sansón thus plans to command Don Quixote to return
home and not to leave his house until he received further orders from his conqueror. He takes with him as
squire a neighbor and friend of Sancho Panza, one
Tomé Cecial, who by his own conversation furnishes a
notable example of Cervantes' method of indirect portraiture. Knights and squires meet at night in a grove,
and the dialogues which ensue are among the happiest
inspirations in *Don Quixote*. Notably that between
Sancho and Tomé Cecial gives Cervantes further opportunity to indulge in delightful wit and that humorous
art of pen-picture of which we are speaking. The two
squires enter into a discussion of their lot, they analyze

the character and ambitions of their masters, they weigh the promises which have been held out to them to induce them to become squires-errant. But Cervantes is unquestionably at his best in the animadversion of these two rustics on their respective families, on the duties which ought to keep them at home and the hollow prospects which have drawn them away into deserts and highways. Their conversation takes place over an improvised spread consisting of wine and a generous meat-pie brought by the provident Tomé in his saddle-bags. The gratification of Sancho may be imagined, who, as we saw, was not at all in sympathy with Don Quixote's principle "that knights-errant must sustain themselves on dried fruits and the herbs of the fields." In the drawing of Tomé Cecial and his master, in the battle which follows between the two knights and in the defeat of Sansón, Cervantes is especially happy, and again shows his rare gift of mingling burlesque with a realism expressed in minute pictures of Spanish life.

A notable example in which Cervantes supplements the direct manner of delineation just referred to, by means of self-description on the part of the character, thus fusing his two methods, may be found in the remarkable picture of Don Diego de Miranda. The portrait of this gentleman whom Don Quixote meets upon the highway is the most finished effort of its kind in the romance. Don Diego's outward appearance is first presented:

As they were engaged in this conversation they were overtaken by a man who was following the same road behind them, mounted on a very handsome grayish mare, and dressed in a loose cloak of fine green cloth, with tawny velvet facings, and a cap of the same velvet. The trappings of the mare, likewise of mulberry color and green, were of the hunter's fashion. He carried a Moorish cutlass hanging from a broad green and gold baldric; the buskins were of the same make as the baldric; the spurs were not gilt, but lacquered green, and so brightly polished that, matching as they did the rest of his apparel, they looked better than if they had been of pure gold. . . .

In appearance he was about fifty years of age, with but few gray hairs, an aquiline cast of features, and with an expression between grave and gay; and his dress and accoutrements showed him to be a man of good condition. What he in green thought of Don Quixote of La Mancha was that a man of that sort and shape he had never seen; he marvelled at the length of his hair, his lofty stature, the lankness and sallowness of his countenance, his armor, his bearing and his gravity—a figure and picture such as had not been seen in those regions for many a long day. [II, 16.]

There is hardly a detail lacking in this picture of "the man in green," and the effect is greatly heightened by the opportune contrast with the appearance of Don Quixote. The one all color, admirably garbed, upon a fine horse, the other with his old armor, and the gray tone of the dusty highway, sallow and mounted upon a bony nag. Then follows the description of the character of Don Diego by himself, in which Cervantes carefully suits the inner to the outer man:

"I, Sir Knight of the Rueful Countenance, am a gentleman by birth, native of the village where, please God, we are going to dine today; I am more than fairly well off, and my name is Don Diego de Miranda. I pass my life with my wife, children, and friends; my pursuits are hunting and fishing, but I keep neither hawks nor greyhounds, nothing but a tame partridge or a bold ferret or two; I have six dozen or so of books, some in our mother tongue, some Latin, some of them history, others devotional; those of chivalry have not as yet crossed the threshold of my door; I am more given to turning over the profane than the devotional, so long as they are books of honest entertainment that charm by their style and attract and interest by the invention they display; though of these there are very few in Spain. Sometimes I dine with my neighbors and friends, and often invite them; my entertainments are neat and well served, without stint of anything. I have no taste for tattle, nor do I allow tattling in my presence; I pry not into my neighbor's lives, nor have I lynx-eyes for what others do. I hear mass every day; I share my substance with the poor, making no display of good works, lest I let hypocrisy and vain-glory, those enemies that subtly take possession of the most watchful heart, find an entrance into mine. I strive to make peace between those whom I know to be at variance; I am the devoted servant of Our Lady, and my trust is ever in the infinite mercy of God Our Lord." [II, 16.]

This manner of self-revelation on the part of Don Diego may sound a trifle sanctimonious, yet we must keep in mind the author's method of treating the characters whose nobility and high spiritual worth he portrays down to the most insignificant trait. Inasmuch as Cer-

vantes permits Don Quixote to meet every kind of person
on the world's highway, it seems to give him a double
pleasure as artist and novelist to introduce to the reader
this noble Spaniard of lofty and exemplary virtues. By
this very principle of variety, the canvas of his novel
became a mirror of his times and every conceivable type
found its proper place upon it.

In the first part of *Don Quixote,* the background of
the knight's adventures is, almost in every case, relatively slight. The event, the scene, the number of characters involved are simply planned. The most elaborate effort may be called that which depicts the occurrences at the inn to which Don Quixote and his friends
have returned from the Sierra Morena. The variety
which Cervantes has imparted to the knight's sojourn in
this "enchanted castle," is notable, but the simplicity
of the picture has been preserved by the natural sequence
of adventures, such as would be customary at any much
frequented halfway house. In the second part Cervantes
gave free rein to his chief gift, his inventive and de-
scriptive faculty. It would be impossible to give an
adequate idea of the elaboration of his canvas, of the
background against which are thrown the adventures of
the second part of *Don Quixote.* No painter of hunting
scenes or garden fêtes could with his brush have added
more details of color, of costume or of grouping of the
personages than Cervantes did with his pen. But the
chief difference naturally lies in the animation and

motion of the scenes in *Don Quixote* in which dialogue and description are admirably balanced.

One of the most successful pictures is that of the wedding-feast of the rich peasant Camacho. From the moment that Sancho is attracted by the odor of the viands (*cf.* p. 259) which are being prepared for an unlimited number of guests to the hour of Don Quixote's leave-taking the reader is drawn into its gaieties and becomes one of the guests. Even Don Quixote and Sancho are no longer isolated, but are fused with the story of Basilio's and Quiteria's love and the hoax played on the wealthy Camacho. No detail has been omitted. Aside from the natural background and the chief participants, there are descriptions of costumes and dances, of the food and the varieties of merriment. The scene which meets Sancho's gaze will serve to give the spirit and richness of the whole episode:

The first thing that presented itself to Sancho's eyes was a whole ox spitted on a whole elm tree, and in the fire at which it was to be roasted there was burning a middling-sized mountain of faggots, and six stew-pots that stood round the blaze had not been made in the ordinary mould of common pots, for they were six half wine-jars, each fit to hold the contents of a slaughter-house; they swallowed up whole sheep and hid them away in their insides without showing any more sign of them than if they were pigeons. Countless were the hares ready skinned, and the plucked fowls that hung on the trees for burial in the pots, numberless the wildfowl and game of various sorts suspended from the branches that the air might keep them cool. Sancho counted more than sixty wine skins of over six gallons each, and all filled, as it proved afterwards, with generous wines. There were, besides, piles of the whitest bread, like the heaps of corn one sees on the threshing-floors. There was a wall made of cheeses arranged like open brick-work, and two cauldrons full of oil, bigger than those of a dyer's shop, served for cooking fritters, which when fried were taken out with two mighty shovels, and plunged into another cauldron of prepared honey that stood close by. Of cooks and cookmaids there were over fifty, all clean, brisk and blythe. In the capacious belly of the ox were a dozen soft little sucking-pigs, which, sewn up there, served to give it tenderness and flavor. The spices of different kinds did not seem to have been bought by the pound but by the quarter, and all lay open to view in a great chest. In short, all the preparations made for the wedding were in rustic style, but abundant enough to feed an army. [II, 20.]

Another adventure handled with supreme skill is that of the puppet theatre of Ginés de Pasamonte, in which Don Quixote views a representation of the romance of Don Gaiferos and the beautiful Melisendra. This episode, which ends in the amusing attack made by Don Quixote on the puppets, whom "by enchantment" he takes to be the real personages, is another happy fusion of burlesque and reality. It does not have the lavish artistic finish of the wedding of Camacho, but it has, on the other hand, more sparkle and irresistible spontaneity. The reader moves again in the midst of a number of living human beings, he becomes a guest at the inn at which the scene takes place, he hears the laughter and characteristic speech of the participants. Nothing in *Don Quixote* could give us a better idea of how Cervantes introduced what he himself must have experienced, for he, no doubt, had often watched the coming and going of travelers at roadhouses; and among them he may have seen some strolling showman, like Ginés de Pasamonte, with his theatre of puppets, whose advent stirred up the neighboring villages and gathered together all those types of old and young which Cervantes delighted in depicting.

In the course of the first part of *Don Quixote* the knight repeatedly promises his squire that his services are to be recompensed by the governorship of some island, which is an imitation of incidents in the romances of chivalry, especially in *Amadis of Gaul,* and *Palmerin of England,* and in the second part these prospects of Sancho are fulfilled. To accomplish this and, incidentally, prepare the ground for a number of adventures, Cervantes contrived the most comprehensive of all his "inventions," the visit of his two protagonists at the country residence of a Spanish nobleman. On this estate Don Quixote meets with a variety of experiences, and the Duke, his host, bestows upon Sancho the governorship of his longed-for island. The sojourn of the two heroes with the Duke and Duchess, including the incidents of Sancho's tenure of office, consumes twenty-eight chapters (30-57), and is the most elaborately wrought out portion of the history of *Don Quixote.*

In it every vein of the whole work, whether grave or gay, finds expression, and no résumé could hope to do it full justice. On the whole, burlesque predominates, and in a number of episodes, such as the pretended flight of master and servant through the air on the magic wooden steed Clavileño, or the midnight battle between Don Quixote and some intruding cats, Cervantes reverts to the broader humor and farce of the first part. The long series of hoaxes played on the knight and his squire is somewhat overdone; it leaves thè impression that the opportunity offered at the Duke's house for comic adventures has been a trifle abused. The sojourn results in another unfortunate drawback: it makes mere mechanical instruments of the Duke and Duchess through whose orders or connivance burlesques, pretended duels, amorous advances by love-sick damsels, disguises and masquerades become possible. Thus, in the midst of a marvelously contrived extravaganza, the characters of the host and hostess have no prominent qualities or striking individual virtues; and the reader is allowed to infer that this noble pair is too much given to deceiving Don Quixote and laughing at his discomfitures to appreciate his great spiritual worth. When the adventures are over, Don Quixote is the one who comes out of his experiences with most dignity. Yet this apparent defect is inherent in the whole episode. Cervantes could not lose sight of his protagonists, and the prominence which both Don Quixote and Sancho retain throughout the twenty-eight chapters spent on the Duke's domain will account for the one-sided delineation of the host and hostess. It is wholly unreasonable to surmise that Cervantes purposely desired to portray nobility in an unattractive light, by holding up as an example a nobleman and his wife whose occupation is idleness, and whose spirit at best is that of frivolity and selfishness. Without these wealthy and aristocratic personages who could be made the tools with which to realize the comedy and burlesque of Don Quixote's prolonged visit under their roof, the whole plan of these adventures becomes impossible. The Duke and Duchess, however imperfectly drawn, are an indispensable feature of the whole.

But this stricture cannot diminish the achievement attained by this particular portion of *Don Quixote,* from which we have already had occasion to quote various passages. Nowhere in the entire work is there greater variety or a more surprising richness of diction and beauty of style. These twenty-eight chapters represent all Spain as only Cervantes could depict it; they contain information which throws light on matters of dress and current customs, they embody interesting reminiscences of his reading, they are extremely happy in their balance of romance and fact. Every type of narrative or of dialogue of which Cervantes was capable may be found: there are formal discourses dealing chiefly with subjects of chivalry, there is a noble scene in which Don Quixote prepares the rustic Sancho for his duties as governor by giving him a code of manners consisting of wise counsels for both body and spirit; there are amusing letters which pass between Sancho and his master, and between Teresa Panza and her husband. The conversations which occur at every moment are managed with rare skill and retain all their freshness and flavor.

Sancho is brought into the limelight on numerous occasions, but his wit finds its fullest expression during his brief tenure of office as governor of the "island Barataria," a little village on the domain of the Duke. There he dispenses justice, makes the round of the entire island to cleanse it of evil-doers, pronounces judgment on the vices and abuses of the citizens and, in general, displays a knowledge of what constitutes the foundation of a sound republic. His governorship comes to an untimely end, partly through the pangs of hunger imposed on him by an official doctor who restricts his diet, and partly through a burlesque battle fought with hostile invaders of his island. In the latter scene he is very roughly used and decides that the cares of government are not meant for his shoulders. After renouncing the honors of office he seeks out his companion, Dapple the ass, and both again regain their ancient liberties. A striking success is achieved by Cervantes in a clever contrast between the harassed governor, Sancho Panza, and the freed peasant, who, when relieved of all worries, is found seated with a friend under the open sky, eating and drinking and forgetting in an old-time conversation the heavy duties imposed by his late exalted position. The wings of his ambition have fallen away, and he will henceforth be content with his simple lot. In the mean-

time Don Quixote, too, has grown weary of the life of
ease at the Duke's palace, and he welcomes the return of
his much-loved squire, that both may set out once more
in quest of adventures.

This is the climax of the second part of *Don Quixote*.
When Cervantes had finished fifty-eight chapters, presumably in the summer or autumn of 1614, he became
acquainted with a book which has ever since been one of
the puzzles of Spanish literature. This was a work pur-
porting to be a sequel to the history of *Don Quixote*.
It was printed at Tarragona in 1614, and the author
called himself Alonso Fernández de Avellaneda, a genuine name, according to some critics, but according to
others, a pseudonym which remains unsolved today. In
the preface this publication makes a scurrilous attack
upon Cervantes, who seems to have offended some of his
contemporary dramatists, notably Lope de Vega, by the
criticisms which he had voiced in the first part of *Don
Quixote*. The inference is, therefore, permissible that
the unknown author was taking up the cudgels in defense
of others; incidentally he derided Cervantes for his age
and his crippled arm, and spitefully boasted that he
would deprive him of all profits which might be derived
from the genuine second part. The book was written by
a man of no mean ability, but it is spoiled by the base
spirit which dictated it, and by the commonplace conception which the writer has of the character of the two
protagonists. He was utterly incapable of grasping the
ethical charm of Cervantes' narrative, nor could he imi-

tate the beauty and variety of the style which characterizes the first part. Cervantes was deeply wounded and
no less troubled about his own second part, which was
not yet concluded. But in the defense he limited himself to a few refutations which he inserted in the remaining chapters of *Don Quixote*, and to a noble statement of his position in the preface. Few of his self-
revelations tell us more of his character. Unquestionably the best answer to the attack would be the appearance of the genuine second part, and to its completion
Cervantes now devoted his time. His unknown critic
had adopted part of his scheme of adventures, announced
at the close of the first part, and Cervantes felt obliged
to change the last stage of Don Quixote's journeyings.
Instead of taking him to Saragossa as he had planned,
he made his goal Barcelona, and no doubt abandoned
some material which could no longer be used in the new
itinerary. These enforced alterations are at times noticeable in the unevenness of the closing chapters, but
the termination of Don Quixote's career is fully worthy
of the whole book. He is finally overthrown in single
battle by "The Knight of the White Moon," none
other than the wag Sansón Carrasco in disguise,
who, after his defeat narrated above, had sallied forth
again in quest of the Knight. According to the conditions of the challenge, the vanquished must lay aside his
arms, withdraw to his own village for the space of a year,
or for as long a time as may be enjoined upon him by
the victor. Don Quixote thus returns, a defeated man,

from his last adventure. A charming touch is added to
this episode of the knight's discomfiture by the manner
in which the tables are turned for master and servant.
While the knight is downcast, it is now the squire who
consoles him by his buoyancy and hopefulness:

Sancho strove to comfort him, and among other things he
said to him, "Hold up your head, señor, and be of good cheer
if you can, and give thanks to Heaven, that if you have had a
tumble to the ground you have not come off with a broken rib.
As you know, 'it is all a matter of give and take,' and, that
'there is not always bacon to hang in your chimney'; a fig for
the doctor, for there is no need of him to cure this ailment.
Let us go home, and give over going about in search of adventures in strange lands and places. Rightly looked at, it is I
who am the greater loser, although it is your worship who
has had the worse usage. With the government I gave up all
wish to be a governor again, but I did not give up all longing
to be a count; and that will never come to pass if your worship gives up becoming a king by renouncing the calling of
chivalry. . . ." [II, 65.]

This final defeat, however, is with consummate skill
turned into a spiritual victory, and the idealism, the
self-purification achieved by wandering and toil, even
as in the case of the author himself, stand out triumphant at the close:

Don Quixote could not shake off his sadness. His friends
called in the doctor, who felt his pulse and was not very well
satisfied with it, and said that at all events it would be as well

for him to attend to the health of his soul, for that of his body was in a bad way. Don Quixote heard this calmly; but not so his housekeeper, his niece, and his squire, who fell weeping bitterly, as if they had him lying dead before them. The doctor's opinion was that melancholy and depression were bringing him to his end. Don Quixote begged them to leave him to himself, as he had a wish to sleep a little. They obeyed, and he slept at one stretch, as the saying is, more than six hours, so that the housekeeper and niece thought he was going to sleep forever. But at the end of that time he woke up, and in a loud voice exclaimed: "Blessed be Almighty God, who has shown me such goodness. In truth his mercies are boundless, and the sins of men can neither limit them nor keep them back!"

The niece listened with attention to her uncle's words, and they struck her as more coherent than what usually fell from him, at least during his illness, so she asked: "What are you saying, señor? Has anything strange occurred? What mercies or what sins of men are you talking of?"

"The mercies, niece," said Don Quixote, "are those that God has this moment shown me, and with him, as I said, my sins are no impediment to them. My reason is now free and clear, rid of the dark shadows of ignorance that my unhappy constant study of those detestable books of chivalry cast over it. Now I see through their absurdities and deceptions, and it only grieves me that this destruction of my illusions has come so late that it leaves me no time to make some amends by reading other books that might be a light to my soul. Niece, I feel myself at the point of death, and I would fain meet it in such a way as to show that my life has not been so ill that I should leave behind me the name of a madman; for though I have been one, I would not that the fact should be made plainer at my death. . . . All that nonsense that until now has been a reality to my hurt, my death will, with Heaven's help, turn to my good. I feel that I am rapidly drawing near death; a truce to jesting; let me have a confessor to confess me and a notary to make my will; for in extremities like this, man must not trifle with his soul." [II, 74.]

As is natural, before the end his thoughts turn to Sancho Panza, the partner of his many adventures, and the chief victim of his illusions:

"It is my will that, touching certain moneys in the hands of Sancho Panza, whom in my madness I made my squire, inasmuch as between him and me there have been certain accounts and debits and credits, no claim be made against him, nor any account demanded of him in respect of them; but that if anything remain over and above, after he has paid himself what I owe him, the balance, which will be but little, shall be his, and much good may it do him. If, as when I was mad I had a share in giving him the government of an island, so, now that I am in my senses, I could give him that of a kingdom, it should be his, for the simplicity of his character and the fidelity of his conduct deserve it." And then, turning to Sancho, he said: "Forgive me, my friend, that I led you to seem as mad as myself, making you fall into the same error I myself fell into, that there were and still are knights-errant in the world."

"Ah," said Sancho, weeping, "don't die, master, but take my advice and live many years; for the most foolish thing a man can do in this life is to let himself die without rhyme or reason, without anybody killing him, or any hands but melancholy's making an end of him. . . . Besides, you must have seen in

your books of chivalry that it is a common thing for knights
to upset one another, and for him who is conquered today to be
conqueror tomorrow."

"Very true," said Sansón, "and good Sancho Panza's view of
these cases is quite right."

"Not so fast, señores," said Don Quixote; "there are no birds
in last year's nests. I was mad, now I am in my senses; I was
Don Quixote of La Mancha, I am now, as I said, Alonso
Quixano the Good; and may my repentance and sincerity restore
me to the esteem you used to have for me." [II, 74.]

Thus, then, comes Don Quixote's end, and the reader
feels in the tranquil scene, that as in the death of Samson Agonistes,

> Nothing is here for tears, nothing to wail
> Or knock the breast; no weakness, no contempt,
> Dispraise or blame; nothing but well and fair,
> And what may quiet us in a death so noble. . . .
> His servant He, with new acquist
> Of true experience from this great event,
> With peace and consolation hath dismissed,
> And calm of mind, all passion spent.

Cervantes, having laid his hero away in the grave,
now feels assured that no presumptuous or malicious
story-teller can again profane his name and honorable
career by making him sally forth on another expedition;
the protagonist would henceforth be his own:

For me alone was Don Quixote born, and I for him; it was his
to act and mine to write; we two together make but one, not-

withstanding and in spite of that pretended writer who has ventured or would venture with his great, coarse, ill-trimmed ostrich quill to write the achievements of my valiant knight. . . . The two expeditions which he has already made, so much to the enjoyment and approval of everybody to whom they have become known, in this as well as in foreign countries, are quite sufficient for the purpose of turning into ridicule the adventures of the whole set of knights-errant. . . . And I shall remain satisfied, for my desire has been no other than to deliver over to the detestation of mankind the false and foolish tales of the books of chivalry, which, thanks to that of my true *Don Quixote,* are even now tottering and doubtless doomed to fall forever. Farewell.

From the reference which Cervantes makes to the reception of the story of *Don Quixote* in foreign countries we may infer that he had before his death the satisfaction of learning that his work was meeting with universal esteem. But he would have received with incredulity the assertion that it was to be translated into more languages than any book excepting the Bible, that scholars were to devote a lifetime to writing commentaries on it, that it was to be prized through all the years as one of the world's great books. Among English-speaking people *Don Quixote's* reception has been especially gratifying. Both parts were not only translated almost immediately after their appearance by Thomas Shelton, but the first edition of the original on a luxurious scale was printed in London in 1738, and the first annotated edition was issued at Salisbury by Dr. John Bowle in

1781. Commentaries and translations have succeeded one another up to the present day.

The direct influence of *Don Quixote* on the subsequent history of the novel in Spain and in foreign countries is difficult to trace and was probably slight. Its realism affected the conception of fiction in a subtle and inconspicuous manner, but that particular feature was never pointed out and openly emphasized as were its humor and burlesque, and these are precisely its inimitable qualities. As a result, the travesties which it inspired have won little fame, and are hardly remembered. English authors who are occasionally associated with *Don Quixote*, such as Henry Fielding, or Smollett, can hardly be said to have appreciated the full value of the work as a contribution to literary esthetics, or grasped the meaning of its achievement as a world novel. *Don Quixote* created no school of fiction; it was the expression of the personality and experiences of a rarely gifted individual. Works of such caliber can be imitated only in isolated traits, and the scope of the romance was comprehended only after a long lapse of time. Its art could not be copied successfully, and Cervantes produced no disciples, because his work does not readily fall apart into definable patterns or models, or resolve itself into routine principles.

A novel like *Don Quixote* is one of those rare products, the completeness and comprehensiveness of which makes a precise definition of its philosophy and its artistic formula gratuitous. Cervantes is an enchanter under whose hand an ever-changing series of impressions and pictures of human life succeed one another without any carefully premeditated framework or any logical pursuit of the original theme. His sympathetic presentation of human shortcomings leads us to the obvious inferences that the conditions of life are generally ridiculous rather than intolerable, that men are stupid and misguided rather than wicked, while the fantastic construction which the visionary knight lays upon this unintelligible world suggests the importance of becoming squarely acquainted with it. An abiding reconciliation with the irremediable ills which come to all men can be found only in an ever cheerful attitude toward life, in the manifold and mysterious resources which lie in human character itself. Cervantes had struggled like the great majority for goals which he never reached, and concluded that the very illusions which pursue all men may at times compensate them for never attaining the heart's desire.

We may remember how in the license prefixed to the second part of *Don Quixote* the censor tells us that one day in the presence of foreign diplomats he mentioned the story of the resourceful knight, which he happened to be reading at the time, and adds: "I offered to take them to see the author of the book, to which they agreed with a thousand manifestations of eagerness. They questioned me in detail concerning his age, his profession, the quality of his person, and the quantity of his purse, and I was obliged to admit that he was old, that he was a soldier by profession, a gentleman, and, as regards quantity, that he was poor. To this one replied quite seriously in the following words, 'To think that Spain does not keep such a man in abundance out of the public treasury!' And another gentleman added the following subtle thought: 'If necessity forces him to write, pray God that he may never have abundance, so that, though he himself remain in poverty, he may, by means of his works, enrich the whole world.' "

CHAPTER IX

TWO transcendant gifts characterize the works of Cervantes, his imagination and his style. In the *Journey to Parnassus* (1614), Mercury, Apollo's messenger, twice addresses the aged author as a "rare inventor"; and in numerous passages of his writings Cervantes emphasizes the importance which he attaches to qualities of style, such as musical diction, careful selection of words and phrases, and, above all, the avoidance of confusion or obscurity. He was, therefore, conscious of having both gifts. As regards his inventive art, the matter or contents of the fiction which he composed, we have learned that his principles were never concretely and consistently set down. He speaks several times of restricting the admission of episodes and occurrences to those based upon verisimilitude; they must be possible and probable. Yet in conforming to these words, as we shall see especially when we come to examine his last plays and the *Persiles and Sigismunda,* Cervantes gave himself the widest latitude. He was often forced to restrain his own fancy, we may presume, because of the great pleasure which he derived

from taxing the inexhaustible resources of his art.   As
a result both his invention and diction are very uneven,
nor are they consistently fused throughout his greatest
books, the *Don Quixote* and *The Exemplary Novels*.   In
both of these works the most perfect specimens of his
achievement may be found; nevertheless, taken all in all,
the rare inventor dominates in *Don Quixote,* while the
stylist or the conscious literary artist is in the ascend-
ancy in *The Exemplary Novels*.   Both are the genuine
Cervantes, but the gift of the first has a more universal
power of appeal, the second demands a more cultivated
appreciation.   The unconscious relation which Cervantes has established between *Don Quixote* and the reader,
no matter of what nationality he may be, makes his book
in so many ways the foremost and the most comprehensive of all works of fiction; though *Don Quixote* derives
its tone, its color and peculiar charm of wit and humor
from the Spanish soil, still its qualities are sufficiently
self-interpretative to awaken a response in all mankind.
The *Novels* are more local, more intensely Spanish in the
subtlest sense; they are compactly filled with matter
which requires that the attention be constantly fixed on
Spain, and, quite generally, on the life and customs of
the Spaniard during the Renascence.   Apart from this,
their technical excellence, their workmanship as manifested in the balance and beauty of presentation and in
the noble and varied Spanish in which they are composed, require detailed and profound study.   The *Novels*
are, therefore, on the whole, finer and more exquisite

literature than *Don Quixote,* although the latter will
always remain the more inspired creation. Moreover, in
the case of the *Novels* Cervantes' method of composition
may be better controlled because of the chance preser-
vation of two of them, *Rinconete and Cortadillo,* and *The
Jealous Estremaduran,* in manuscript versions which
antedate the printed form by a number of years. The
original copies appear to represent a kind of first draft
which Cervantes showed to friends; the published versions reveal a more careful reformatory process, a desire
for elaborate polish of style; as is natural, the revised
form is not always as felicitous as the first spontaneous
expression. A single illustration will suffice. The closing paragraph of *The Jealous Estremaduran,* according
to the manuscript version (1606?), has the following
form, and shows that its unadorned simplicity was no
longer acceptable to Cervantes:

Isabella remained tearful, a widow and rich; and when Loaisa
was hoping that she would fulfil the command which he already
knew that her husband had inserted in his will, he found that
within a week she entered, as a nun, one of the most secluded
convents of the city. He, in despair and humiliated, thereupon,
according to current talk, took part in a famous expedition
which at that time Spain was undertaking against the heretics.
On that occasion it was definitely learned that he was killed
by an harquebus which exploded in his hands, the proper chastisement for his loose life. The parents of Isabella remained
sad, but wealthy; the servants of Carrizales had enough to dine
and sup, without deserving it; the woman González remained

poor and defrauded by her evil thoughts; and all who hear of this affair ought to profit by it, and not trust in tornells or servants, if they are to have any confidence in duennas with long head-dresses. The said affair, although it appears feigned and untrue, actually happened.

In the reformed version (1613), this passage was made to read:

Leonora remained a widow, tearful and rich; and when Loaisa was hoping that she would fulfil the direction which he already knew that her husband had inserted in his will, he found that within a week she entered, as a nun, one of the most secluded convents in the city. Disappointed and fairly humiliated, he emigrated to the Indies. The parents of Leonora felt very sad, although they consoled themselves with what their son-in-law had left and bequeathed to them in his will. The servants consoled themselves after the same manner, and the slave and the slave-girls with their liberty, while the malicious duenna remained poor and defrauded of all her evil expectations; and I was left animated by the desire to arrive at the end of this incident, example and mirror of the little use there is in trusting to keys, tornells, and walls when the will remains free, and of the little reliance that is to be placed in few and unripe years, if in their ears are instilled the exhortations of those duennas who wear black and abundant mourning, and white and long head-dresses. Only I do not know for what cause Leonora did not put more energy into clearing herself, and giving her jealous husband to understand how pure and without offense she had been on that occasion; but excitement tied her tongue, and the rapidity with which her husband died afforded no opportunity for her defense.

The deepest pleasure may be derived from a perusal of the *Novels*, but to the average reader of foreign speech the difficulty of understanding them throughout is at once apparent. The local flavor, wholly aside from the particular atmosphere of the epoch which the *Novels* reflect, loses much of its charm in translation; the individuality or beauty of phrase can be rendered only imperfectly, and the delineations of types and customs as well as the descriptions of scenery lose some of their animation, freshness and warmth of color. Cervantes himself was greatly opposed to the translation of modern works, and may have feared that his own writings would greatly suffer thereby. In *Don Quixote* he characterizes them in a very telling way:

It seems to me that translation from one language into another, if it be not from the queens of languages, the Greek and the Latin, is like looking at Flemish tapestries from the wrong side; for though the figures are visible, they are full of threads that make them indistinct, and they do not show with the smoothness and brightness of the right side. [II, 62.]

From this it will be evident also why the *Novels* have not been translated as frequently as *Don Quixote*, and why they are much less known to the English-speaking peoples.

The stories, which are twelve in number, were probably ready for press in July, 1612, but owing to the delay of certain necessary licenses to print, they were not published until the late autumn of 1613. The date of composition of each tale cannot be readily determined, but it is likely that most of them were written after the publication of the first part of *Don Quixote*. Three or four of them may have been sketched during the years which preceded the issue of Cervantes' master work, but we may assume that all of them received their final form shortly before they were presented to the official censor in 1612. From the style as well as from internal evidence they are, therefore, the work of his most mature years, when he reached the sixties, and a just estimate of their unsurpassed qualities of undiminished power, of flexibility and variety, is certain to concede to them an enviable rank for all time. It matters not, then, that Cervantes' genius ripened late, for in that gradual and harmonious blending of his personality and experiences he required years to be born, and found himself crowned in his old age with the spirit of youth.

In the absence of any portrait to place upon the first leaf of his *Novels,* and to satisfy those who desired to know "what face and figure were his who dared to appear before the eyes of the public with so many inventions," Cervantes gives us in the preface a charming pen-picture of himself:

He whom you here behold with aquiline visage, with chestnut hair, smooth and unruffled brow, with sparkling eyes, and a nose arched, although well proportioned, a silver beard, although not twenty years ago it was golden, large moustache, small mouth, teeth not important, for he has but six of them and those in ill condition and worse placed because they do not correspond the one with the other, the body between two extremes, neither large nor small, the complexion bright, rather white than brown, somewhat stoop-shouldered, and not very nimble on his feet; this, I say, is the portrait of the author of the *Galatea* and of *Don Quixote de La Mancha,* and of him who wrote the *Journey to Parnassus* in imitation of Cæsar Caporal of Perugia, and other words which wander up and down, astray, and perchance without the name of the writer. He is commonly called Miguel de Cervantes Saavedra. *

Cervantes then proceeds to tell us that he was the first to essay the writing of novels in the Castilian tongue, to which assertion we have had occasion to refer before in discussing some of the forms of fiction which preceded him. The statement could be taken solely as an indication of the slight regard which he felt for the talent of earlier novelists, and, therefore, as a mere personal opinion, were it not corroborated by the true state of the literary art of the sixteenth century. We saw how difficult it is to relate the esthetic formula of Cervantes to narrative fiction, notably to the various unfinished types of story-telling which found occasional expression during the years in which his genius matured. In the short story there was practically nothing worthy of the name,

* In 1911 the existence of a genuine portrait of Cervantes was announced to the public; it has since been accepted as authentic by the Royal Spanish Academy, but its history is somewhat obscure and unsatisfactory.

As regards the name Saavedra, which Cervantes added to his usual designation, its origin has not been definitely ascertained. There is some evidence that his father Rodrigo was also known under the form Cervantes Saavedra.

and as a proof of this judgment, nothing has survived in popular favor. Cervantes himself says: "The many novels which may be found in print in Spain are all translated from foreign languages, while these are my own, neither imitated or stolen; my imagination engendered them, my pen gave them birth, and they are growing steadily in the arms of the press." The allusion here is plainly directed at the various miscellanies, or collections of wholly unoriginal tales, more properly called yarns, which derive their material almost entirely from Italian sources, foreign jest books, compilations of exempla, fables, scattered legends or classical commentaries. *The Book of Tales,* by Timoneda (1576), is a fair specimen of what was foisted upon the reader as fiction. The greater part of its contents was copied without taste or judgment out of Italian *novellieri.* The style is purely conversational, without any conception of polish, beauty of phrase, or specific choice of word. Nor were such tales ever designated by the word "novel." The term was new to the Spanish language, and had been introduced for the first time during the Renascence in connection with some translations from Boccaccio.

Cervantes' vast superiority over all of his predecessors was apparent to his contemporaries, some of whom called him "our Spanish Boccaccio." This characterization is superficial and misleading, for the art of *The Exemplary Novels* does not at once reveal any similarity to that of the *Decameron.* The two conceptions of novel writing as evinced by these remarkable works differ not only in expression, but in their manner of selecting material for fiction. Boccaccio, as well as other Italian novelists, was unquestionably known to Cervantes, and his *Decameron*, in particular, must have influenced the *Novels;* yet the differences are far more evident than the similarities. As was the case with the *Lazarillo* and the *Celestina,* the style and contents of the tales of Boccaccio comprise features which the genius of Cervantes was bound to reject. They have nothing in common with his literary art, or with his peculiar ethical and esthetic points of view. One of the principles of his narrative, on which he has insisted in the most unequivocal terms, emphasizes the inappropriateness of all that is vile and ugly to an art destined to ennoble and charm. Cervantes was incapable of drawing detailed pictures of licentiousness, of those baser passions and impulses not born of a serene contemplation of life. "One thing I shall venture to affirm," he says in his preface, "that if by any chance the reading of these novels should induce anyone who may peruse them to entertain an evil desire or thought, I would rather cut off the hand with which I wrote them, than offer them to the public." This does not imply a narrow-minded or puritanic point of view on the part of Cervantes. He deals with vice and corruption in such stories as *Rinconete and Cortadillo,* with sensual passion in *The Jealous Estremaduran* and *The Force of Blood,* but the processes of his art touch these matters so delicately that they never form a crass climax or prominent manifestation as in some of the tales

of Boccaccio. The positive qualities of the great Italian,
his conspicuous humanism, his wide interests in all
classes of people, his cultivated style, are above praise
and were, no doubt, appreciated by Cervantes. But they
are not always the characteristics most in evidence; his
genuine nobility and refinement are not precisely the
traits which continue his popularity among average readers of the present day; for those who are permitted to
obtain a copy of his *Decameron* from behind lock and key
by means of which the public morals are safeguarded in
our libraries, are not, as a rule, apt to search out the
inoffensive story of *Patient Griselda* for their pastime.
In this sense not a line of Cervantes was ever written to
stimulate the passions, and the preface of his *Novels*
will again give the object which he always had before
him:

The amorous phrases which you will find in some are so
virtuous and so in keeping with Spanish ideas and Christian
discourse that they will not avail to move to evil imagining
the careless or careful person who should read them. I have
bestowed on them the name of "exemplary," and if you look
well to it, there is not one of them from which you could not
derive a profitable example. If I did not fear to dwell too long
on this matter, perchance I could have shown you the savory
and honest fruit that may be derived as well from all of them
put together as from each one by itself. My design has been
to place in the market-place of our commonwealth a truck-table
[a kind of pool] at which everyone can succeed in entertaining
himself without fear of injury, I mean without hurt to mind

or body, because virtuous and agreeable exercises rather benefit than harm. Surely people are not always at church, the oratories are not always occupied, men are not always taken up with affairs, however urgent they may be. There are hours of recreation when the harassed spirit may rest. For this purpose avenues are planted, fountains are sought for, slopes are leveled, and gardens are cultivated with care.

This passage reveals succinctly the purpose of Cervantes and the spirit of beauty and harmony which controlled his art. It would, nevertheless, be a false conclusion to infer from his statement that he allowed his compositions to be dominated by an intrusive and prominent moral. He was too great an artist to yield to the control of any mawkish or ill-suited sentiments, and his rejection of sensual or base features is not a concession to public opinion, but an unconscious and natural repudiation prompted by his sound and clean spirit.

The sensuous element of Boccaccio's art has frequently been condoned because of the freedom of manners current in the society of his day, and by the fact that the majority of his tales are not original and merely retained the defects of coarse or crude sources. The first explanation given may be sound, but the second reflects on Boccaccio's manner of selecting or creating his material; it opens the question of how largely he conformed his work to the taste of his readers. Regarding Cervantes it may be asserted that, as in *Don Quixote,* he attempted to overcome the popularity of the romances of chivalry, so in his *Novels* he wished to create a new kind of narrative, and, incidentally, elevate the public. He had no Spanish model to go by, and by a free creation preferred to prescribe to the pleasure of the reader rather than allow an untutored taste to dominate him. On this ground alone, then, that the contents and the style of the *Novels* are to be ascribed almost wholly to his inventive art, the palm for originality would go to Cervantes. On the other hand, Boccaccio's stories, though less his own, have a wider range than the *Novels* of Cervantes because of their greater scope and latitude in what may be depicted, and their ampler dramatic effort which so forcefully presents crime, horror and grim tragedy. Of these there is practically no example in the works of Cervantes, nor could they form a part of his portraiture, which includes, at the most, moving and pathetic scenes.

In view of the independence of Cervantes as regards the general contents of his *Novels*, a comparison of certain qualities of his narrative style with similar traits in Boccaccio will be worth while. Both display resourcefulness in holding the attention of the reader. This is accomplished by continuous progress in the tale, by variety and action, although we must not forget that there are also in both a number of elements which seem extremely insipid today, but which probably did not fail to engage the interest of the readers in the days of the authors. Both are unsurpassed in the expression of the joy of living, in the love of all that relates man to the fullness of existence, in understanding the range of our passions for good and evil. We must except, however, in the case of Cervantes, those fields which are debatable for an art that he believed ought to shun extremes. Moreover, Cervantes' spiritual equilibrium and sincere religious beliefs prevented him from approaching with cynical irreverence and scorn for our finer sensibilities questions of faith, or customs and institutions established by his church. The stories of both novelists present a vigorous delineation of scenes and of men, although Cervantes is the more careful and painstaking artist of the two, surpassing Boccaccio greatly in the portraiture of his chief characters, in those determining peculiarities of an individual which place him living before the reader; he excels in the detailed description of his background, as for example, where he reproduces the salient features of an inn, the interior of a house, or local customs manifested in the movement and animation of a street. The canvas of Boccaccio's *Decameron* naturally contains very many more characters than that of the *Novels,* because of the numerical superiority of his one hundred over Cervantes' twelve stories; but the majority of his personages are shadowy beings, mere instruments created to carry out the plot. In Cervantes, however, the number of minutely drawn individuals is striking, as may be seen when we examine such novels as *Rinconete and Cortadillo, The Jealous Estremaduran* or *The Colloquy of the Dogs.*

As regards certain outward features of the styles of Cervantes and Boccaccio, the apparent similarities are often due to the natural resemblance in the genius of the Spanish and the Italian languages. Much may also be explained from the culture of their respective epochs, from the influence of humanism and of classic ways of phrase-building prompted by a growing assimilation of traits from ancient writers. Both are masters of eloquence, capable of great flexibility and of noble and harmonious diction, and both are inclined to an occasional display of fine writing. Boccaccio, by far the better educated and more learned man, makes this fact clearly manifest in his works. But his verbal exuberance, his ample use of figured style, which may also be ascribed to his schooling, form a noticeable contrast to the self-restraint, and the simplicity and directness of popular speech for which Cervantes is noted. From the modern point of view compression of the narrative is not a virtue of either writer; for in those days an extension of time was always readily granted to permit a writer to dwell upon matters which awaken no response today. Finally, the individual merits of the *Decameron* and of the *Novels,* no less than their marked differences, may be explained by the relative ages of the authors when they composed them: Boccaccio was in his best years, Cervantes had already passed the threshold of old age.

No résumé of the *Novels* can hope to give an adequate idea of the peculiar charm which often lies in simple details, in dialogues, or descriptions of scenes or manners. But it will be possible to review their characters sufficiently to show their relative worth. To the taste of the modern reader they are far more uneven than could have been the case when they were composed. There are pages which seem singularly pale when compared with those lifelike delineations to which the *Novels* owe their fame. The portions which have lost their vitality today are those which are most closely related to fiction as it was generally known in the sixteenth century; on the other hand, the freshness of some of Cervantes' portraitures and the careful drawing of contemporary customs are wholly derived from his original vein of narrative.

The first story, *The Little Gypsy*, is probably the best-known of the collection on account of the universal interest in gypsies, and because of the skill with which it fuses popular elements of love and adventure. During the romantic movement it was, moreover, proclaimed by various critics, notably in Germany, as a model of story-telling, and the praise voiced at that time has been occasionally repeated. Preciosa, the heroine, a pretty gypsy girl of fifteen, is in reality of noble birth; and although she has been brought up from her infancy among wandering gypsies, her character has retained its innate superiority:

Preciosa grew up to be the most unique dancer that there was in all gypsydom and the most lovely and clever that could be found, not among gypsies, but among those whom fame could proclaim to be lovely and witty. Neither sun nor breeze, nor all the inclemencies of heaven, to which, more than any other people, gypsies are exposed, were able to mar her countenance or imbrown her hands; and, what is more, the rough upbringing which fell to her lot discovered nothing in her except that she was born with greater qualities than any gypsy, for she was extremely civil and well spoken. With all this she was somewhat forward, yet not so as to betray any symptoms of immodesty; rather while she was lively, she was so modest that in her presence no gypsy, old or young, dared to sing improper songs or utter words which were not seemly. Finally the grandmother recognized what a treasure she had in her grandchild, and, consequently, the old eagle resolved to take the eaglet out to fly and teach her to live by her claws. Preciosa came forth rich in carols, couplets, staves, sarabands and other verses, especially ballads, which she sang with particular grace, and her crafty grandmother perceived that such ditties and graces would form a most powerful attraction in a girl so young and beautiful, and would do much to increase her gains.

The novel deals largely with the activities of the gypsies in town or country; there are graceful descriptions of dances, of gatherings in private houses or upon the street, to see the attractions of the little gypsy girl. A youth, the son of an aristocratic house, falls in love with Preciosa, and, abandoning his home and career, follows the gypsies and becomes one of them. Neither their speech nor the life of their camps has much that is convincingly wild or characteristic of a nomadic race, and Cervantes unquestionably modified the real life of gypsies by mingling it with the atmosphere of romantic fiction, such as pastoral literature, which he knew so well and had never wholly laid aside. Toward the close the

story makes prominent a number of features which may
be found in the Renascence tale of love and adventure,
and which are derived chiefly from Byzantine and subsequent medieval literature.   These are the well-known
themes of the lost child of exalted lineage which grows
up in a lowly station and is recognized at the opportune
moment by means of a birthmark, or the trinkets and
clothes which it wore when lost.   The recognition scene
as usual, represents the climax, and a happy ending
unites the lovers and restores Preciosa to her parents.
Aside from bits of vivacious dialogue, and some sparkling scenes of merriment and song, the style of *The Little
Gypsy* is to be highly commended.   But the fanciful
plot can be classed rather with that of two or three other
novels of Cervantes' collection, which contain similar
traditional elements of fiction, and which, therefore, do
not represent the highest level reached by his art.

These least original stories of the collection are *The
Liberal Lover, The Spanish-English Lady, The Two
Damsels,* and *The Lady Cornelia.   The Liberal Lover,*
which may be founded on an early sketch by Cervantes
in novel form, rehearses one of his favorite themes, the
experiences of a Spanish captive among Mohammedan
peoples.   The composition is a good example of adventure story, in which the author has given free play to
his fancy; although there are improbable occurrences
and coincidences in it, the autobiographical details lend
to the contents the same interest that attaches to the related plots of his dramas, *Pictures of Algiers* and *The*

Prisons of Algiers, and to the story of the Captive in
Don Quixote. In *The Spanish-English Lady* also, the
unique interest of the plot for us depends on a few
reminiscences of the author's experiences. The narrative rehearses the pathetic lot of Isabel, a lass of seven
who is taken to London "among the spoils which the
English carried off from the city of Cadiz." An involved love-story follows in which, after many hardships,
the lovers are at last reunited in Spain. The weakness
of the story is apparent as long as Cervantes is on unknown ground, in England and dealing with English
society, but when his chief characters are once more on
Spanish soil events and personages are convincingly
drawn. *The Two Damsels* is a double love-story, consisting of numerous improbable adventures and coincidences. The main theme, that of the maiden disguised
as a man and wandering abroad in search of her unfaith-
ful lover, gave Cervantes little opportunity to express
himself in his real vein, and the course of the narrative
did not invite him to a truthful picture of real life. It
is very probable that he was influenced by contemporary
plays, which frequently contain the part of a disguised
or wandering damsel. In *The Lady Cornelia* Cervantes
makes the Italian cities of Bologna and Ferrara the background of his story without, however, relating its atmosphere to Italian manners; the few Italian names which
occur are not sufficient to give the tale a foreign tone.
The plot deals with a clandestine marriage, the enmity
between the husband and his wife's brother, the vicissi-

tudes of mother and infant, and, finally, the intercession of two noble Spaniards, through whom all obstacles to happiness are overcome. There are some scenes described with vigor and in an animated style, but the plot as a whole is too dependent upon unusual episodes to let it rank among Cervantes' best work. Thus in the stories just reviewed the manifest shortcomings, in spite of the originality of the plots, are two: the assimilation of certain fiction elements of an older school, which even Cervantes could not recreate, and the over-indulgence in pure invention. As has been stated before, in connection with his earlier works, the attempts to depict amorous scenes are unsatisfactory, because they required a kind of speech entirely foreign to Cervantes' robust genius. The models which suggested the traditional touches were the Greek romances, Italian novels or Spanish stories derived from them. Nevertheless, the fact that numerous related novelistic features were incorporated into the Spanish drama of the Golden Age, must disarm extreme criticism, for it constitutes an additional proof of the popularity of these themes of universal fiction which Cervantes was impelled to imitate in his *Novels*.

Somewhat related in character to *The Little Gypsy* is *The Illustrious Kitchen-maid,* the heroine of which, Costanza, lives like Preciosa in a humble station, but turns out to be of noble birth. Yet if we except the *dénouement* which, as in *The Little Gypsy*, recounts the history of Costanza's infancy, her exposition as a babe, her education under the care of the innkeeper's wife, and the usual recognition scene, this story of love and adventure is, as such, Cervantes' most successful effort. No female character in all his works has been painted with more care and affectionate interest on the part of the author. No detail is lacking to give us Costanza's dress, her long auburn tresses, her simple ornaments, her neatness, her modest and demure behavior. The freshness and charm which the narrative has preserved are derived in particular from the scenes and dialogues in which life and action predominate. The story has for a background Toledo, replete with so many inexhaustible attractions born of the character of its people and their picturesque environment. As a consequence, the chief merit of *The Illustrious Kitchen-maid* lies in its comprehensive description of the occupations of the inhabitants, of life upon its steep and crooked streets, its great square or market-place, or at "the Inn of the Sevillan," which is the center of the story. The whole canvas is an ample one, including many types from almost every station of life. Notably the traffic at the hostelry is sketched in a most vivid way, and we see before us the innkeeper and his wife, the two young heroes disguised as muleteers in order to be near Costanza, the serving wenches and a gay panorama of related personages. The story is enhanced by a number of episodes in the picaresque vein, and by graceful and witty narratives which place before the reader's eyes scenes of public amusement, dance and song, some of which are in the great humorist's best manner.

The history of the two young vagabonds, *Rinconete and Cortadillo,* is a genre picture of the highest order. The two lads, Pedro del Rincón and Diego Cortado, meet at a roadhouse on their way to Seville; like Lazarillo de Tormes they are of humble origin and learn at an early date to make their way by their wits. Their pictures are minutely drawn:

The one was between fourteen and fifteen years of age, and the other was not over seventeen. Both were engaging youths, but were very tattered, ragged, and ill-clad. Neither wore a cloak, their breeches were of linen, and their stockings were bare flesh. It is true that their shoes redeemed the matter, because those of the one were sandals as worn as they were old, and those of the other full of holes and without soles, so that they served him rather for fetters than for shoes. The one wore a green sportsman's cap, the other a hat that had no band, low in the crown and with a broad flap. Over his back and girt about his chest the one carried a shirt of the color of chamois, and he had gathered up the tails and thrust them into one of its sleeves. The other was free from encumbrances and baggages, except that in his bosom was to be seen a great bundle, which, as afterwards appeared, was a collar of the kind called starched walloon, starched with grease and so wholly threadbare that it appeared all threads. In it were wrapped up and preserved sundry playcards of an oval shape, for from use the pips had become worn out, and that they might last longer they had been pared, and the cards were in consequence of that shape. They were both sunburned, their nails were edged with dirt, and their hands were not very clean. The one had half a sword and the other a knife with a yellow handle of the kind used by herdsmen.

After each has recognized the calling of the other, they decide to join forces, and make their own whatever portion of the globe may be susceptible to cheating and robbery. They seal their new partnership by successfully duping the first newcomer at cards, and then set out for Seville. This famous seaport was the great emporium of the age, and in the midst of its many activities they soon exercise their skill in market-place and thoroughfare. Presently they make the acquaintance of Monipodio, "the father, master, and protector of thieves" and the most striking character of this rogue's comedy. The boys are introduced by another knavish youth into the courtyard of his little house and note with care all the objects to be seen there, as well as some that are visible in adjacent rooms. Nothing is omitted in the remarkable picture, from the rushes on the floor to the bad print of Our Lady on the wall and a basin for holy water. Numerous types of the underworld, each one characterized in a line or two, now enter to see the great Monipodio, who descends after a slight delay "as eagerly expected as he was favorably looked upon by that virtuous company":

He appeared to be about forty-five or forty-six years of age; he was tall; his face was swarthy, his eye-brows met; his beard was black and very thick; his eyes were deepset; he wore no coat, and through the opening of the shirt a forest was visible, so much hair had he on his breast. He had a cloak of baize drawn about him nearly down to his feet, which were thrust into shoes left unfastened. His legs were covered by linen pantaloons, broad and wide down to the ankles. His hat was of the gypsy kind, with a bell-shaped top and a broad flap. Across his shoulder and breast he wore a belt in which was stuck a broad short sword of a famous make. His hands were short and hairy, his fingers were fat, and his nails bent and clinched; his legs were concealed, but his feet were enormously broad and swelled by bunions. In short, he looked the most uncouth and ill-favored barbarian in the world.

The two lads now agree to serve under his banner, and Cervantes continues to paint the activities of all the members of this circle of worthies with exquisite satire enlivened by his best wit and humor. Its ramifications extend over the whole city and in the net of its corruption are caught men from every walk of life, including, of course, the police itself. Upon one occasion a constable comes to the door of Monipodio to complain that a purse belonging to a relative had been stolen, and since "the officer of the peace is a friend" the statutes of this academy of thieves demand that the money be returned forthwith. Women no less than men are delineated with most striking individual touches; no painter of Spanish custom has equalled the delicate irony with which Cervantes brings out the physical and moral traits of these shady personages, their rivalries, their passions, their vices. The records of their crimes are mingled with seemingly inconsistent acts of piety, with routine conformity to the teachings of religion, thus throwing over their lives the mantle of a mock-respectability. All this is drawn with inimitable humor and that interest in every phase of life which characterizes Cervantes' greatest pages; the acquaintance displayed throughout with infinite sides of Sevillan customs would seem miraculous, if we did not remember Cervantes' power of observation. It is, moreover, apparent how much more skilfully the roguish features of the story are handled than in the dry and unillumined style of *Lazarillo* or in the heavy and inelastic manner of *Guzman de Alfarache*. At the close of the story he hints that he may write a continuation of "the life and miracles of Rinconete, as well as those of his master Monipodio." Such a sequel would have been most welcome, for nothing that Cervantes has penned contains in so compact a form an equal wealth of popular speech, including rogues' slang, of vivacious imagery and delicate satire. Unfortunately the story of *Rinconete and Cortadillo* is most difficult to render in English, for no foreign version can give an adequate idea of its whimsicalities and its peculiar local flavor.

In *La Galatea* Cervantes had already included some tales which partake of the nature of short stories. But they contain nothing strikingly original, and are worthy of consideration chiefly because of their select diction and polish. In *Don Quixote* the story of *Ill-advised Curiosity* attempted for the first time a narrative dealing with the more intricate moral relations between men and women, with those subtler motives which result in definite actions and resolutions, and conduct to good or evil ends. But the plot was not of Cervantes' invention, and its lack of solid content was not remedied by spinning out its slender threads to a tiresome length. There are, however, among *The Exemplary Novels* three widely different tales, which most successfully place before the reader amorous intrigues, exhibitions of depravity and vice, most minutely drawn pictures of the weak or corruptible nature of men and women. These three, *The Force of Blood, The Jealous Estremaduran* and *The Deceitful Marriage,* contain Cervantes' most studied exposition of a profound and detailed analysis in the form of a plot. And since his esthetic formula rejected extreme portraitures of sin and passion, these aspects of our baser nature are painted with great skill and, we may add, with remarkable delicacy for a time which permitted liberties rarely attempted in stories of our own day.

The Force of Blood is a tale drawn with the most somber colors; yet the repellent subject, the abduction of an innocent maiden by a powerful young nobleman, is wholly redeemed by its forceful and convincing style. This theme of violence and injustice founded upon the action of "a gentleman to whom wealth, illustrious descent, a perverted inclination, extravagant license and loose companions led to do things and indulge in outrages which disgraced his quality, and earned him the reputation of a libertine" was put on the stage in numerous plays of unsurpassed power by Lope de Vega, and its dramatic possibilities are approached by Cervantes in his story. The quiet opening makes an ad-

mirable contrast with the tragedy which immediately
follows:

On a hot summer night an elderly hidalgo with his wife, his
little son, a daughter sixteen years of age, and a maid-servant
was returning from refreshing himself by a stroll on the bank
of the river at Toledo. The night was clear, the hour was
eleven, the road was solitary and the pace was slow, so as not
to pay in weariness the price that the pleasure derived from the
river or the meadows at Toledo brings with itself. With the
confidence which the excellent policing of the city and its orderly
population inspire, the good gentleman and his respected family
were walking without a thought of any mischance befalling
them; but most of the mishaps that happen to us are unexpected: and quite contrary to their expectation a misfortune
overtook them which destroyed their peace, and entailed on them
many years of sorrow.

At this point the daughter is seized and carried off by
the young aristocrat and his band of ruffians. Her ruin
having been accomplished, it remained for Cervantes'
art to develop and conclude his plot in accordance with
those principles which he has so often made clear, that
there is a balance between all extremes, that injustice
must be offset by virtue and evil overcome by good.
Thus the family of the man who commits the wrong, and
that of the girl who has been wronged, are brought together by her child in a series of moving situations which
demonstrate the force of blood-relationship. The ultimate redemption of the man from his crime is the result
of the noble fortitude and piety of the heroine, and the

solution of all difficulties is found in their marriage and the consequent happiness of all. This ending, no doubt, has something of the commonplace in it, and betrays the ordinary concession to poetic justice rather than close adherence to the facts of life. But Cervantes did not have the tragic instinct which carried dramas through to irretrievable calamity and defeat, showing aspects of life which he could not harmonize with his unshakeable, however ill-founded belief that right must triumph over wrong.

In *The Jealous Estremaduran* the theme of amorous passion is again introduced, and applied to the wily intrigues "of an idle and vicious youth, and the wickedness of a treacherous duenna, combined with the inadvertence of a girl solicited and over-persuaded." It is the story of a young Sevillan who corrupts the youthful wife of an old man; and in the development of his narrative Cervantes omits no details of the house and its inmates. His purpose was not only to demonstrate again the failure of such unequal marriages, but to give a most careful portrait of the idiosyncracies of an old husband. The latter treats his wife, Leonora, like a caged bird, lest the temptations of the outer world prove her undoing, and by his irrational procedure brings about precisely what he wishes to avoid. At the close he explains his actions to Leonora's parents, the evident moral pointed by the story being that lock and key are of no avail when the will remains free and virtue can be overcome:

I tried to guard this jewel which I chose, and you gave me, with the greatest precautions which were possible for me. I raised the walls of this house; I closed the view from the windows looking to the street; I doubled the locks of the doors; I placed a tornell as in a convent of nuns; I banished perpetually from the house everything that bore the semblance or the name of man. I gave her servants and slaves to wait on her, nor did I refuse them or her whatever they chose to ask of me; I made her my equal; I shared with her my most secret thoughts; I handed over all my property to her. All these were deeds conducive, if I was right in my reckoning, to my living in secure enjoyment, without disturbance, of what had cost me so much, and to her endeavoring not to give cause that any kind of jealous fear should enter into my thoughts. But as it is not possible by human exertion to ward off the chastisement which the divine will desires to inflict on those who do not rest their desires and hopes wholly and entirely upon it, it is no wonder that I have been cheated in mine, and that I have myself been the fabricator of the poison which is robbing me of life.

The sensitiveness of Cervantes to adverse criticism may account for a change which he made in the original version of this tale before giving it to the press. According to the earlier manuscript copy already mentioned, Leonora is seduced, but in the revised version she displays opportune courage, and the efforts of her deceiver are unable to vanquish her. This substitution stultifies the aim of the story and constitutes an inartistic blemish, since for Leonora's defeat the rest of the tale was to be merely the foundation. From Cervantes' own plea in the preface it is apparent that he shrank from the climax which he had built with such unusual power, lest his story prove unworthy of the title exemplary.

The third tale of our group, *The Deceitful Marriage,* is built upon the simple theme which Cervantes expresses in these words: ''He who is accustomed to deceive another must not complain if he himself is deceived.'' With the same careful attention to details of the background and to traits of character, Cervantes develops his brief satire, yet not without humor nor yet without a touch of cynicism that is rare in his point of view. The subject matter, no doubt, justifies this change of tone, for it is taken from the underworld, and deals with the deceitful intrigue of a soldier who marries a woman of questionable character in order to fleece her; but who is himself tricked and humiliated, since she proves not to possess any of the property which she has paraded as her own. The picture of the soldier putting on airs amid his newly acquired comforts forms a humorous contrast with the ensuing revelation in which he is disabused:

For six days I enjoyed my honeymoon, amusing myself in the house like the spendthrift son in the home of his rich father-in-law. I trod on luxurious carpets; I slept upon linen sheets; I lighted myself with silver candlesticks. I breakfasted in bed; I got up at eleven; I dined at twelve and at two I took the siesta on the dais. Doña Estefanía and the serving-girl danced attendance on me. My man, whom I had hitherto found lazy and stupid, became as active as a deer. The moments that doña Estefanía was missing from my side, she was to be found in the kitchen, wholly occupied in preparing dishes that would tickle my palate and arouse my appetite. My shirts, collars and handkerchiefs smelled like a new Aranjuez of flowers, being dipped in perfumed water and orange blossom which was thrown over them.

Cervantes, who saw with such clear vision the defects of human society, makes evident in this incisive piece of criticism that the deplorable mixture of good and evil which exists in all leads to shame and poverty only—as in the case of the soldier—where vicious desires and selfish aims bar the road to virtue.

Two masterpieces of the greatest originality remain, *The Licentiate of Glass* and *The Colloquy of the Dogs*. These stories demonstrate the flexibility of the term novel as used by Cervantes, for both are psychological narratives, devoted to a microscopic analysis of various phases of human society.

The Licentiate of Glass is a story without a heroine, for it is entirely devoted to the biography of Tomás Rodaja, a young student at Salamanca of great brilliancy and application, whose checkered career of extensive study and travel is suddenly interrupted by a strange malady. This is brought on by a poison given to him in the guise of a love-philtre:

Tomás remained in his bed for six months, during which he dried up, and became a thing of skin and bone, as the saying is, and showed that all his senses were deranged. Although every possible remedy was applied, only the bodily illness was cured, but not the ailment of the understanding, because, although he was in good health, he was mad with the strangest madness that had ever yet been seen among the fancies of lunatics. The unhappy man imagined that he was entirely made of glass, and under this delusion, when anyone came near him, he used to utter piteous cries, entreating and supplicating him with rational words and sentences, that he should not approach him, because he would break him, for he was not really and truly as other men, but was all of glass from head to foot.

In the intellectual biography of the Licentiate which now follows, Cervantes presents another study of partial insanity, recalling that of Don Quixote; this consists of a portraiture based upon the concentration in one character of peculiar idiosyncracies which attract to him all kinds of fellow beings, and enable him by his strange combination of madness and wisdom to extract from the world which gathers around him the substance upon which to build his pithy analysis of life. In other words, the Licentiate as a sane man would never have had the associations and experiences which spring from his madness, and which alone afford him the opportunity of judging his fellow men. There can be no question, moreover, that Cervantes wished to symbolize by the "glassy" state of Tomás's mind or spirit a supersensitiveness, a greater power of receiving impressions of the world which surrounded him, and, because of his intellectual brilliancy, of formulating a more incisive estimate of the qualities and defects of human society. This idea is clearly brought out by Tomás's desire that all

should speak to him from a distance, and by his assertion
that his answers to every question would reveal more
understanding because he was made of glass and not of
flesh and blood:

"Glass," he said, "is a subtle and delicate material: the soul
acts through it with more promptitude and efficiency than through
the body, which is heavy and earthy." Some desired to try if
what he said was correct, and so they asked him many difficult
questions, to which he replied readily with the greatest acuteness of intellect, a thing which excited wonder among the most
lettered men in the university and in the professors of medicine
and philosophy, who perceived that in a man possessed by such
an extraordinary hallucination as to suppose that he was made
of glass, so great an understanding was lodged, that he replied
to every question with propriety and acuteness.

Inasmuch as Tomás's madness is harmless, he walks
freely through the city, and in the course of these customary rambles Cervantes has an opportunity to review
the whole life of the municipality. The situation upon
which Tomás is called to pass judgment he usually sums
up briefly in a phrase or two, often by means of a retort
to a question. All subjects, intellectual, moral or social,
are touched in his discourses, and one or two examples
may suffice to show his manner of dealing with them.
When asked to give his opinion of poets, he first praises
the good, and then speaks of the sham poets:

"What of the bad, the prattlers? What can be said except
that they are the idiocy and arrogance of the world?" And he

further added, "Indeed it is a sight to behold one of these fledgling bards, when he wishes to repeat a sonnet to those who surround him; the excuses that he makes to them, saying: 'I beg your worships to listen to a little sonnet which I composed last night on a certain occasion, which in my opinion, although it is of no value, has something or other—I can't say exactly what—pretty about it!' Upon this he purses his lips, arches his eyebrows, ransacks his pockets, and from a thousand other papers, greasy and half-tattered, among which lurk a thousand other sonnets, he extracts the one which he desires to declaim, and at length repeats it in a mellifluous and affected tone. If by chance those who listen to it do not praise it, being either shy or ignorant of what is expected of them, he says, 'Either your worships have not understood the sonnet, or I have not known how to recite it, and so it will be well to repeat it again, and I beg your worships to pay more attention to it, for really, really the sonnet deserves it,' and he turns to repeating it as at first, but with new gestures and new pauses."

Of apothecaries he says that there were those "who from not having the courage nor the daring to say that anything was wanting in their shops which the doctor prescribed, for the things that they lacked substituted others which in their opinion possessed the same virtue and quality, although this was not so, so that the medicine being ill-compounded had the contrary effect of that which, if well made up, it would be likely to exercise."

This leads him to discuss physicians, and after praising skilled and honorable practitioners, he describes the quacks and dwells on their danger to the commonwealth:

"The judge can pervert or delay justice for us; the lawyer maintain for his own interest our unjust demand; the merchant drain away our property; finally, all persons with whom of necessity we have dealings can do us some harm, but to take away our lives without being liable to the fear of punishment is possible for none. Only the physicians can kill us, and kill us without fear and without interference, without unsheathing any sword but a prescription; and there is no discovering their misdeeds, for they are at once buried beneath the earth. I remember that when I was a man of flesh, and not of glass as I am now, a sick man dismissed a physician of the second class in order to be cured by another. The first took care, four days afterwards, to pass by the shop where the second had his prescriptions dispensed, and asked the apothecary how the sick man whom he had left was getting on, and if the other doctor had prescribed any purge for him. The apothecary replied that he had by him a prescription for a purge that the sick man had to take on the morrow. He asked the apothecary to show it to him, and seeing that at the end of it was written *Sumat diluculo* [to be taken at dawn], he said: 'All that this purge contains satisfies me, except it be this *diluculo,* for it is extremely harmful.'"

A special interest attaches to the story of the Licentiate, because of the autobiographical touches drawn from the early travels of Cervantes. After two years of madness Tomás is cured by a skilful monk, and, finding that the populace does not care to listen to his sane wisdom as it once did to his aphorisms when he was crazed, he decides to become a soldier in Flanders, and at his death leaves a reputation for prudence and valor.

In *The Colloquy of the Dogs* Cervantes likewise reaches the highest level of psychological narrative. It consists of the application of a conversational tone to an analysis of the widest possible array of experiences. During the Renascence many humanists, among them Erasmus, had used the form of the dialogue in sententious or philosophic discussions of a comprehensive range of subjects, showing thereby a genuine relationship to the classics in both thought and frame. The *Colloquy of the Dogs* is probably the greatest example of its kind which the age has produced. As its chief interlocutors Cervantes presents two watch-dogs, Berganza and Cipión, who are attached to the service of a hospital at Valladolid. After many vicissitudes and wanderings, both find themselves employed in the task of gathering alms for a charitable order, and their conversation, overheard one night, is preserved in our colloquy. Most of it is put into the mouth of Berganza, who relates his life first, Cipión agreeing that if their miraculous gift of speech is retained for another night, he, too, will rehearse his canine career. As a number of passages from their colloquy have already been quoted (p. 35, 126, 172), it must suffice here to give a brief review of the panorama which Berganza causes to pass before the listener. His services in town and country have been many, since he has been associated with humankind of every walk of life. He has had as master a butcher of the slaughter houses of Seville, and has thus become acquainted with the lower world of that great city; he has guarded the flocks of shepherds; he has been a member of the family of a Sevillan merchant and through his sons has become the favorite of students; subsequently he has lived in the company of a police officer, of soldiers and of gypsies, and he has, therefore, had the widest opportunity of getting information about many phases of typical Spanish life. Berganza now proceeds to dissect for us all the types that he has encountered, and we consequently have a canvas which by its ample proportions is worthy to be placed by the side of *Don Quixote*. Indeed, it may be said that owing to the wide application of its wisdom, to the balance between the extremely easy flow of its conversational style and its compact and pithy form, *The Colloquy of the Dogs* ranks among the greatest creations from the pen of Cervantes.

The Exemplary Novels were turned into French in 1615, shortly after their publication, and an Italian version appeared in 1626. But no faithful and complete English translation was made until our own day, when Norman Maccoll undertook the task (1902). This is sufficient evidence that acquaintance with them in England was never more than superficial. Their influence in Spain was noticeable during the seventeenth century, but it was transitory, for, like *Don Quixote*, they are inimitable. Certain authors, such as Lope de Vega, Montalbán, Tirso de Molina, Liñán y Verdugo, and María de Zayas, were impelled by Cervantes' example to attempt the form of the short story, but not one of them

attained the excelling qualities of the great master, or
caught the subtle tone of his narrative. They could not
copy his style or imitate his pictures of life, and, as a
rule, they produced romantic and wholly unconvincing
results. The only novelist who rises above the average
achievements of the century is Tirso, known best as a
dramatist, by his creation of the character of Don Juan,
and famous for his humor and wit. Strangely enough
The Exemplary Novels of Cervantes became the happy
hunting ground of playwrights of various nations,
French, Spanish and English, during the seventeenth
century; yet to our modern taste they contain but little
that seems fit to be put upon the stage. As a matter of
fact, their best features were hardly ever imitated, and
precisely those amorous or fantastic episodes which were
based on invention and not life, served as a basis for a
number of plays, such as Fletcher's *The Fair Maid of
the Inn,* taken from *The Illustrious Kitchen-maid,* or
his *Chances,* derived from *The Lady Cornelia.* In
these later garbs Cervantes would frequently have failed
to recognize the originals from which they purported to
have sprung.

It is perhaps futile to hope that *The Exemplary Novels*
may ever be more widely known among English-speaking people. As late as the eighteenth century they were
still considered noteworthy landmarks in fiction by literary circles, but they hardly left a trace of their classic
qualities of keen vision and harmonious diction. Since
then they have gradually faded from the knowledge of

the reading public, and Cervantes' name is remembered only in connection with *Don Quixote*. It would be well worth while, nevertheless, to bring out the *Novels* singly in a form which may appeal by its lightness rather than its bulk. Such a publication might serve to reveal the numerous marvels of Cervantes' rare imagery and of those life-like dialogues which to all who know his works place *The Exemplary Novels* with his enduring achievement.

CHAPTER X

E left Cervantes in the summer of 1604, at
Valladolid, where he was making the preliminary arrangements required to print the first
part of *Don Quixote*. When he removed to
that capital is uncertain, but in June, 1605, his residence
was established, temporarily at least, in a modest quarter
of Valladolid, on the Calle del Rastro. There he occupied some rooms on the first floor of a house still standing. If this compressed lodging was indeed his, it is
difficult to understand how he could have maintained
at his side at the same time his wife, his two sisters, his
daughter, a niece, and a maid-servant. Yet the fact that
all these members of the Cervantes' family were living
together has become known through an unfortunate
event which occurred on June 27, 1605. On that date,
shortly before midnight, a nobleman of Valladolid, one
Don Gaspar de Ezpeleta, was mortally wounded in a
duel near the door of Cervantes' home. His cries were
heard by Cervantes and a young neighbor who together
carried him up to the room of some fellow lodgers, where

he expired without revealing the name of his assailant.
The magistrate in charge of the case at once began his in-
vestigations among the numerous women of the families
who lived under the same roof, in order to learn whether
any one of them had been implicated in Ezpeleta's death.
From the records his procedure seems awkward, and his
questions brought out only a mass of contradictory evidence which served to prejudice him against the neighborhood in which Cervantes lived. The most harmful
testimony, given by a certain widow, was directed against
Cervantes' daughter, and although the reader of the incomplete, yet bulky and tedious records of the case remains fully convinced that all prejudicial assertions
against Isabel de Saavedra, and indirectly against other
members of Cervantes' family, repose on gossip and
hearsay, the episode continues to be perplexing and pain-
ful. It is possible, at least, to affirm that the duel was
wholly unrelated to the Cervantes' family. Ezpeleta was
apparently an indigent nobleman who indulged in commonplace, amorous intrigues, and his assassin had, unquestionably, avenged himself for a purely personal injury.

The entire misfortune, from Cervantes' point of view,
may be laid at the door of an idle community of women,
who seem to have had little more to do than pry into their
neighbor's business and carry slander to willing ears,
who watched the coming and going of every visitor, and
without knowing his business were capable of inferring
every evil. The little that we know in particular of

Isabel de Saavedra does not make her a woman of attractive character, and it would no doubt require an irrational Don Quixote to break a lance in her behalf. But it is only fair to recall her obscure origin, her slight education, her humble surroundings. She seems to have been self-willed and unloveable, still it is not believable that, while living in the company of her aunts and cousin, who testified to her unassailable character, she should have been guilty of wrongdoing. Fortunately the whole affair has very little connection with Cervantes himself, but it demonstrates once more that no happy fate had tied him to this household of women and that poverty still held sway at his hearth. His wife, doña Catalina, was absent at the time of the Ezpeleta tragedy, although she had apparently been a member of the household shortly before its occurrence. Her more common residence may still have been Esquivias, at least until Cervantes' definite removal to Madrid. The exact date of this change is not known, for during the three years which elapsed between the summer of 1605 and that of 1608 he again disappears from view, and conjectures as to his occupation are futile. From the latter date, however, to the time of his death (1616), his chief abode was at Madrid, now definitely the capital of Spain. From time to time, he made a journey to Esquivias.

His own household was gradually diminished in numbers: his sister, Andrea, was carried off by a fever in 1609, and we must take for granted that she left her daughter, Costanza, in her brother's care. Cervantes

frequently introduces this name in his novels, giving it
to some of his choicest characters, such as the heroine
of *The Illustrious Kitchen-maid,* to the little gypsy,
Preciosa, whose real name is Costanza, and to an attractive maiden in the *Persiles.* It would be pleasant to infer from this that a real bond of affection united uncle
and niece. Costanza was unmarried at her death, which
occurred in 1624. Cervantes' sister Magdalena died in
1611, a pious spinster, who left a hazy record of complaints directed at various times against a number of
men who seem to have abused either her kindness or
her credulity. His natural daughter, Isabel de Saavedra,
was twice married. By her first husband she had a
daughter, Isabel Sanz del Águila, who was born about
1607 and died before reaching her fourteenth year. The
tangled career of Isabel de Saavedra involved her in various lawsuits regarding peculiar property rights, which
are filled with dark phases, and, no doubt, caused her
father worry and sorrow, but they need not concern us
here. Toward the close of Cervantes' life she is mentioned
less and less; and his household seems thus to have been
reduced to his wife and niece. Doña Catalina de Salazar
survived her husband by more than ten years, for she
died in October, 1626, at the age of sixty-one. We have
no means of judging how well suited they were to one
another; Cervantes' poverty and incessant quest of some
position in which to make a living kept them apart for
many years, with only occasional intervals of reunion, as
far as we know. There are no indications whatsoever

of any conjugal disagreement or infelicity, yet it would be interesting to learn whether doña Catalina fully understood the genius of her husband. From the writings of Cervantes it is impossible to infer that he had any enthusiastic regard for the average woman's character; the delineation of an occasional maiden attractive for her youth and beauty is offset by the much-repeated assertion that women are frail creatures, given to tale-bearing, and much in need of vigilance and protection. To be sure, there is no ill-will against womankind to be noted in Cervantes, but perhaps an indirect confession lurks in his writings that his household, notably the members of his own family, had been something of a cross to bear.

In Madrid Cervantes' tasks presumably were those routine ones which enabled him to earn money. But during this period he also found time to complete his *Don Quixote* and *The Exemplary Novels*, besides a number of additional works. It is also probable that he had the leisure, as far as his poverty permitted, to meet various literary men, and that his own name was becoming widely known among the writers of the day. But to him the world of letters was out of joint, and as he had desired to set right the popular taste in fiction by means of *Don Quixote*, so through another work, *The Journey to Parnassus*, his longest poetic effort, he launched a review, partly satirical, partly humorous, and not infrequently dull, of the lyric and dramatic poets of his time. The verdict of many critics as well as that of the years has

been that this long poem in *terza rima* is not a masterpiece; and James Young Gibson's vivacious translation
is a rare example of how a foreign version may here and
there surpass the original in poetic quality. Cervantes'
work was suggested by an Italian poem of Cesare Caporali of Perugia, likewise entitled *A Journey to Parnassus,* and printed in 1582. Cervantes had completed the
eight chapters of which the poem consists in or before
1613; a prose *Postscript* was added in 1614, and the
whole work saw the light before the end of the same
year.

The Journey to Parnussus is a maturer counterpart
of *The Song of Calliope* (p. 98), a roster of the poets
whom Cervantes knew, by name at least, toward the close
of his life, but who, for the most part, have been wholly
forgotten since. Cervantes represents himself as setting
out in search of Parnassus, and begins with a humorous
reference to his own poverty, to the fruitless life at Madrid and the literary surroundings with which he was out
of sympathy:

> . . . for the poet's travelling weight to bear
>   The task is light, and any beast is good
>   To carry it; for no valise is there.
> Yea, 'tis God's truth, that though a poet should
>   Inherit wealth, he straightway doth incline
>   To lose it, not increase it; 'tis his mood.
> The reason of this fact I do divine,
>   That thou, great Sire Apollo, dost infuse
>   Into their minds a goodly share of thine;

And as thou dost not mingle, nor confuse
  The same with business matters of the day,
  Nor on the sea of commerce vile dost cruise;
So they, whate'er their themes, severe or gay,
  Concern them not with trade or balance-sheet,
  But o'er the spheres prefer to wing their way;
Limning, perchance, of Mars some bloody feat
  On foughten field, or else among the flowers
  The deeds of Venus, amorous and sweet;
Bewailing wars, or piping in Love's bowers,
  With them life passes like a dream of earth,
  Or as the gamblers spend the fleeting hours.
Poets are made of clay of dainty worth,
  Sweet, ductile, and of delicacy prime,
  And fond of lingering at a neighbor's hearth;
For e'en the wisest poet of his time
  Is ruled by fond desires and delicate,
  Of fancies full and ignorance sublime;
Wrapped in his whimsies, with affection great
  For his own offspring, he is not designed
  To reach a wealthy, but an honored state.
So let my patient readers henceforth mind—
  As saith the vulgar impolite and coarse—
  That I'm a poet of the self-same kind;
With snowy hairs of swan, with voice of hoarse
  And jet-black crow, the rough bark of my wit
  To polish down Time vainly spends its force;
Upon the top of Fortune's wheel to sit,
  For one short moment, hath not been my fate,
  For when I'd mount, it fails to turn a whit;
But yet to learn if one high thought and great
  Might not some happier occasion seize,

I travelled on with slow and tardy gait.
A wheaten loaf, with eight small scraps of cheese,
    Was all the stock my wallet did contain,
    Good for the road, and carried with great ease.
"Farewell," quoth I, "my humble home and plain!
    Farewell, Madrid, thy Prado, and thy springs
    Distilling nectar and ambrosial rain!
Farewell, ye gay assemblies, pleasant things
    To cheer one aching bosom, and delight
    Two thousand faint, aspiring underlings!
Farewell, thou charming and deceitful site,
    Where erst two giants great were set ablaze
    By thunderbolt of Jove, in fiery might!
Farewell, ye public theatres, whose praise
    Rests on the ignorance I see becrown
    The countless follies of unnumbered plays!"

From Cartagena Cervantes is borne to his destination in an allegorical galley sent by Apollo under the command of Mercury, who is to bring to Parnassus all the good poets whom he can muster. With their assistance, Apollo will have the forces required to do battle with all the wretched poetasters who threaten his abode. By means of this device Cervantes has an opportunity of naming the talents which he deems worthy of this honor; but his choice is difficult to explain today, and the satire or praise is meaningless where we do not have the two most important factors of the situation, the character of the poet's work and the personal relation between him and Cervantes. It is evident that most of the latter's estimate is not based on an objective point of view. *The Journey to Parnassus* is, nevertheless, a work of importance, partly because like everything that Cervantes has written, it contains some illuminating disclosures about himself and his work, and partly because it is a bond which, by its references and criticisms, unites him more closely to the literature of his times. It contains occasional passages of eloquence and of formal beauty, but as a whole it is a *tour de force,* the effort of which is betrayed now and then by the monotony of the rhyme.

The prose *Postscript,* from which we have had occasion to quote in connection with Cervantes' earlier activities as playwright, is in the master's best vein; it is the perfection of light dialogue and quiet humor. It is also of great importance in a study of his last contributions to the stage, and discloses that his interest in the theatre had not abated at the end of his first dramatic period. But a quarter of a century had sped since then and Cervantes was to realize with keen disappointment that his ambitions to become a successful playwright, which had remained unfulfilled in the past, were to be crowned with as little success in his last years upon a completely revolutionized stage.

The Journey to Parnassus would seem to be better fitted by its contents than any other work of Cervantes, to give us a complete picture of his friendships, or to afford definite information on his connection with the literary circles of Madrid during his last years. Yet it is possible to gather from it surprisingly little of all that we would know. Although Cervantes' occasional treatment of a poet, as in the case of the famous Quevedo, makes it apparent that a friendly feeling animated the characterization, there is to be found but rarely one of those joyful and spontaneous records of a deep friendship. There is sufficient evidence that he had a number of intimates, but the conclusion from his own words in *The Journey to Parnassus,* as well as from a number of prefaces, is that he was not whole-heartedly one of any circle of writers. This is, after all, entirely to Cervantes' credit; for it makes evident not only that he dwelt upon the outskirts of the active world of letters, but that he had no interest in the rivalries and enmities of his contemporaries; his reputation was established, and he could afford to stand apart from what each new day brought forth. It is a pleasure to know, at least, that towards the close of his life he had two patrons who were instrumental in relieving him from his poverty. In the preface of the second part of *Don Quixote* he pays them a glowing tribute:

Long life to the great Count of Lemos, whose Christian charity and well-known generosity support me against all the strokes of my hard fortune; and long life to the supreme benevolence of his Eminence of Toledo, Don Bernardo de Sandoval y Rojas; . . . these two princes, unsought by any adulation or flattery of mine, of their own goodness alone, have taken it upon them to show me kindness and protect me, and in this I consider myself happier and richer than if Fortune had raised me to her greatest height in the ordinary way.

We do not know the extent of Cervantes' intimacy with these two prominent men, nor the exact nature of their benefactions, but we can assume that they enabled him to devote his time to his pen, and for that reason alone the Count of Lemos and the Archbishop of Toledo deserve our lasting gratitude.

In the summer of 1615 Cervantes made the customary arrangements for the publication of a volume entitled, *Eight Plays and Eight New Interludes Never Acted.* The collection was published presumably toward the end of the autumn of the same year. With the exception of six of the interludes, all of the compositions are written in verse. The eight dramas are each in three acts, thus conforming to the definitive construction which became the law during the Golden Age of Spanish letters. When Cervantes abandoned his literary career temporarily in 1587, he, no doubt, had in his possession a number of finished or unfinished plays; and during the years which intervened between his two active dramatic epochs (1587-1608?), he seems to have found time occasionally for some new productions. It would be unwise to suppose that all these efforts were wholly cast aside. Be all this as it may, whether his material was entirely new, or, in part at least, based upon what he had written years before, Cervantes was now desirous of placing before the public a new contribution to the stage. In the preface to the volume he speaks of his renewed ambitions:

Some years ago I returned to my former happy occupation,

and, believing that the world was still the same as when my praises were abroad, I again composed some plays. But I found no birds in last year's nests; I mean, I did not find stage managers who demanded them, although they knew that I had them; and so I laid them aside in a box and consecrated and condemned them to perpetual silence. Opportunely a dealer in books informed that he would buy them from me if a prominent manager had not told him that much was to be expected from my prose, but from my verse nothing. If I must confess the truth, I was certainly pained to hear it, and I said to myself: "Either I have changed into another person, or the times have greatly improved, which is contrary to what generally happens, for the ages past are always extolled." I again cast my eyes over my plays, and over some interludes which were shelved with them; I saw that neither were too bad to come out of the shadow cast over them by the critical manager into the light of other managers less finicky and better informed than he. Finally I grew tired of the whole business and sold them outright to the above book-seller, who has printed them as you here see them. He paid me reasonably well; I gathered up my money calmly and without any further arguments with actor-folk.

The contents of this volume are thus all that we possess of Cervantes' second dramatic period. The question arises at once why they were unacceptable to the critical manager. The answer has been given by posterity: with the exception of the eight interludes, which belong to Cervantes' enduring work, the plays could hardly have been successful on any stage, and today most of them are tedious reading. Cervantes himself does not seem to have been aware of their glaring defects, for in his preface he says: "I wish they were the best in the world, or, at least, sufficiently good; you will judge for yourself, reader; and if in your opinion they have any merit, and you perchance run across that critical manager, tell him to mend his ways, for I offend no one. And let him take note that my dramas contain no patent or concealed absurdities, and that the verse is of the kind demanded by plays."

Let us briefly examine the eight dramas. Their titles are, *The Gallant Spaniard*, *The Mansion of Jealousy*, *The Prisons of Algiers*, *The Blessed Vagabond*, *The Grand Sultana*, *The Labyrinth of Love*, *The Pleasant Play*, and *Pedro de Urdemalas*. It is difficult to determine precisely when they were composed, since it is necessary to judge entirely by internal evidence, by the style and versification. The oldest is probably *The Mansion of Jealousy*, with a sub-title, *The Forests of Ardenia;* it is possible that Cervantes recast an early play which he called *The Forest of Love* and mentioned in the *Postscript* of *The Journey to Parnassus*. The plot is throughout irrational and extravagant; it was suggested by Ariosto's *Orlando* and presents the rival passions which Roldán and Reinaldos felt for the fair Angélica, passions, which, like the play, lead nowhere. The only readable portions are some merry scenes enlivened by the song and dance of shepherds. It is inconceivable that Cervantes should have written this play, so full of the "patent or concealed absurdities" which he condemns, during the period of his great prose creations.

The Grand Sultana may also be based upon an older
play, *The Grand Sultana* (or Turkish Lady), likewise
mentioned in the *Postscript;* but in that case the composition was probably rewritten thoroughly, to judge
from the versification alone. It is the history of Catalina
de Oviedo, who, although married to the Grand Turk,
remains faithful to the Christian church. The amorous
scenes between Christian captives, and the slight comedy
added by the clownish wit of Madrigal do not atone for
the complete lack of dramatic fitness of the plot. *The
Labyrinth of Love* likewise seems to belong in part to
Cervantes' earlier period, partly because of the pre-
dominance of long and heavy verses, but also because of
the fantastic and improbable contents. These consist of
a false accusation against the heroine Rosamira, a theme
common in Italian fiction, and carrying in its wake the
well-known train consisting of imprisonment, disguises,
and duels, which all terminate in the usual demonstra-
tion of the heroine's innocence. In *The Prisons of Algiers,* Cervantes presents another example of play, which,
like his *Pictures of Algiers,* deals with an amorous intrigue between Christian slaves in Africa. As was the
case with the prose stories of *The Captive* and *The Liberal Lover, The Prisons of Algiers* contains many touches
very evidently based on personal recollections. We have
had occasion to mention *The Gallant Spaniard* in connection with possible autobiographical details (p. 54),
because one of the chief characters is called Saavedra,
and the plot has for a background the African country

which Cervantes knew so well. *The Blessed Vagabond*
is a good example of how a most satisfactory introductory act may be nullified by the two following. In spite
of this fact, this drama seems to belong entirely to Cervantes' last period. It is the history of a student of
Seville, who in the first act is admirably presented as an
arrogant brawler and ruffian, but withal a man of honor,
and a prince of good fellows among his devoted follow-
ers. The atmosphere in which he moves is that of
Rinconete and Cortadillo, and we meet again some of
the life-like types of the rogue's domain. But the hero
renounces the world, and having entered a Dominican
monastery in Mexico he leads a saintly life for two acts
which are as dull and undramatic reading as the first is
vivacious and entertaining. The two remaining dramas,
The Pleasant Play and *Pedro de Urdemalas* are, on the
whole, the most readable of the volume and justify the
belief that they were written within the period of Cervantes' prose masterpieces. *The Pleasant Play* is conceived throughout in the spirit of the lighter interludes,
but the chief comic elements are to be found in the actions of the minor characters rather than in the main
plot, which is exceedingly slight. It consists of two
interwoven love affairs that come to naught, and by their
failure constitute an unusual ending to which Cervantes
calls attention in the last verses:

> Thus it came to pass in this story;
> At its close none are married,

Some because they do not wish to be,
Others because they cannot. . . .
Therefore without any matrimony
Ends this pleasant play.

On the other hand, the courtship of the maid-servant Cristina by two amusing rivals, Ocaña and Torrente, furnishes the best scenes of this genuine comedy. A number of delightful pictures of open-air gaiety furthermore serve to bring out the humor and wit of the secondary characters. The hero of *Pedro de Urdemalas* is one of the more completely drawn characters in Cervantes' extensive gallery of witty and roguish types. The play is a loosely connected series of scenes which deal with the humorous adventures of Pedro, and bring him into contact with a large number of personages, in particular, peasants, magistrates of a little village, gypsies and strolling actors, who are all drawn in Cervantes' best manner. The play is also enhanced by dancing and merry incidents.

It would be futile to go into the character of the verse or the structure of these dramas. Passages of real poetic merit exist, but they are not numerous, and a fair, objective estimate of Cervantes' *Eight Plays* is that they are the product of a man who is neither a facile and pleasing versifier, nor by instinct a dramatist. Foreigners who insist on spying out the demerits in both language and construction, generally do so at the risk of being told by fervent devotees of Cervantes that they do not grasp

the secret qualities of Spanish; they thus unwittingly
antagonize those admirers of his who are not contented
with the achievement of a *Don Quixote* and the *Novels,*
but who must perforce find in him also a great playwright. But the verdict of the general reader has for
three centuries allowed Cervantes' volume of plays to
gather dust unmolested, and the sounder criticism of
specialists has made no effort to rate them as masterpieces. The technique of Cervantes did not extend to the
successful composition of ambitious three-act plays, and
the stage manager who expressed the opinion so unwel-
come to the author, assuredly knew his business well.

The failure of Cervantes to win a hearing on the stage
during his last years, and his disappointment in the nature and direction of the theatre at the beginning of the
seventeenth century are intimately allied. There can be
no doubt that when he temporarily abandoned writing
for the stage in 1587 he was by the routine of his daily
occupations unable to follow the steps by which the crude
drama of the eighties progressed and developed into its
most flourishing state and produced its noblest and most
artistic creations. When Cervantes found an opportunity in the first part of *Don Quixote* to express his opinion
of the stage, he showed little sympathy for what was to
be heard and seen in the theatres. Lope de Vega and
his abler disciples and imitators were at that time creating a really acceptable dramatic art, because they substituted possible, compactly built plots related to actual
Spanish life and genuine, spontaneous sentiments for

stilted, unreal actions and unnatural, exaggerated emotions; even where the "new art" dealt with subjects
known to the old, it revealed a greater knowledge of
psychologic truth and a finer taste in diction. The older
compositions which had enjoyed favor in the days when
Cervantes was writing his *Pictures of Algiers* labored
under the great disadvantage of being written for the
most part by men of scant poetic gifts. Their verse is,
with few exceptions, labored and rarely reveals genuine
emotion or plastic beauty. But by the genius of Lope
above all others, the dramatic instrument which had been
used was remoulded at one stroke; the warmth and color
which he gave his plays, the facility and flexibility of
his verse, the richness and variety of his diction, the
harmony between his language and the subject matter,
and finally, the wide range of his plots created a new
model for the drama, just as the achievement of Cervantes had pointed a new way for fiction. Lope was, moreover, able to give his art a triumphant career by his
creative power. As Cervantes admitted, the number of
plays written by the "monster of nature" was nothing
less than miraculous. It was, therefore, natural that
among the innumerable and multifarious subjects which
Lope and his school treated, some were not fitted for the
stage by their romantic or undramatic nature. On the
other hand, there were those, whose name is legion, which
deal in a convincing, realistic fashion with certain phases
of contemporary society, and reproduce with truth and
vivacity the language of the Spanish people. Yet in his

strictures Cervantes chose to be severe with the particular plays which show most defects, but which are by
no means as numerous as those upon which Lope's fame
rests; he preferred to praise the old-fashioned compositions belonging to his first period at the expense of the
new living art, simply because his heart was with the
older school of which he had once been a part. We may
assume that the passage in *Don Quixote* was written
about 1602 or 1603; Cervantes first characterizes the
Spanish drama in general:

While the drama, according to Tully, should be the mirror
of human life, the model of manners, and the image of the
truth, those which are presented nowadays are mirrors of nonsense, models of folly and images of lewdness. For what greater
nonsense can there be in connection with what we are now discussing than for an infant to appear in swaddling clothes in the
first scene of the first act, in the second a grown-up, bearded
man? Or what greater absurdity can there be than putting
before us an old man as a swashbuckler, a young man as a
poltroon, a lackey using fine language, a page giving sage
advice, a king plying as a porter, a princess who is a kitchen
maid? What shall I say of their attention to the time in which
the action they represent may or can take place, save that I
have seen a play where the first act began in Europe, the second
in Asia, the third finished in Africa, and, no doubt, had it been
in four acts, the fourth would have ended in America, and
so it would have been laid in all four quarters of the globe? If
truth to life is the main thing the drama should keep in view,
how is it possible for any average intellect to be satisfied when,
the action being supposed to pass in the time of King Pepin or

Charlemagne, the principal personage in it is made out to be the Emperor Heraclius who entered Jerusalem with the cross and won the Holy Sepulchre, like Godfrey of Bouillon, there being years innumerable between the one and the other? Or, what shall we say, if the play is based on fiction, and historical facts are introduced, or bits of what occurred to different people and at different times mixed up with it; all, not only without any semblance of probability, but with obvious errors that from every point of view are inexcusable? And the worst of it is, there are ignorant people who say that this is perfection, and that anything beyond it is affected refinement. [I, 48.]

Cervantes then proceeds to regret the impressions such plays must make among foreigners "who scrupulously observe the laws of the drama," and that a well-ordered government ought to demand higher standards of plays, even if they are intended only as a harmless amusement:

For after listening to an artistic and properly constructed play, the hearer will come away enlivened by the jests, instructed by the serious parts, full of admiration at the incidents, his wits sharpened by the arguments, warned by the tricks, all the wiser for the examples, inflamed against vice, and in love with virtue. In all these ways a good play will stimulate the mind of the hearer be he ever so boorish or dull; and of all impossibilities the greatest is that a play endowed with all these qualities will not entertain, satisfy, and please much more than one wanting in them, like the greater number of those which are commonly acted nowadays. Nor are the poets who write them to be blamed for this; for some there are among them who are perfectly well aware of their faults, and know thoroughly what they ought to do. But as plays have become a saleable commodity, they say, and, with truth, that the players will not buy them unless they are after this fashion; and so the poet tries to adapt himself to the requirements of the actor who is to pay him for his work. And that this is the truth may be seen by the countless plays that a most fertile wit of these kingdoms has written, with so much brilliancy, so much grace and gaiety, such polished versification, such choice language, such profound reflection, and, in a word, so rich in eloquence and elevation of style, that he has filled the world with his fame. Yet, in consequence of his desire to suit the taste of the actors, they have not all, as some of them have, come as near perfection as they ought. Others write plays with such heedlessness that after they have been acted, the actors have to fly and abscond, afraid of being punished.

The preface to Cervantes' *Eight Plays*, which was written ten years or more after the passage just quoted, shows more genuine and frank admiration for Lope's genius, and more appreciation of the Spanish theatre in general, as represented by those "who helped Lope to raise the great framework of the drama." From this noticeable change of heart it is evident that Cervantes was now willing to make concessions to the new stage, but it is, nevertheless, inconceivable that in the *Eight Plays* which he had offered to the public, he was hoping to keep abreast of "the latest vogue." Not one can be considered an imitation of Lope, and if Cervantes actually attempted to copy his style, he reveals absolutely no understanding of Lope's method, and his mis-judgment and inconsistency in this connection will always remain perplexing. In the second act of *The Blessed Vagabond* Cervantes goes so far as to retract the demands made in *Don Quixote*, namely, that the rules of art be observed, for he introduces Comedy in person, and lets her say:

The times change all things and perfect the arts, and to improve what has been imagined is no difficult task. I was fair in times gone by, and today, if you look well, I am not bad, even if I do not comply with the grave precepts of the ancients. Present usage is not subject to art; . . . now the drama is a map upon which you may see London and Rome not even a finger's length apart. It matters nothing to the listener that I pass in a moment from Germany to Guinea without leaving the stage; for thought is winged, and by it you can accompany me wherever I go.

The most ardent defender of the romantic drama could have said no more. But whatever may be the demerits of Cervantes' plays, there can be no doubt that his great flexible genius would have adapted itself more to the course taken by the new art, if he had had still many years ahead of him to develop his gifts as a playwright.

One of the brightest pages in the achievement of Cervantes will always be found in the eight brief *Interludes* which were included in the same volume. In these one-act farces he returns to his proper mode of self-expression, to humorous dialogue and that incisive realism which presented the characters he knew best. *The Divorce Court* is a sparkling scene which presents the average domestic infelicity by means of various couples who seek separation for scores of different reasons. *The Vagabond-Widower* presents another picture of the rogue's type and of low life, the most admirable examples of which are his *Rinconete and Cortadillo* and the first act of *The Blessed Vagabond*. *The Election of the Magistrates of Daganzo* is a witty travesty of the procedure of small villages, and of the ambitions of the rustic candidates who discuss their own qualifications and desire to justify their aspirations to being chosen. *The Watchful Sentinel* presents the amusing rivalry of a soldier and a sacristan for the hand of an attractive kitchen-wench at whose doors they keep vigil. *The Feigned Basque, The Cave of Salamanca,* and *The Jealous Old Man* are based on themes of disguise or deception, the last dealing with the contrivance of a young wife to introduce her lover into the house in the presence of her aged husband. The action has numerous parallels among the fabliaux, and in Italian fiction, and represents Cervantes' most unveiled attempt at realism. *The Miraculous Play* is based upon a medieval anecdote, the display of a pretended picture upon what is in reality a bare canvas. The objects displayed are supposed to be visible only to those born in legitimate wedlock. The gaping public naturally sees nothing, and the humor— of a thoroughly medieval and Renascence kind—lies in

the deception of those who have always considered themselves to be the sons of their fathers.   In all of these
life-like scenes Cervantes continued the popular vein of
Lope de Rueda, who in his farces had left the models of
admirably drawn pictures of everyday incidents.   The
Interludes are essentially of the people, and afforded to
Cervantes the very best opportunity, not only of imitating some dialogue or scene he might have witnessed in
village or city, but of presenting some commonplace
theme dear to the people because of its wit and of its
truthful analysis of human shortcomings.

The volume of *Eight Plays* and the second part of
Don Quixote were to be the last of Cervantes' works
printed during his lifetime.   He had various unfinished
manuscripts upon his table, for he speaks in his last
prefaces of his hope to complete *The Illustrious Bernardo, The Weeks of the Garden,* and a second part of
La Galatea.   How far these efforts were advanced is not
known; but one work he completed before his death, *The
Hardships of Persiles and Sigismunda: A Story of the
North.*   This romance is written in four books and seems
to have occupied his time intermittently after 1608 or
1609; on April 19, 1616, he penned a beautiful and
touching dedication for it, addressed to his patron, the
Count of Lemos, four days before he breathed his last.
The book was presumably seen through the press by
Cervantes' widow, and was published in the spring of
1617.   It has been rarely reprinted since the seventeenth
century, but some of its scenes were imitated, as was

the case with the *Novels,* by playwrights both in Spain and in foreign countries. Before 1700 ten editions came out, and it was twice translated into French in 1618, into English, from the French, in 1619, and into Italian in 1626. The most recent translation into English, by Miss Stanley (1854), is defective and unsatisfactory. Since the seventeenth century *Persiles and Sigismunda* has, with the exception of a brief interval of superficial popularity, slept an unmolested sleep upon its shelf. This exception was the period of romanticism, especially in Germany, where a number of prominent critics and poets sang its praises in extravagant terms. They justly praised Cervantes' imagination, his inventive power and the beauty of his style, but they failed to point out that in his last creation the great master had abandoned the vein with which his name was to be linked, that of clear and admirably balanced realism, for fantastic and wholly improbable imaginings.

The story of *Persiles and Sigismunda* is of interest because of its violent contrast with *Don Quixote* and the *Novels.* It begins in the middle, and during the course of its development gradually makes known the beginning. This device was taken from Heliodorus, with whom, Cervantes says in the preface to the *Novels,* "he is bold enough to compete." The hero, Periandro, has been captured by pirates; the vessel is wrecked; Periandro alone survives, and is taken up by another boat under the command of the Danish prince Arnaldo. The latter happens to be cruising in search of a maiden,

Auristela, whom he obtained from some pirates, but who unfortunately had again been abducted by others. Periandro, who is trying to discover the whereabouts of this same Auristela, acquaints Arnaldo with the object of his quest, professing at the same time to be her brother. In the disguise of a maiden Periandro is then sold to some barbarians upon an island on the assumption that they have Auristela in their possession. The savage, Bradamiro, falls in love with the supposed girl. Auristela, disguised as a boy, and her old nurse are quite naturally found where they were thought to be. When the lot of the captives is about to be decided, a quarrel arises among the savages, which ends in a general carnage and the devastation of the island by fire. Periandro and Auristela, however, are saved and conducted to a cave, where their rescuer, a Spaniard who for a long time has been an inhabitant of the island, relates the history of his adventures. All then set out together for another island, where they meet an Italian, Rutilio, who also tells the story of his life. Shortly after the termination of his narrative a shipwrecked Portuguese singer is picked up, and we get another tale of adventure, all in the best manner of Cervantes. The wanderers now reach an island, Golandia, where the whole party finds opportune shelter. Shortly thereafter we make the acquaintance of several newcomers, whose arrival leads to the chance reunion of a number of long-separated wanderers. In the meantime, Prince Arnaldo has again arrived upon the scene and demands Auristela in marriage from her feigned brother, Periandro. The reply is a vague acceptance of the offer, coupled with the request for a delay until Auristela has completed a pilgrimage to Rome in fulfilment of a certain vow. The. wanderers, therefore, set out once more; another shipwreck follows, and Periandro and Auristela are again separated. By following the adventures of the maiden, we learn of the experiences of various travelers wandering over northern seas, and incidentally of the festivities held at the court of King Policarpo. Periandro, we are told, has taken part in various games, and astonished all the spectators by his superior skill; he especially impresses the daughter of the king. The very next shipwreck lands Auristela and her companions on the island of King Policarpo, where the lovers are again reunited. Complicated love affairs follow, the narration of which by the author is interrupted several times by the autobiography of Periandro, who recalls former adventures of himself and Auristela, both by land and sea, thus bringing the story up to the actual moment of their wanderings. The king in the meantime plans to get possession of Auristela, but the whole party manages to escape to another island. Here there are numerous leave-takings; the hero and heroine together with a few of their friends finally set out for Lisbon, where they arrive without any further mishap. Here ends the second book and with it the naïve and irrational first half of the romance. The pilgrims now undertake an interesting journey through Spain, France and Italy. Numerous adventures, or short tales, love affairs, all related in a manner very characteristic of Cervantes, are introduced. In due time we hear of the early history and of the true relation of Periandro and Auristela, together with the origin of their pilgrimage to Rome. Finally, Auristela having fulfilled her vow, and all other difficulties having been overcome, she and Periandro, who are in reality a prince and princess with the names Persiles and Sigismunda, are happily married and return to their northern home.

In order to rehearse the mere skeleton of the story, it has been necessary to omit all secondary episodes and minor characters. The résumé is, therefore, bound to be somewhat dry and lifeless. In spite of the utter improbability, and even impossibility, of all that happens in the first two books, there are passing moods during which we can read some of their pages with genuine pleasure. Many a boy of eighteen has attempted the composition of a yarn of this type, and we may assume that Cervantes was at heart younger when he wrote *Persiles and Sigismunda* than at any period of his life. It would likewise be unwise to condemn this romance after one hearing. Cervantes put more of himself, of his experiences, of his reading, of his personality into this tale than into anything else that he wrote. It was, if we may infer so much from his own statement, the production for which he himself had the most genuine affection, for in his dedication of the second part of *Don Quixote* he calls the *Persiles* "either the worst or the best which I have composed for entertainment in our language. And I am sorry that I said the worst, because, according to the opinion of my friends, it will be the best possible." We need not detain ourselves in discussing the evident inconsistencies in the great genius of Cervantes, who criticized the drama of his contemporaries for absurdities which abound in his own plays, and who, at the same time that he was writing some of the greatest chapters of *Don Quixote,* was capable of composing the childish adventures to be found in the first two books of the *Persiles.* Still, if we look closely, this last self-contradiction is inherent in the characteristic gifts of Cervantes, in his very art, which came to him naturally and without effort; so that, as a consequence, his superb imagination, his inventive power, were left without the restraint or discrimination which more highly trained, but less inspired, talents can at critical times impose upon themselves. The key-note to these discrepancies with the principles of his art, which advocated only what was probable and admitted the impossible, may be found in *Don Quixote* itself. Near the close of the first part Cervantes gives what may be taken for a curious preliminary sketch of just such a romance as the *Persiles.* In the midst of the analysis of the romances of chivalry the following opinion attributed to the Canon stands out; we are told that—

he found one good thing in them, and that was the opportunity they afforded to a gifted intellect for displaying itself; for they presented a wide and spacious field over which the pen might range freely, describing shipwrecks, tempests, combats, battles, portraying a valiant captain with all the qualifications requisite to make one, showing him sagacious in foreseeing the wiles of the enemy, eloquent in speech to encourage or restrain his soldiers, ripe in counsel, rapid in resolve, as bold in biding his time as in pressing the attack; now picturing some tragic incident, now some joyful and unexpected event; here a beauteous lady, virtuous, wise, and modest; there a Christian knight, brave and gentle; here a lawless, barbarous braggart; there a courteous prince, gallant and gracious; setting forth the devotion and loyalty of vassals, the greatness and generosity of nobles. Or the author may show himself to be an astronomer, or a skilled cosmographer or a musician, or one versed in affairs of state, and sometimes he will have a chance of coming forward as a magician if he likes. [I, 47.]

Some of these elements of fiction can be found in the average romance of chivalry, but an example of practically all of them exists in the *Persiles,* although confined chiefly to the first two books. The remaining two are, with the exception of those features which had to be continued from the earlier portion, in Cervantes' best narrative vein. As long as his chief personages were wandering aimlessly, driven by blind chance over the seas and islands of the north, Cervantes had to make use of his imagination and of the nonsense which he found in books of travel, such as Torquemada's miscellany entitled *A Garden of Rare Flowers.* And nothing could be stranger or more ridiculous than the customs ascribed by this book to the peoples of northern

Europe. Cervantes also found material in the Byzantine romances, especially in Heliodorus, in chronicles of the Indies, in cosmographies and quaint maps of the world, "in which Rome and London were separated only by the length of a finger," in Virgil's *Æneid*, in Plutarch's *Morals,* in Pliny's *Natural History,* and, finally, in various Italian novelists. In short, no other work of Cervantes so thoroughly betrays his method of composing, his reading, his type of mind, his charming personality as does the *Persiles.* It is likewise filled with details drawn from his own life; it pictures the author as looking back over his long and romantic career, and embroidering fact with fancy; it combines in the frankest and most innocent manner conceivable irrational incidents and the soundest observation of genuine life and manners. The improbable portion deals with such things as the strange flora and fauna of northern islands, never beheld by mortal eyes; the sane part is based upon reliable experiences in Cervantes' own Spain. The style of the *Persiles* is more uniformly excellent than that of any other work, and nowhere has Cervantes surpassed it in clearness and grace of diction, in the careful choice of his vocabulary. The romance is also characterized by a nobility of sentiment and that serenity of spirit to be found in one who has risen above the whirl of existence.

The *Prologue,* in particular, is in Cervantes' happiest manner, and will always retain a special charm and sweetness from the fact that it was composed not long before his death. Its tone is most distinctive in its whimsical and pathetic personal touches:

It happened recently, my dear reader, that I was coming home with two friends from the famous town of Esquivias, famous for a thousand reasons, one for its illustrious families, and another for its very illustrious wines, when I heard behind us one approaching with great speed; for he seemed eager to catch up and shouted to us not to give our beasts the spur. We waited for him, and presently a student came up mounted upon a she-ass. He was entirely dressed in grey, wore leggings, round-toed shoes, a sword with a chape, and a starched walloon collar with bands; the truth is that of the latter he only had two, because the collar slipped to one side every moment and he had the greatest difficulty to keep it straight. When he had come up with us, he said: "Your worships are unquestionably on the track of some sinecure or prebend at Madrid to judge from your haste. . . ." To this one of my friends replied, "The hack of my friend, Miguel de Cervantes, is to blame, it has such a long pace." No sooner did the student hear the name of Cervantes than he dismounted, and, dropping his saddle-pad on one side and his valise on the other—for he was travelling with all this display—he rushed at me, seized my left hand and exclaimed: "To be sure, this is the sound cripple, the widely famous, the joyous writer, and, in short, the delight of the muses." Whereupon I, out of courtesy and as an answer to his extravagant praises, put my arms around his neck, completely ruining his collar in the act, and said: "That is the mistake which many commit through ignorance, for I am Cervantes and none of the trifling things you call me; go back for your ass, and let us travel together the rest of the way in pleasant conversation." We proceeded, and the discussion turned on my illness, the good student destroying my illusions at once by saying: "The disease you describe is dropsy, and all the water of the ocean won't cure you, no matter how fresh you get it. Drink less, Señor Cervantes, and don't forget how to eat; that will cure you without the aid of any other medicine." "So others have told me," I replied, "but I am as fond of drinking as though I had been born only for that; my life is nearing its close, and, to judge by the beat of my pulse, it will cease by next Sunday at the latest. You have met me at an unfortunate hour, for no longer shall I have an opportunity to show you my gratitude for your kindness." Here we reached the city and entered by different ways. . . . I again embraced him, we parted, and he left me, having given my pen a rare occasion for writing more entertaining pages. But all times are not alike; perhaps some day I may pick up the broken thread and say all that remains unsaid. Farewell jests, farewell fancies, farewell merry friends, for I am dying and desire to see you soon contented in the next life.

And in his deeply moving dedication to the Count of Lemos, dated four days before his death, he says:

I would that those ancient rhymes. famous in their time, and beginning
        "With my foot already in the stirrup,"
were not so ápposite in this letter of mine, for with these very words I can begin and say,
        "With my foot already in the stirrup,
          In the agony of death,
          Noble Lord, I address these words to you."

Yesterday I received extreme unction, and today I pen this dedication; the time is brief, my agony increases, hopes diminish, and yet withal I protract my life beyond my desire to live; for I should like to have it prolonged until I have greeted your excellency and welcomed you back to Spain. . . . Many works still remain unfinished. . . .

Cervantes' death fell on April 23, 1616; he was carried to his grave by some brothers of a Franciscan order which he had joined, and buried without display in a convent of Trinitarian nuns on the Calle de Cantarranas, not far from his last residence on the Calle del León. Unfortunately his exact resting-place can no longer be identified, and his body has become mingled with our universal mother earth, as his work has been fused with the spirit of all mankind.

The literary achievement of Cervantes may be clearly divided into those works which the world is willing to leave unread, which, for the lack of a better term, may be called his minor works, and those into which he lavishly poured the wealth of his personality and genius, and which belong to the world's master works. Posterity knows but little of Cervantes' *Galatea,* his *Eight Plays,* his *Persiles* and his miscellaneous verse. Their fate is unjustly shared, at least in foreign countries, by his masterly *Exemplary Novels.* On the other hand every nation has accepted his *Don Quixote* as the sum and epitome of his accomplishment. This estimate of a book which belongs to all peoples is entirely natural and just: no author can hope to make the same great conquest with two works. But a fuller and more equitable verdict must be passed on his inferior writings than can be inferred from their universal neglect. The secondary compositions of a great writer like Cervantes not only contain many of the positive and abiding qualities to be found in his best known pages: they may relate him to his time, to its literary activities, to its everyday thoughts and interests more intimately than his chief creations. This is the case with Cervantes' lesser works, which stand far less aloof from the world of contemporary letters than his *Novels* or his unique *Don Quixote*.

La Galatea was a reflection of the taste of the sixteenth century, the expression of a genre in fiction which we should regret to miss. This pastoral is our first specimen of Cervantes' style; its short stories give a fair idea of his best manner, and it forms, all in all, the foundation for any study of his art. The dramas of his first period, of which we unfortunately have only two, go a step farther in that they reveal much more of his creative vigor and personality. Without pointing an untried way, or adding any noteworthy features to the dramatic methods of his early contemporaries, Cervantes nevertheless infused into these compositions a deeper tone by the loftiness of his sentiments, by his piety and love of country; he also manifested a novel sense of balance, which avoided the extremes of undramatic horror and of colorless delineation. His eloquent but restrained rhetoric, his genuine pathos and his acquaintance with the human heart are not satisfactory substitutes for a genuine dramatic talent, but they stand out among all the creations of the older stage. The *Eight Plays* left to us from his second period are uniformly deficient in technique and versification, and constitute, on the whole, a contribution of less artistic value than the first two. A number of isolated scenes, which vivaciously and convincingly present pictures of real life, fail to redeem the fantastic and romantic features which too often dominate the plots. These *Eight Plays* of Cervantes, therefore, have no intimate relation with the best dramas of the seventeenth century; a comparison between them and the poetic and spontaneous creation of Lope de Vega discloses neither a successful, nor even a conscious imitation on the part of Cervantes, and the slight resemblances in their manner are entirely external. Cervantes selected for his last dramatic compositions novelistic themes, and the choice once more demonstrates that he could not oppose the dictates of his genius, which expanded and moved unhampered only in the realm of prose fiction. On the other hand, the *Eight Interludes* will survive as sparkling examples of his good-natured humor and restrained satire, of his life-like dialogue, and of his gift of succinct analysis of the common people. The *Persiles* represents the farthest extent to which Cervantes allowed his great inventive art to go. There is to be found in every great writer an extreme expression of his esthetic creation, which frequently represents an unconscious abuse of his gifts, and in the *Persiles* Cervantes allowed his imagination to roam without the restraint of what in lieu of a better phrase we must call his artistic common sense. Yet the work is being more and more prized as the great repository of his most peculiar gifts, and because it admits more side-lights on his personality, on his technique and manner of composition than his greater works. It also contains some of the most perfect pages of his literary style.

It would be futile to discuss the merits of Cervantes' miscellaneous verse, in particular, his *Journey to Parnassus* and the metrical portions of *La Galatea*, in order to detect in them a portion of his enduring achievement. His most fervent devotees seem disinclined to exclude his poetic efforts from among his best work; at all events, they see in them only superior qualities which objective critics have been unable to discover. The willing admission that an occasional passage or poem has genuine merit does not satisfy them, as it seems to damn his poetic gifts with faint praise. The discussion, therefore, is like that which took place over the barber's basin; to some it was an interesting but not unusual piece of metal; to Don Quixote it was an enchanted helmet of pure gold in spite of its defects, and no argument could shake that conviction "to the day of judgment."

The attainment evident in his master works, *The Exemplary Novels* and *Don Quixote* stands written in-

delibly in the history of fiction, and every word of
encomium must seem inadequate. The *Novels* would
undoubtedly attract a wider reading public among us
if it were more generally known to what extent they
are a priceless document on the civilization of the Spanish Peninsula. All Spain is there. Indeed, the title
would be more accurate and, no doubt, more attractive,
if it could be changed into *Pictures and Manners of the
Spanish People.* Cities and individuals alike have received the breath of life and will continue to survive for
us on these extraordinary pages. Here is Madrid, there
is Seville, there is Toledo, each drawn with its most
significant aspects, and everywhere we meet with the
unmistakable spirit of the Spanish people as a whole.
And if we seek out the portraits of single men or women,
how fruitful our quest becomes! All the various types
that a traveller of the sixteenth century could have met
are to be found, from the diversified examples of the
aristocracy down to the father-confessor of a gang of
thieves. No historian of the Spanish people can do
without the precious details to be found in Cervantes'
Novels. And if the book is not read as generally as it
deserves, even by the Spaniards themselves, it is, nevertheless, regarded by them with reverence. Just so a
famous old edifice in the midst of a modern community
may be held in high esteem and cherished for its beauty
of structure and ornamentation; it may only from time
to time be scrutinized more carefully by the casual
passerby, and infrequently inspire imitation in other

builders, because its influence is exerted in a more subtle manner. But if the passerby lingers to examine it, the imagination of the race and the history of an epoch gone by will assume body and life, and he will see before him a landmark of the past which can stir only noble national pride, and which is bound to keep alive solely high standards for all constructive work of the future.

Don Quixote, on the other hand, has become a part of the literary conscience of the world, and, therefore, possesses the rare fame of being known, at least by name, to countless persons who have not had the leisure to peruse it. Perhaps this is the common lot of the great books of mankind, which we are contented to call the repositories of the best fruits of our earthly life, of the records of progress made by our toil, our faith, our hopes and our discomfitures: we find time to turn their pages only at rare intervals. Still they have become sufficiently fused with the world's culture to survive in the subconscious realm of cultivated men and women, and in every community there are some who, impelled by simple devotion, or by the nature of their tasks, read our masterpieces, and thus help to keep alive their influence.

Don Quixote has an advantage over most famous works, in so far as its wit and humor lure the reader at the outset; and, having obtained his good will, they can proceed without further drawback to induce him to discover the fulness and variety of its serious human imagery. It would, therefore, be a mistake to suppose that only the gaiety and laughter of *Don Quixote* give the work its vitality; the book rests also on a very complete and perennially fresh interpretation of life: and such an interpretation requires the normal leavening of pathos, of sorrow, of broken purposes. Petrarch has said in a profound verse, "Naught else but tears on earth prevails" (null' altro che pianto al mondo dura); yet the beauty of Cervantes' romance lies precisely in the avoidance of the extremes of grief and joy, in an admirable fusion of features which stir laughter and compassion. Fortunately the world is everywhere so constituted that it can prize the nobility of soul exemplified in *Don Quixote,* and that fortitude which gives his failure the aspect of victory; we may recall Pandora's buoyant lines in Moody's *Fire-bringer:*

> Of wounds and sore defeat
> I made my battle stay;
> Wingèd sandals for my feet
> I wove of my delay;
> Of weariness and fear,
> I made my shouting spear;
> Of loss, and doubt, and dread,
> And swift oncoming doom
> I made a helmet for my head
> And a floating plume.
> From the shutting mists of death,
> From the failure of the breath,
> I made a battle-horn to blow
> Across the vales of overthrow. . . .
> O hearken where the echoes bring,

> Down the grey disastrous morn,
> Laughter and rallying!

This simplest of philosophies, the philosophy of
courage, to sing and to serve, speaks from the pages of
Don Quixote; it combines by the rarest of processes perfected esthetic and ethical points of view; it is characterized throughout by a serene atmosphere free from
all exaggerated emotion and that dramatic presentation
of life which admits the voices of pessimism and despair.
It is certain that Cervantes was unaware of such tragic
depths as lie in Gloucester's cry:

> As flies to wanton boys are we to the gods,
> They kill us for their sport.

Nor could the resilient nature, the unreasoning but none
the less noble faith of Don Quixote have grasped the
overwhelming force of a despair which prefers death to
life, and yearns

> To shake the yoke of inauspicious stars
> From this world-wearied flesh.

Wherever we find incidents which terminate in disillusionment or misfortune, we note also the accompanying counsel of stoic patience and courage. This is nowhere more beautifully expressed than on one of the
last pages which Cervantes penned:

We cannot call that hope which may be resisted and overthrown by adversity, for as light shines most in the darkness, even so hope must remain unshaken in the midst of toil; for to despair is the act of cowardly hearts, and there is no greater pusillanimity or baseness than to allow the spirit, no matter how beset by difficulties it may be, to yield to discouragement. ["Persiles and Sigismunda," I, 9.]

Don Quixote, which embodies this sentiment, is thus by the great simplicity of its thought, by the ease with which it may be comprehended, a book for the average person, and so for every man. It voices those qualities from which humanity draws its noblest inspirations, an unclouded faith in God and His world, spiritual poise, and the triumphant heroism that greets the unseen with a cheer.

BIBLIOGRAPHY

I. TRANSLATIONS

DON QUIXOTE DE LA MANCHA :—SHELTON.—*The History of Don Quichote*. The First Part. [London, 1612 ?] *The Second Part of the History of the valorous and witty Knight-Errant, Don Quixote de la Mancha*. London, 1620. Reprinted in the *Tudor Translations*, London, Nutt, 1896.

MOTTEUX.—*The History of the renown'd Don Quixote de la Mancha*. Publish'd by Peter Motteux. London, 1700. This translation has been frequently reprinted; it is included in Everyman's Library; a commendable edition is that issued at Edinburgh, William Patterson, 1879, with a biography of Cervantes and notes by Lockhart.

ORMSBY.—*The Ingenious Gentleman Don Quixote of La Mancha*. With Introduction and Notes by John Ormsby, 4 vols., London, 1885. Reprinted by Gowans and Gray, Glasgow, 1901, in *The Complete Works of Miguel de Cervantes Saavedra*, edited by James Fitzmaurice-Kelly, and by Dodd, Mead, and Company in New York.

WATTS.—*The Ingenious Gentleman Don Quixote of La Mancha*. With Notes and a new Life of the Author, by Henry Edward Watts, 5 vols., London, Bernard Quaritch, 1888.

Shelton's translation, often too far from the original, makes pleasant reading on account of its quaint and archaic speech. Motteux borrows from predecessors, but presents an attractive version, also characterized by excessive freedom. Ormsby is to be recommended because of the sincerity and faithfulness of his text. Watts is also praised by many critics for his careful and erudite study of the original.

THE EXEMPLARY NOVELS :—MABBE.—*Exemplarie Novels*. In Six Books. (Containing six novels only: *The Two Damosels*,

The Ladie Cornelia, The Liberal Lover, The Force of Bloud, The Spanish Ladies, The Jealous Husband.) Turned into English by Don Diego Puede-Ser. London, John Dawson, 1640.

KELLY.—*The Exemplary Novels of Miguel de Cervantes Saavedra,* by Walter K. Kelly. London, Henry G. Bohn, 1846. Not to be recommended.

MACCOLL.—*Exemplary Novels of Miguel de Cervantes Saavedra.* Translated by N. Maccoll; Gowans and Gray, Glasgow, 1902, 2 vols., in *The Complete Works of Cervantes,* edited by Jas. Fitzmaurice-Kelly.

LORENTE.—*Rinconete and Cortadillo,* Boston, Four Seas Company, 1918.

LA GALATEA:—OELSNER-WELFORD.—*Galatea.* Translated by H. Oelsner and A. B. Welford, Gowans and Gray, Glasgow, 1903. In the *Complete Works of Cervantes,* edited by Jas. Fitzmaurice-Kelly.

A JOURNEY TO PARNASSUS:—GIBSON.—*Journey to Parnassus,* Composed by Miguel de Cervantes Saavedra. Translated into English tercets with Preface and illustrative Notes by James Y. Gibson. London, Kegan Paul, Trench and Co., 1883. The Spanish text is included.

NUMANTIA:—GIBSON.—*Numantia:* A Tragedy translated from the Spanish with Introduction and Notes by James Y. Gibson. London, Kegan Paul, 1885.

PERSILES AND SIGISMUNDA.—*The Travels of Persiles and Sigismunda. A Northern History.* Anonymous. Translated from a French version. London, 1619.

STANLEY.—*The Wanderings of Persiles and Sigismunda. A Northern Story.* Translated by Louise D. Stanley. London, J. Cundall, 1854.

II. EDITIONS

COLLECTIONS:—ROSELL-HARTZENBUSCH.—*Obras Completas,* Madrid, Rivadeneyra, 1863-4 (12 vols.).

BONILLA-SCHEVILL.—*Obras Completas,* in progress of publication; with Prefaces and Notes. Madrid, 1914—. Eight volumes to date, including *La Galatea* (2 vols.), *Persiles y*

Sigismunda (2 vols.), and *Ocho Comedias y ocho Entremeses* (4 vols.).

Don Quixote:—The Hispanic Society of America.—Facsimile edition of the first two issues of Madrid, 1605, and the first of 1615 (3 vols.).

Clemencín.—*Don Quixote,* with commentary, Madrid, 1833-39 (6 vols.).

Fitzmaurice-Kelly and Ormsby.—*Don Quixote,* London, 1899-1900 (2 vols.).

Cortejón, Givanel Mas and Suñé Benajes.—*Don Quixote,* with commentary. Madrid, 1905-13. (6 vols.).

Rodríguez Marín.—*Don Quixote,* with commentary. Madrid, 1911-13 (8 vols.). Another edition in large format, Madrid, 1916 (6 vols.).

Clemencín is noted for the first exhaustive study of the romances of chivalry. Cortejón gives the variants of all important editions, and elucidates many Spanish customs. Rodríguez Marín is well versed in Spanish poetry and folklore, and explains numerous obscure passages.

The Exemplary Novels:—Brockhaus.—*Novelas Ejemplares,* Leipzig, 1883.

Cuervo.—*Cinco Novelas Ejemplares,* Strassburg, 1908.

Rodríguez Marín.—*Novelas Ejemplares* (six novels in two volumes), with commentary. Madrid, 1914-17.—*El Loaysa de "El celoso Estremeño,"* Sevilla, 1901.—*Rinconete y Cortadillo,* Madrid, 1905 (both novels with introduction and notes).

Amezúa y Mayo.—*El Casamiento engañoso y el Coloquio de los Perros* (with commentary), Madrid, 1912.

Miscellaneous Verse:—Ricardo Rojas.—*Poesias de Cervantes* (with introduction and notes), Buenos Aires, 1916.

III. WORKS OF REFERENCE

Fitzmaurice-Kelly.—*Historia de la Literatura española* (revised edition), Madrid, 1916; full bibliography, pp. 383 ff.

Fernández de Navarrete.—*Vida de Miguel de Cervantes Saavedra,* Madrid, 1819.

Rius.—*Bibliografía crítica de las Obras de Cervantes*, 3 vols., Madrid, 1895-1905.

Pérez Pastor.—*Documentos cervantinos hasta ahora inéditos*, 2 vols., Madrid, 1897-1902.

León Máinez.—*Cervantes y su Epoca*. Jérez de la Frontera, 1901.

Fitzmaurice-Kelly.—Prefaces in *The Complete Works of Cervantes*, Glasgow, 1901-3.

Cotarelo y Mori.—*Efemérides cervantinas*, Madrid, 1905.

Cejador y Frauca.—*La Lengua de Cervantes*, 2 vols., Madrid, 1905-6.

Fitzmaurice-Kelly.—*Cervantes—A Memoir*, Oxford, 1913.—In Spanish, Oxford Press, 1917.

Rodríguez Marín.—*Documentos nuevos cervantinos*, Madrid, 1914.

Bonilla.—*La Vida corporativa de los Estudiantes españoles en sus Relaciones con la Historia de las Universidades*, Madrid, 1914.

Cotarelo y Valledor.—*El Teatro de Cervantes*, Madrid, 1915.

IV. STUDIES AND ESSAYS

Sainte-Beuve.—*Don Quichotte*, "Nouveaux Lundis," t. VIII, 1864.

Morel-Fatio.—*Le "Don Quichotte" envisagé comme peinture et critique de la société espagnole du XVIᵉ et du XVIIᵉ siècle* in "Études sur l'Espagne," 1st series, Paris, 1895.

Pereda.—*El Cervantismo* in "Esbozos y Rasguños," 2nd edit., Madrid, 1898.

Crothers.—*Quixotism* in "The Gentle Reader," Boston, Houghton Mifflin, 1904.

Menéndez y Pelayo.—*Cultura literaria de Miguel de Cervantes*, "Revista de Archivos," May, 1905.

Woodberry.—*Cervantes* in "Great Writers," New York, McClure, 1907.

Turgenev.—*Hamlet and Don Quixote: the two eternal human types*, "Current Literature," 42. 1907.

Havelock Ellis.—*Don Quixote* in *"The Soul of Spain,"* Boston, Houghton Mifflin, 1913.

Bonilla.—*Cervantes y su Obra*, Madrid, 1916.

INDEX

A

academies, Italian, 96.
Achilles Tatius, 174.
Acquaviva, 50, 51, 57.
Æneid, 173, 360.
African campaign, disaster of, 65.
Agramante, 233.
Alba, Duke of, 44.
Albert, Archduke, 27.
Alcalá de Henares, 3.
   during Cervantes' boyhood, 7ff.
   Magistral Church, 5.
   Plaza de Cervantes, 4.
   remains, 3.
   Santa María, church of, 4.
Alcalá, University of, 5ff, 16.
   argumentation and dispute, 8.
   Bachelor of Arts, 8.
   boarding-houses, 11, 12.
   College Church, 5.
   curriculum, 7.
   ecclesiastical character, 8.
   effect on early education of Cervantes, 16.
   Hall of Ceremonials, 6.
   humanities, 8.
   Latin language, 8.
   number of students, 6.
   pastimes, 12-13.
   remains, 5.
   removal to Madrid, 5.
   sports, 13.
   stepping-stone to careers, 9.
   student life, 9ff.
   subjects taught, 8.
   theatrical performances, 14.
   Trilingual College of San Jerónimo, 8.
Alcázar, Baltasar del, 100.
Alemán, Mateo, 15.
Alexandra, 148.
Algiers, 75.
   departure from, 89.
allied forces at Lepanto, 60, 62.
Amadis of Gaul, 194, 196, 202, 239, 278.
Amaranta, 137.
Ameto, 105.
Andalusia, 154, 166.
Angora, 27.
apothecaries, 324.
Apothegms, collections of, 174.
Apuleius, 174.
Araucana, 99.
Arcadia, 105, 111.
Archbishops of Toledo, 5.
Ariosto, 233, 342.
Aristotle, 8, 170.
Armada, invincible, 156.
arms and letters, 99.
Arnaute Mamí, 73, 74.
Artidoro (Rey de Artieda), 116.
arts, 192.
Astrée, 111.
attack on Cervantes, 282.
autobiographical details in works, cf. Cervantes.
Azores, 95.

377

B

"Barataria," 281.
Barbarigo, Agostino, 60.
barber's basin, 217.
Barreiros, 6.
Basilio, 260.
Bazán, Álvaro de, cf. Marqués de Santa Cruz, 60, 95.
Bella, Antonio de la, 86.
Berganza, 326.
Blanco de Paz, 85, 86, 88, 89.
Blessed Vagabond, 344, 352.
Boccaccio, 105, 299ff.
Boiardo, 217.
books of travel, 169.
Bourgeois Gentilhomme, 269.
Bowle, Dr. John, 288.
Byzantine romances, 360.

C

Calisto and Melibea, cf. *Celestina,* 102.
calle de Cantarranas, 363.
calle del León, 363.
calle del Rastro, 330.
Camacho, 258, 260-2, 276-7.
Caporali, Cesare, 298, 333.
Cardenio, cf. *Don Quixote,* 239.
Carlos, Prince, 50.
Carmelites, 30.
Catalina de Oviedo, 343.
Cave of Salamanca, 352.
Celestina, 102, 103, 176, **177ff,** 262, 265, 300:
  delineation, 178.
  dialogue, 178.
  influence, 181.
  large canvas, 177.
  primitive passions, **178.**
  humanism, 180.
  translations, 177.
  urban realism, 184.
Cervantes, Andrea de **(sister),** 86, 93, 94, 332.

Cervantes, **Juan de (grand-father),** 19.
  advocate, 23.
  career, 22ff.
  city attorney, 23.
  death, 22.
  law-suits against, **24-5.**
  Licentiate, 23.
  judge, 23.
  magistrate, 23.
  malfeasance, 26.
Cervantes, Loisa de (sister), 30.
Cervantes, Magdalena de (sister), 34, 93, 94, 162, 333.
Cervantes, Maria de (aunt), 20.
Cervantes, Miguel de, 3ff.
  academic life, 168.
  achievement, 363ff.
  acquaintance with classics, 169ff, 174.
  acquaintance with prominent men, 99.
  activities (1566-7), 38.
  aloofness from intellectual forces, 168.
  art, 179, 218, 300, 302, 303.
  association with stage, 134.
  autobiographical details, 38, 44.
  baptism, 4.
  baptismal document, 4.
  birth, 4.
  birthplace, 3.
  campaigns, 165.
  candidate for posts in Indies, 158.
  captivity, 165.
  captured by pirates, 73ff.
  career of arms and letters, 33.
  certificate of ransom, 87
  chamberlain, 50.
  character, 88, 283.
  choice of career, 93.
  commissary, 154.

compared with Boccaccio, 300ff.
cynicism, 320.
daughter, cf. Isabel de Saavedra, 162.
death, 363.
debt to government, 160.
defense against Avellaneda, 283.
deficit in accounts, 160.
departure from Algiers, 89.
departure for Italy, 50, 56.
departure from Italy, 65, 71.
dialogue, gift of, 266.
discrepancies in art, 358.
document on family, 50.
document on captivity, 87.
dramatic art of first period, 146.
dramatic works, 134, 341; see "drama" and Eight Plays.
duel, 51, 52, 54, 56, 57, 116.
education, 35-7, 91.
eloquence, 305.
employment by government, 160.
enlistment as soldier, 43.
escape from punishment, 52.
excommunication, 156.
externals of career, 38.
family, 3, 16, 21, 31, 331.
first literary venture, 95.
first to write novels in Castilian, 298.
flight from Spain, 51, 52, 54, 116.
foreign diplomats on, 290.
garrison duty, 64.
gifts, 292.
growth of genius, 153.
hidalgo, 18.
home life, 28.
household, 133.
imagination, 169, 354.
in debt, 94.
information on family and birth, 49.
inventive art, 292.

irony 180.
Italian campaigns, 57.
Italian culture and literature, 66ff.
Italian influence, 175.
Italian sojourn, 65.
Lepanto, 61, 62.
literary career interrupted, 136.
lyric art, 124.
marriage, 131, 132.
merits as soldier, 65.
method of composition, 294-5, 360.
migrations of family, 16.
military service, 38, 43, 56, 57, 59, 71, 95.
mind, 153, 167, 168.
new psychology, 154.
occupation in Seville, 162.
pastoral, judgment on, 125, 127.
philosophy, 175, 289-90, 370.
playwright, 150.
plots to escape, 77, 80, 84, 85.
poet, 49.
poetic gifts, 366.
portrait, 297-8.
poverty, 333.
poverty of family, 22, 93, 130.
publications, earliest, 48.
pursuit of letters, 129.
ransom, 86ff.
reading, 360.
relation to intellectual life, 167.
religious beliefs, 303.
reminiscences of Italy, 71.
residence at Valladolid, 330.
resources of art, 293, 303.
return to Madrid, 45, 47, 51, 89, 93.
revenue collector, 160.
routine occupation, 133, 153, 154.
salary, 155.
satirist, 97, 129.
second dramatic period, 341.

self-criticism, 247.
simplicity, 305.
sisters, 30. cf. Andrea de Cervantes, Loisa de Cervantes, Magdalena de Cervantes.
slave, 76ff, 88.
stoicism, 153, 370.
students, 7.
studies interrupted, 48, 50.
style, 175, 198, 218, 265, 294, 305, 354.
success as dramatist, 136.
theatre, 158.
theories on early education, 33.
tragic instinct, 318.
training, 37.
Universities, 7, 168.
Vega, Lope de, and drama of Cervantes, 348ff.
verdict on *Don Quixote*, 287.
versification of early plays, 147.
wanderings, 155, 165.
whereabouts, 33, 37, 49, 164.
women of family, 27, 31.
Cervantes, Rodrigo de (brother), 26-7, 28, 37, 71-2, 79, 93, 94, 95, 130.
Cervantes, Rodrigo de (father), 4, 15ff, 17, 22, 34, 37, 38, 50, 93, 130:
character of *Captive's* father, 39.
financial state, 35.
imprisonment for debt, 19.
incompetence, 30.
law-suit, 19.
médico cirujano, 16.
nobility of family, 18.
personal property, 21.
poverty, 18, 39.
Cervantes, Rodrigo de (great grandfather), 23.
Chances, 328.
Chapter of Seville, 156.
Charles V., 55.

Chaucer, 120.
Christian powers, 58.
chronicles, 169, 360.
Cipión, 326.
cirujano, 17.
Cisneros, Cardinal Ximénez de, 5.
City School, Madrid, 47.
Civilization, contemporary, 175.
Clareo and Florisea, 174.
Classics, influence of, 49.
Clavileño, 279.
Clitophon and Leucippe, 174.
collections of apothegms, 174.
College of Jesuits, Seville, 35: curriculum, 37.
study of classics, 37.
Colloquy of the Dogs, 9, 35, 185, 304, 321, 326-7.
ample canvas, 327.
analysis of experiences, 326.
classics, 172.
Galatea, 126.
model dialogue, 326.
Spanish life, 327.
Colonna, Marco Antonio, 58.
Comedy of Confusion, 137, 138.
conceptos (concetti), 124.
Constantinople, 87.
Cordido, Diego, 24.
Córdoba, 20.
Cortinas, Leonor de (mother), 20, 33, 34, 35, 37, 38, 86, 93: death, 28, 162.
heroic efforts, 29.
influence, 28.
cosmographies, 360.
Costanza, 332-3.
crafts, 192.
Crisio (Virués), 115.
Cueva, Juan de la, 100.
Cueva y Silva, Francisco de la, 100.
current taste, 180.
Cyprus, 58, 59.

D

Dalí Mamí, 73, 81.

Damón (Laínez), 116.
Dapple, 215, 227, 248.
Decameron, 299ff.
Deceitful Marriage, 316, 320-1.
devotees of Cervantes, 366.
dialogues, 311.
Dialogues, of Lucian, 174.
Dialogues on Love, 118.
    influence on Cervantes, 118.
Diana, 105.
Diana in Love, 106ff.
Diego de Miranda, see *Don Quixote,* 254, 272-5.
disguise, 309.
Divorce Court, 16, 352.
Don Quixote, 63, 293, 334, 353, 363, 368-9:
    action in Part I, 252.
    analysis of Part I, 246ff.
    apology of Don Quixote for actions, 256.
    "Arabic" author, 213.
    arms and letters, 234.
    art, 289.
    autobiographical details, 40-3, 82, 234.
    background, 165.
    balance between dialogue and description, 276.
    balance in events of life, 229.
    burlesque, 205, 217, 279.
    canvas enlarged, 212.
    canvas of romance, 232.
    Cardenio, 239.
    change of itinerary, 283.
    character of hero, 176.
    classics, 171.
    combat with Biscayan, 222.
    combat with lion, 254.
    commentaries, 249, 288.
    concessions to critics, 251.
    conversation of two squires, 271-2.
    contemporary society, 266.
    contrast between knight and squire, 216.
    contrasts, 227ff., 258.
    corruption in office, 26.

date of printing, 203.
death of hero, 287.
defects, 233.
delineation of personages, 267.
delineation of woman, 242.
development, 206.
development of hero's saner nature, 252ff.
discourses, 234.
discussion, 253.
Don Quixote and Sancho, 215, 263-4.
Dorotea, 239.
drama, 147, 234.
Duchess, 264.
Duke and Duchess, 256, 278ff.
elaboration in Part II, 275.
eloquence, 262.
enchantment, 245.
equanimity of hero, 231.
essentials of romance, 249.
fame, 368.
Fernando, 239.
final defeat and return, 283.
first defeat, 210.
first experiences, 208.
first return, 211.
first sally, 209, 211.
flocks of sheep, 218.
foundation laid, 165.
full meaning, 217ff.
funeral procession, 232.
Galatea, 110, 111.
Galician carriers, 228.
galley slaves, 233.
goatherd, adventure with, 236ff.
helmet of Mambrino, 223ff.
hero needs a companion, 212.
highest level of Part I, 244.
history of fiction, 193.
humanistic qualities, 262.
humor, 217, 227.
idealism, 213.
inception of *Don Quixote,* 176.
influence, 289.

in foreign countries, 288.
inn, 217, 227, 275.
innkeeper, 208, 232, 243.
interpretation of life, 369.
"island" Barataria, 281.
library, 212-3.
limitations of theme, 251.
literary art, 166.
love stories, 238.
Luscinda, 239.
madness, 211, 257.
magician, hostile, 213.
main purposes, 205.
manuscript ready, 166.
Marcela, 236.
material for comedy, 230.
novelistic incidents, 235.
original conception, 205, 207.
plans for third sally, 246.
preface, 204ff.
preliminary arrangements, 330.
preparations of hero, 208.
prison, supposed origin in, 161.
publication of Part I, 203; Part II, 250.
puppet theatre, 277.
realism, 289.
regeneration of protagonists, 257.
relative merits of two parts, 251.
ritual of arming, 209.
romance of chivalry, 197.
second return of hero, 245.
second sally, 213.
serious parts, 233.
shepherds, 232.
Sierra Morena, 232.
simplicity, 371.
sojourn at palace of Duke, 278ff.
spurious history of Don Quixote, 282.
story of Cardenio, 239ff.
strolling actors, 266.
termination of career, 283,

traditional elements, 241.
translations, 288.
types and individuals of Part II, 253.
types of adventure, 216ff.
typographical errors, 249.
unevenness, 283.
variety, 221.
virtues, 257.
vocabulary, 244.
Dorador, El, 80.
Doria, Andrea, 60.
Dorotea, cf. *Don Quixote,* 239.
Dorotea, 125.
drama, 136, 310, 346ff.; see *Eight Plays.*
dramas of the eighties, 151-2.
dramatists, contemporary, 146.
Dulcinea, 239.
D'Urfé, 111.

E

Eclogues of Garcilaso, 104.
Egmont, 44.
Eight Interludes, 365.
Eight Plays, 340ff., 363, 364-5; see "drama."
    analysis, 342.
    composition, 340.
    defects, 351.
    failure, 346.
    Preface, 134, 340.
    second dramatic period, 341.
    technique, 346.
    versification, 345.
Election of Magistrates of Daganzo, 352.
Elegy on death of Queen, 48.
Elizabeth of England, 156.
enjoyment of reader, Cervantes' aim, 201.
Erasmus, 326.
Ercilla, 99, 170.
Espinel, 99.
Esquivias, 131, 153, 162, 164, 332,

Essex, **163.**
Exemplary Novels, 293ff., **334,**
  363, 366, 367-8:
  amorous intrigues, 316.
  abduction, 316.
  adventure type, '308.
  autobiographical details, 308.
  clandestine marriage, 309.
  date, 297.
  defects, 310.
  delicacy, 316.
  delineation, 316, 364.
  descriptions, 304.
  dialogue, 308.
  document on Spain, 367.
  imitations, 328.
  influence, 327.
  local flavor, 296.
  models, 310.
  originality, 303.
  portraiture, 304.
  Prologue, 62, 301.
  redemption of criminal, **317.**
  résumé, 305ff.
  satire, 320.
  Spain, 293.
  sparkling scenes, 308.
  tradition, 308.
  translation, 296, 327.
  types of character, 367.
Ezpeleta, Gaspar de, 330ff.

F

fabliaux, 352.
Fair Maid of the Inn, 328.
Famagusta, 59, 61.
family of Cervantes at Alcalá,
  33:
  at Madrid, 34.
  at Seville, 34.
  at Valladolid, 33.
Feigned Basque, 352.
Fernández de Avellaneda, 282.
Fernando, cf. *Don Quixote,* 239.
fiction, 200.
fiction of good and evil women,
  119.
Fielding, 289.

Figueroa, Costanza de (niece),
  94.
Figueroa, Francisco de, 100,
  124.
Figueroa, Lope de, 62.
Filida's Shepherd, 100, 107ff.
Fire-bringer, 369.
Flanders, 43, 44, 45, **47, 56.**
Fletcher, 328.
flocks of sheep, 217.
Force of Blood, 300, **316-7.**
Forest of Love, 137, 342.
Forests of Ardenia, 342.
Franciscan order, 363.
Freire, Simón, 160.

G

Gaiferos, Don, 277.
Galatea, 98, 101ff., 110, **111,**
  126, 315, 353, 363, 364:
  autobiographical details, 117.
  bucolic compositions, 124.
  contemporary popularity, 111.
  date of composition, 108.
  discussions by shepherds, 118.
  examples of discussions, 120.
  germs of Cervantes' gifts,
    128.
  influence, 125.
  metrical forms, **123.**
  origins, 103.
  scholastic features, **118.**
  story, 109ff.
  spirit, 109.
  tragic episodes, **113-4.**
Galen, 21.
Gallant Spaniard, 54, 343.
galley slaves, 239.
Gálvez de Montalvo, 100, 107,
  108, 110, 116.
Garcilaso, 49, 103, **107,** 123.
Garden of Rare Flowers, 359.
Gibson, J. Y., 163, 335.
Gil, Juan, 86, 141.
Ginés de Pasamonte, **277.**
golden age, 234.
Golden Ass, 174.

Goletta, 59, 64.
Grand Sultana, 137, 343.
Gran Turquesca, la, 137.
Griselda, Patient, 301.
Grisóstomo, 236.
Guzmán de Alfarache, 15, 315:
  on University of Alcalá, 15.
gypsies, 307.
Gypsy Girl, 180.

H

Haedo, Diego de, **81.**
Hamet, 63.
Hassán, 75, 80, 81, 85, 86, **87.**
Hebreo, León, 118, 120.
Heliodorus, 174, 360.
Hero and Leander, **173.**
Herrera, 99, 124.
hidalgos, 21.
Holy Brotherhood, 222.
Holy League, 59, 64.
Homer, 114, 173.
Horace, 170.
Horn, 44.
humanism, 192, **305.**
humanists, 326.

I

Ill-advised Curiosity, 243, 315.
Illustrious Bernardo, 353.
Illustrious Kitchen-maid, 180,
  185, 310-11, 328, 333:
  Costanza, 311.
  descriptions, 311.
  picaresque vein, 311.
individualism of Spaniard, **194.**
Inquisition, 21, 24, 49, 88.
Interludes, 340, 351-2.
Isabel de Valois, 48.
Isabella, 148.
Italian cities, 46.
Italian fiction, 352.
Italian novelists, 360.
Italian novels, 310.
Italy, 45, 49.
  departure for, 50, 56.

departure from, 65, 71.

J

jail in Seville, 160.
Jealous Estremaduran, 185, 300,
  304, 316, 318-20:
  change in original, 319.
Jealous Old Man, 352.
jealousy, 118.
jest books, 103, 299.
Journey to Parnassus, 124, 292,
  334ff., 342:
  allegorical gallery, 337.
  autobiographical, 98, 338.
  contemporary literature, 338.
  eloquence, 338.
  Postscript, 137, 150.
Juan de Austria, 60, 61, 64, 65,
  73, 95.

K

Knight of the Cross, 202.
Knight Platir, 202.
knights-errant, 216.

L

Labyrinth of Love, 343.
Lady Cornelia, 308-9, 328.
Laínez, 100.
Lauso (Cervantes), 116.
Lazarillo de Tormes, 102, 103,
  176, 184ff., 300, 312, 315:
  bald style, 184.
  cynicism, 184.
  firmness of outline of char-
    acters, 185.
  history of realism, place in,
    185.
  importance, 184.
  individuality of characters,
    189.
  masters, 185, 187, 190.
  relation to life, 185.
League of Breda, **44.**
Legend of Good Women, 120.
Leiva, Sancho de, 71.

Lemos, Count of, 250, 339-40, 353, 362.
León, Luis de, 99, 124, 170, 195.
Leonardo de Argensola, 100, 148ff.
Leonor de Cortinas, cf. Cortinas, 4.
Lepanto, 43, 60, 63, 132.
Letter to Mateo Vázquez, 77, 83-4.
Liberal Lover, 59, 308, 343.
library of Don Quixote, 106, 110, 176.
Licentiate of Glass, 45, 321ff.:
  autobiographical details, 325.
  intellectual biography, 322.
  life of city, 323.
  mind of hero, 322.
  study of partial insanity, 322.
  Italian influence, 67.
Liñán, 98.
Liñán y Verdugo, 327.
literary activities of Madrid, 98.
literary men, 334.
Little Gypsy, 47, 52, 306.
López de Hoyos, 48.
love, nature of, 118.
Low Countries, 27.
Lucian, 174.
Luscinda, cf. *Don Quixote,* 239.

M

Maccoll, 327.
Madrid in 1580, 96.
Mambrino, 217.
Manrique, Jorge, 49.
Mansion of Jealousy, 342.
maps, 360.
Marcela, cf. *Don Quixote,* 236.
Margarita, 54.
Marqués de Santa Cruz, 60, 62, 63, 95, 156, 157.
Marquesa, 60.
Matchless Arsinda, 137.
Maurice of Nassau, 27.
Medina Sidonia, Duke of, 163.
Melisendra, 277.

memorial to King, 59, 93, 95, 158.
Messina, 60, 62.
Metamorphoses, 173.
minor works, 363.
Miraculous Play, 352.
Mirror of Chivalry, 202.
miscellanies, 103, 169, 299.
models, literary, 102.
Modoni, 63.
Molière, 269.
Moncada, Miguel de, 60.
Monipodio, 313.
Montalbán, 327.
Montemayor, 105ff., 116.
Montesinos, cave of, 40.
Moody, 369.
Morals, 360.
Musaeus, 173.
Mustafa Pasha, 59.
mystics, 118, 119.

N

Natural History, 360.
Naval Battle, 136, 138.
naval battle (Lepanto), 59.
Navarino, 59, 63.
Navarro, 135.
neo-platonism, 118.
neo-platonists, 118.
Netherlands, 44.
"new art of Lope de Vega," 347.
Nicosia, 59.
Nieuport, 27.
novel, development of, 193.
novellieri, 299.
Numantia, 136, 138:
  heroism depicted in, 145.
  patriotic qualities, 141ff.
  personification of lofty ideas, 146.
  plot, 142ff.
  popularity, 142.
  defects of early plays, 146.
Numantians (Spaniards), 141.
Núñez de Reinoso, 174.

O

Odes to the Armada, 157:
  patriotic fervor, 157.
Odyssey, 173.
Olivante de Laura, 202.
Only Play, 137.
Oran, 78, 79, 95.
Oriana, 239.
Orlando Furioso, 342.
Orlando Innamorato, 217.
Osorio, Rodrigo, 158:
  contract with, 158-9.
Ottoman empire, 58.
Ottoman fleet, 60.
Ovando, Nicolas de, 94.
Ovid, 173.

P

Palacios de Salazar Vozmediano, Catalina de (wife),
  131ff., 162, 332, 333, 353:
  dowry, 132.
  family, 132.
Palermo, 65.
Palmerin of England, 202, 278.
Pardo, Juan, 4.
pastoral, history of, 103.
pastoral type, 101.
pastorals, writers of, 125.
Patras, gulf of, 60.
patrons of Cervantes, 339.
Pedro de Urdemalas, 344, 345.
Peña Pobre, 239.
Persiles and Sigismunda, 10, 13,
  26, 47, 52, 55, 71, 110, 292,
  333, 353ff., 363, 365-6:
  autobiographical details, 89,
  360.
  character, 357ff.
  dedication, 351, 357, 362.
  inconsistencies, 358.
  preliminary sketch, 358-9.
  Prologue, 360-2.
  sources, 359ff.
  style, 360, 366.
  translations, 354.
Philip II, 27, 44, 48, 50, 58, 60,
  65, 156, 163.

Phyllis, 148.
physicians, 324.
picaresque novels, 11, 184.
Pictures of Algiers, 77, 79, 136,
  138ff., 308, 343; defects of
  early plays, 146.
  patriotic tone, 141.
  personal recollections, 139.
  personifications, 140.
  plot, 139ff.
  religious feeling, 141.
*Pictures of Constantinople and
  the Death of Selim*, 138.
pirates, 72, 117.
Pius V, 50, 58.
Plato, 9, 170.
Plautus, 14.
plays: see "drama"; *Eight
  Plays; Interludes.*
playwrights, 100.
Pleasant Play, 344-5.
Pliny, 360.
Plutarch, 360.
Poem on San Jacinto, 162.
poetic justice, 318.
poetry, 96, 175, 192.
poets, 323.
Poliscene de Beocia, 203.
Polo, Gil, 100, 101, 106ff., 108,
  123.
Ponce de León, Manuel, 62.
popular phrases, 265.
Porras, Gaspar, 138.
Porto das Moas, 27.
Portugal, campaign against, 27.
Postscript, 152, 335:
  best vein, 338.
  theatre, 338.
Prisons of Algiers, 77, 309, 343.
Prize, capture of, 63.
proverbs, 258.

Q

Quevedo, Francisco de, 170.

R

realism, 200.

Redemptionists, 89.
Reggio, 62.
Renascence, 9, 96, 104, 167ff., 192, 262, 293, 299, 308, 326.
Rey de Artieda, 100.
ridicule of pedantry, 171.
Rinconete and Cortadillo, 185, 300, 304, 312ff., 344, 352.
Rodríguez, Alonso, 130.
Rojas, Ana Franca, 130.
Rojas, Fernando de, 177.
romance of chivalry, 102, 192ff., 194ff., 196, 197ff., 202, 203.
romantic movement, 306.
romanticism, 354.
Rome, 57.
royal permit, 38.
Rueda, Lope de, 134, 135, 176, 353.

Ruffino, Bartolomeo, 77.
"rules of art," 149, 351.

S

Saavedra, Fernando de, see *Gallant Spaniard*, 54.
Saavedra, Isabel de, 130, 331, 332, 333.
Saintes Maries, les, 72.
Salamanca, 6, 91.
Samson Agonistes, 287.
Sancha, 29.
Sancho Panza, 29:
  analysis of life, 259.
  character, 214.
  death of master, 286.
  development, 259.
  discussions, 260.
  governor, 252, 278, 281.
  gradual polish, 266.
  intelligence, 259.
  master's defeat, 284.
  moralizing, 262.
  outfit, 215.
  pacifism, 229.
  philosophical squire, 259.
  wife, 29, 245, 267-70.
  wisdom, 264.

Sandoval y Rojas, 339-40.
Sannazaro, 105, 116.
Sansón Carrasco, 247, 250, 270.
Santa Cruz, Marqués de, 60, 62, 63, 95, 156, 157.
Santa Teresa, 194.
Sante Ambrosio, 94.
Sanz del Águila, Isabel, 333.
sayings, 258.
scholars and humanists, 169.
scholastic system, 7.
Selim II, 58, 62.
Seneca, 170.
Serrano, the Bachelor, 4.
Sessa, Duke of, 65, 73.
Seville, 153, 313ff.
Shelton, Thomas, 288.
Shepherds' Calendar, 111.
shepherds, life of, 103.
Sidney, Sir Philip, 111.
Sierra Morena, 239.
Sigura, Antonio de, 51.
Simancas, 50.
Siralvo (Gálvez de Montalvo), 115.
slave trade, 75ff.
Smollett, 289.
societies, literary, 97.
Sol, El, 71ff.
Song of Calliope, 98ff., 335.
sonnets, 77, 97, 129, 162, 163.
Spain, revealed by archives, 21.
Spanish-English Lady, 73, 308-9.
Spenser, 111.
stanzas, 77.
Story of the Captive, 39, 43, 64, 75, 77, 82, 243ff., 343.
students, 10-13.
suit of Valladolid, 23.

T

tears, in pastoral, 114.
Terence, 14.
Teresa Panza, 29, 267.
Theagenes and Chariclea, 174.
theatre, condition of, 129, 136.
theatre, of Cervantes' first period, 149.

theatrical world, 134.
Timoneda, 299.
Tirante, 202.
Tirsi (Figueroa), 115.
Tirso de Molina, 327, 328.
Toledo, 311.
Tomé Cecial, *see Don Quixote*, 271.
Topography and General History of Algiers, 81.
Torquemada, 359.
Torreblanca, Leonor de (grandmother), 20, 22.
household goods, 21.
translation, 173, 296.
Trinitarian nuns, 363.
Trinitarians, 86.
Tunis, 64.
Turk, 57, 58, 59, 61, 63, 64, 100.
Two Damsels, 308-9.

U

Uluch Ali, 63.
"unities," 149.
Urbina, Diego de, 60.
Urganda, 211.

V

Vagabond-Widower, 352.

Valdés, Juan de, 195.
Valladolid, 19, 21, 330.
Vargas Manrique, 97.
Vázquez, Baltasar, 4.
Vázquez, Mateo, 77, 83.
Vega, Lope de, 97, 98, 100, 124, 125, 136, 137, 146, 150, 170, 282, 316, 327, 346, 347, 350-1, 365.
Velázquez, Jerónimo, 129.
Veneziano, Antonio, 77.
Venice, 58, 64.
Vera (or Cabrera), Catalina de (great grandmother), 23.
verse, miscellaneous, 366.
Villalva, 6.
Virgil, 9, 104, 114, 170, 173, 360.
Virués, 100.
Vivar, 98.
Watchful Sentinel, 352.
Weeks of the Garden, 353.
windmills, 217.
wisdom of life, 257.
women, 334.
world of letters, 95, 153.

Z

Zayas, María de, 327.